SECRETS
OF THE
BETHEL SIGNS
AND
WONDERS CULTURE

HOW TO UNLEASH THE SUPERNATURAL
POWER OF GOD IN YOUR LIFE

GREG TAYLOR

© 2019 by Greg Taylor

No part of this book may be reproduced, transmitted or distributed in any form or by any means, electronic or mechanical, including photocopying, recording, or by any information storage or retrieval system, without permission in writing from the author.

Unless otherwise indicated, all Scripture quotations are from the Holy Bible, English Standard Version (ESV), copyright © 2001, 2007, 2011, 2016 by Crossway Bibles, a division of Good News Publishers. Used by permission. All rights reserved.

Quotations marked NASB are taken from the New American Standard Bible® (NASB), Copyright © 1960, 1962, 1963, 1968, 1971, 1972, 1973, 1975, 1977, 1995 by The Lockman Foundation. Used by permission. www.Lockman.org

Quotations marked NIV2011 are taken from The Holy Bible, New International Version® NIV® Copyright © 1973, 1978, 1984, 2011 by Biblica, Inc.™ Used by permission. All rights reserved worldwide.

Quotations marked NKJV are taken from the New King James Version®. Copyright © 1982 by Thomas Nelson. Used by permission. All rights reserved.

ISBN: 978-0-473-48504-7

Third Heaven Publishing
Christchurch, New Zealand

Website: gregjtaylor.com

Special bonus report available: "Women in Ministry: Examining the Case Against Female Leadership in the Church" –
gregjtaylor.com/bethel-book-bonus

DEDICATION

I would like to dedicate this book to three people who have changed my life: Bill Johnson, Kris Vallotton, and Bob Robinson.

Bill and Kris have greatly enlarged my perspective on the supernatural and what is possible with God, while a number of years earlier Bob (one of my former theology teachers at Bible college) influenced me strongly in the development of how I think theologically. Without the contributions of these three men, I would not have been able to write a book like this.

ACKNOWLEDGEMENTS

I would like to firstly acknowledge my parents, Les and Christine Taylor, for their great support throughout the long journey of writing this book. Without this, I could not have completed the project.

Secondly, I would like to recognize Dr. Bob Robinson and Edward Kornkven, both of whom reviewed drafts of the book and provided very useful feedback.

Thanks also to those on the Bethel Church and Laidlaw College staffs who assisted me in various aspects of my research.

CONTENTS

Dedication iii
Acknowledgements v
Preface ix
Introduction xiii
How to Read this Book xxv
Disclaimer xxvii
1. God is Good 1
2. Focused on His Presence 27
3. Partnering with God 43
4. Saints, Not Sinners 61
5. Optimistic and Victorious Eschatology 95
6. Complete Five-Fold Ministry 123
7. Culture of Revival 167
8. Nothing is Impossible! 189
9. Culture of Empowerment 209
10. Culture of Risk 229
Concluding Thoughts 261
Appendix: Signs and Wonders 263
References 267
Endnotes 269
About the Author 291

PREFACE

Over the last two decades, Bethel Church in Redding, California has risen to prominence in the area of supernatural ministry. The blind are receiving their sight, the deaf hearing, and the good news is being preached effectively to a lost and dying world, that is so desperately searching for something - anything - that truly satisfies. What is more, all of this is happening through very ordinary people, both within "church", and to an even greater extent outside of it.

These developments have attracted the attention of believers from all over the planet who are no longer satisfied with living out a boring and powerless Christianity, that is of little relevance to their everyday lives. They are people who are ravenous for the "more of God" that has become the norm at Bethel.

Their excitement about this outpouring of the Spirit happening in Redding has led to them absolutely devouring books by Bethel authors. At the same time, many of them have been going on pilgrimages to the church, hoping to leave with powerful spiritual impartations, and renewed enthusiasm for their faith. Also, every year, more than 2,000 of these people make great sacrifices to totally immerse themselves in the Bethel environment through its ministry school, seeking to become fully activated in signs and wonders ministry.

I was one of those people. In 2014, I went to Redding to study at the Bethel School of Supernatural Ministry (BSSM). And while I was there, I became curious as to why they are so successful at seeing the supernatural manifest, compared to most other churches. After considering this question, I quickly realized that it isn't due to anything special about either the church's physical location or any of its people. What I discovered was that the decisive factor, instead, is Bethel's signs and wonders culture (more on this, in a moment).

The consequence of this is that it is not necessary to visit Bethel and receive an impartation, in order to pick up what they have. While they are a shining example of what is possible with God, He is the ultimate source of everything that happens at this church. His Holy Spirit, which empowers believers in the supernatural, is available to each and every person, no matter where they reside.

Bethel's success in supernatural ministry is due, in large part, to revelation they have received from God, on how to access His miraculous power consistently and utilize it effectively, to fulfill required needs. With these insights, they have constructed a culture in which it is easy for any person to move powerfully in signs and wonders, and live a life of incredible impact on the world. When you become part of this culture, the supernatural becomes natural – which is why people are flocking to Redding in such great numbers.

However, there is nothing that prevents any other group of believers from also applying these insights, to create a similar culture for themselves (in their own context), and thereby moving in this level of power. In fact, it is part of the core mission of the Bethel movement to export their culture and share everything that they have discovered with others, so that they too can be fully equipped in God.

There is one problem, though, and this is that because there are so many of these powerful insights, it would normally take a few years of full immersion in Bethel's culture, to gain a good working knowledge of the vast majority of them. This is why thousands of people are prepared to spend up to three years at the Bethel School of Supernatural Ministry (BSSM). As one of the people who have done this, I can highly recommend making such an investment in yourself. You would not regret it!

But the good news is that it is not essential for you to spend years at Bethel learning these insights, to be able to construct your own similar supernatural culture and see the sort of results that they do. After months of carefully analyzing Bethel's signs and wonders culture, both experientially as a BSSM student, and through the detailed research of many of their published materials, I have established that there are only really a few key components of it (10 to be exact) - which can all be learned relatively quickly and easily. And when you apply these 10 "secrets", you can quite quickly begin forming your own supernatural culture and start seeing God perform incredible signs and wonders through yourself, on a regular basis.

The purpose of this book, therefore, is to identify and explain each of these secrets of the Bethel signs and wonders culture, to give you the tools needed to construct your own supernatural culture. This will enable you and your friends to unleash the supernatural power of God in your own lives and ministries.

INTRODUCTION

In recent decades, the steady decline of the influence of Christianity within Western society has been clear for all to see. For a number of centuries the Church occupied a position at the center of people's lives, serving as a source of community, security, and hope. It is now, however, widely regarded as being an archaic institution that is largely irrelevant to modern-day life in the 21st century. Some even openly mock it these days.

Science has supposedly burst the bubble of the supernatural foundation of our faith that God is real and plays an active role in the world. Believing in Him is now seen as akin to believing in Santa Claus, the Easter Bunny, and the Tooth Fairy – endearing for a child, but completely laughable for any educated adult. The miraculous stories in the Bible are understood simply as myths and fables that belong firmly in the realm of fantasy, rather than documented history.

Meanwhile, there has been a great increase in the number of attractive substitutes to religion for people to spend their limited free time on, which incidentally, science and technology have often made strong contributions toward. Movies, Internet/social media, sports, shopping, and travel now occupy much of people's attention outside of their work lives.

It is hardly surprising, therefore, that many in our society today value churches only in terms of the aid they provide to the poor/disadvantaged, and as venues for weddings and funerals. Despised, though, are the spirituality, fellowship, and general support that they offer.

For a lot of believers, this makes quite depressing reading, as it is a scenario that we are all too familiar with and have been struggling to turn around. Paradoxically, though, some are excited and see it as a sign that we are on the right track, given that this mass falling away from the faith and truth seems to line up with biblical prophecy, regarding the time of Jesus' second coming (2 Thess. 2:3 NKJV; cf. 1 Tim. 4:1).

However, we as the Church have not helped ourselves in promoting what we know still is, and will always be, the greatest message in the world – that of Jesus Christ the Savior of the world (1 John 4:14). We have largely capitulated to the prevailing anti-supernatural culture, and in doing so have sacrificed one of our most important points of difference, the wonderworking God of the impossible, on the altar of another "god" – that of modernity, the humanistic philosophy that arose from the 18th century Enlightenment movement in Europe.

Modernity, which strongly values human intellect, achievement, and self-sufficiency, is one of the chief "gods" of the Western world[1]; it is highly antagonistic toward religious faith and any concept of the supernatural. Modernity says that there is nothing out there greater than us to depend on – meaning that we have to rely solely on ourselves and what we can achieve on our own. In effect, we are our own gods in this man-centered universe (cf. Christianity's God-centered one). This ideology has been a major factor in the secularization of our society and consequently the erosion of the Church's influence.

One aspect of modernity has been quite decisive in it both achieving wide acceptance within society and gaining the Church's acquiescence: its emphasis on science and technological progress – through "modern" science. Over the last few centuries, modern science has flourished enormously and brought unparalleled technological advancements to society, to the great benefit of all. These contributions have won it huge respect and caused many, if not most, people to buy into the philosophy behind it – which is essentially modernity, as the descriptor "modern" suggests.[2]

Of particular significance to our discussion is the fact that modern science has some important presuppositions that are directly contrary to faith and the supernatural – such as materialism (only matter is real), naturalism (everything can be explained in terms of natural processes), and empiricism (we have to be able to verify something through observation, to be able to label it as "true").[3] The presence of these presuppositions[4] has led to modern science overstepping its bounds and making pronouncements in realms far outside of its field of expertise, such as in metaphysical matters. It has been used to explicitly reject the possibility of anything supernatural like the Judeo-Christian Creator God, miracles, and any concept of an afterlife – due to the beliefs that nothing exists other than the physical world (materialism) and that natural processes are ultimately responsible for everything (naturalism), along with science's difficulty in verifying most supernatural claims (empiricism)[5]. This has caused an unnecessary conflict between science and faith, to the point where it is now commonly (but erroneously) accepted that you cannot both believe in science and be a Bible-believing Christian.[6]

Of course, there has been a clear winner between these two positions in the hearts and minds of people. Modern science's esteemed status within our society has ensured that its metaphysical claims have been accepted over those of Christianity. This has enabled its philosophy, modernity, to become embedded into Western culture at the expense of the supernatural Christian faith, whose beliefs and ideas had previously underpinned society.

Theologians and Bible scholars have responded to this situation by coming up with and adopting modernistic-type interpretations of the Bible that downplay the supernatural (e.g. the Jesus Seminar, cessationism), in an attempt to harmonize with modernity and therefore remain "relevant". Most often, though, the issue is not in them outright denying certain aspects of the supernatural, but just that they focus almost exclusively on other areas – especially those that relate to modernistic concerns. For example, they tend to be immeasurably more interested in debating the nuances of Paul's theology than discussing topics like miracles, spiritual gifts, and angels and demons.

John Wimber mentions that an associate of his did an analysis of the 27 most frequently used reference works from the library of a large and prestigious evangelical seminary in the United States. This associate reviewed 87,125 pages from these mostly multi-volume works and found that only 0.08 percent of the pages were devoted to healings, 0.15 percent to miracles, and 0.10 percent to signs and wonders.[7] Wimber therefore correctly concludes that:

> When the high number of verses devoted to healings, miracles, and signs and wonders in the New Testament (especially in the gospels) is compared with the low number of pages written on the same topics in modern theological literature, it is reasonable to assume that modern secularism[8] has influenced Christian scholars.[9]

This lack of emphasis on the supernatural and/or denial of certain aspects of it has had the effect of engraining in theological students, many of whom have gone on to become our pastors and teachers in church, the idea that the supernatural is not an important or normal part of the Christian faith. It should be no surprise then that we hear so little about the supernatural in most churches today, and that it is no longer within the reality of the vast majority of Christians.

What has happened, therefore, is that the force of modernity in the culture and the lack of an appropriate response to it by Christian academics/leaders, have caused believers to doubt some of the supernatural aspects of their faith and instead buy into much of modernity's unbiblical philosophy.

While most of us haven't thrown out the existence of God, the resurrection of Jesus, or the reality of an afterlife in either Heaven or Hell, we have compartmentalized our faith by relegating God and the supernatural to the realm that is normally only experienced after death. This is the error that missiologist Paul Hiebert calls the "Flaw of the Excluded Middle"[10]. Accordingly, our belief in Jesus relates only to the hope of a good afterlife: going to Heaven instead of Hell when we die. And the practice of our faith is limited mainly to the domains of ritual and ethics: attending church on Sunday, reading our Bibles, praying (but not really expecting anything out of the ordinary to happen), and living good lives as morally upstanding citizens.

However, when we get sick we usually rely totally on doctors and medical science.[11] If our finances are tight, we tend to look for ways to reduce our expenses. And when we are seeking a spouse, we might try to expand our social horizons or possibly download some app on our phone. Gone is the idea of a God who heals miraculously, provides supernaturally, and is a divine matchmaker. He is no longer believed to be relevant to any aspect of our lives on Earth, other than perhaps as a comforter in times of trouble (2 Cor. 1:3-4). Essentially, we have chosen a god for this life (modernity – the "god" of science and technology, natural processes, and human self-sufficiency) and another one for the next life (the supernatural God of the Bible).

In reality, our lives on Earth as Christians function just like those of everyone else who doesn't know God, because in practice we're actually believing in the same modernistic "god" as them and expecting similar outcomes. The result is that we don't have a whole lot to offer the non-Christian world as inducements to join us in the faith. They generally do not believe there is an afterlife (or at least not our dualistic concept of one i.e. Heaven and Hell) and therefore are skeptical about any promises related to that. Furthermore, they're not interested in a "new" life in the present that's pretty much the same as theirs – apart from some additional constraints, which they believe would limit their enjoyment of it (e.g. a set of restrictive ethics and various time consuming disciplines).

We excuse ourselves for being unsuccessful at evangelism (or not even trying in the first place) and consequently having half-empty churches, by thinking that the lack of interest in what we're offering is just the response of sinful and unregenerate human beings, who have no ability to discern spiritual truth. But this is a gross misrepresentation of the situation and a complete cop out on our behalf. Jesus in His ministry didn't have any trouble in pulling huge crowds and drawing passionate followers to Himself. Neither did the first apostles after His ascension to Heaven; thriving churches sprung up all over the place in very little time with the proclamation of the Gospel they preached. So what did Jesus and the earliest believers do differently to what is generally done in Christendom today?

Well, they didn't just preach a Gospel of words about a hope beyond the grave. Instead, they preached AND demonstrated a miraculous Gospel of power that relates to every aspect of life now, in addition to what happens after death (1 Cor. 2:4-5, 4:20). They presented a loving and powerful God that is still active in this world, who wants to involve Himself thoroughly in our lives and richly bless us. However, the watered down and powerless Christianity that is being offered to the world today is just plain irrelevant and, to be quite frank, boring to most people. Can we really be surprised that they show so little interest in it and instead chose to live such hedonistic lives? I don't think so.

The problem, though, is definitely not with God, who is, and will always be, the most relevant, interesting, and fun "person" in the whole universe. Nor is it with His Gospel of power, which provides us with everything we need to live incredibly abundant, fulfilling, and significant lives that are attractive to others – both now and in the hereafter (John 10:10). Nothing about either Him or the Gospel has changed since the day of Pentecost in the Book of Acts (Acts 2). Everything that those first believers experienced from that point onward is available to us, and almost certainly a whole lot more!

The issue is in fact with us, in that we have utterly failed to access most of what God has made available to us, as a result of our capitulation to modernity. Consequently, the brand of Christianity that we've presented is far removed from the Earth-shaking movement testified about on the pages of Scripture: our church services are often tedious, our evangelistic efforts are usually repelling, and we generally live quite unremarkable and boring day-to-day lives – leading many to question whether Christians actually have any fun. I strongly suspect that the apostle Paul would be shocked if he was able to see what the Church has become, particularly in respect to how weak and ineffective its witness is, and how downtrodden many of its people are.

God, however, never intended us to live the sorts of mundane, boring, and often defeated lives that many of us are so used to living. Being a Christian, although not always easy, is meant to be exciting and even thrilling – more like a ticket to Disneyland than the cosmic life insurance policy that it has frequently been sold as. There are incredible worlds to discover, which most others are totally unaware of, and epic missions to embark on, which have the potential to change the course of history. And to enable our success, God has bestowed special supernatural powers on us, which allow us to dominate all the forces of darkness standing in our way. I would argue that it wouldn't be too much of a stretch to claim that life as a Christian can be far more exhilarating than even the movies!

This is where we come to the main subject of this book, Bethel Church, in Redding, California, which has discovered the reality of such a life. They utterly reject the idea that our faith should be compartmentalized, such that we practice it only at selected times during the week, and that it relates solely to the afterlife. For them, God wants to be intimately involved in every aspect of our lives right now – including our relationships, work, leisure activities, health, and finances. If something matters to us then it is important to Him. And His desire is not just for us to get everyone into Heaven when they die, by convincing them to become followers of Jesus, but to bring

Heaven to Earth, by transforming every aspect of this world to His will – through His supernatural power working in us.

Since the late 1990s, Bethel church and its ministry school, the Bethel School of Supernatural Ministry (BSSM), have experienced a significant outbreak of signs and wonders, which has been consistently growing throughout the years. Probably just about every major healing miracle that you can imagine has occurred through and for Bethel people[12] at some point, including the curing of many "incurable" diseases like terminal cancer. Pain disappearing from people's bodies has become quite routine. Financial and other miracles of provision are regular occurrences, especially for BSSM students, who are always seeking money for their various school-related expenses and living costs. Miracles over nature, such as the changing of the weather, are not unheard of. And there have even been some instances of the dead being raised.

Aside from the power gifts (healing, miracles, and faith (1 Cor. 12:9-10)), the successful application of the prophetic and other revelatory gifts (1 Cor. 12:10) is also very common. Bethel people are well known for giving very accurate and specific prophetic words.

What makes Bethel quite different from most of the other outpourings of signs and wonders, both past and present, is that it is a grassroots movement that strongly emphasizes the power of God operating through the people rather than just the leaders; and the unleashing of this power outside of church buildings rather than just inside of them. The supernatural has been thoroughly integrated into people's everyday lives, such that the kinds of things we've been talking about are happening everywhere e.g. home, work, and at the mall. And frequently, this leads to people giving their lives to Jesus.

Bethel encapsulates the idea God that originally had, of the Church not being a set of buildings where meetings are held, but a body of people who He has sent out into all the world – to be witnesses of His Son Jesus, the Savior of the world, and builders of His glorious Kingdom on Earth.[13] The main goals of the Bethel leadership team are therefore the same as those Jesus had regarding His disciples: to train and equip those under them in how to live successfully as supernatural believers, and then to send these people out into the world to turn it upside down for the Kingdom (cf. Acts 17:6). This includes the young and the old[14], the rich and the poor, men and women, blacks and whites (and everyone in between), citizens and foreigners, ...

In essence, senior leader Bill Johnson and his team are "body builders" who see their role as being to build big people rather than a big church. While numerical growth is welcomed, expected, and planned for as a normal aspect of the Kingdom (cf. Mark 4:26-29), it has never been the main goal of the movement – at least not since Bill began leading the church in 1996. They are far more concerned with the number of people leaving Bethel trained and equipped, than the number of those there at any given moment. In other words, this is an apostolic movement – which, by definition, focuses on sending rather than gathering people.

The result of this has been that thousands upon thousands of people trained at Bethel have left and gone all over the world. Collectively, they are impacting every major sphere of society for the Kingdom of God, including government and politics, business, education, the arts and entertainment, and popular culture. In the midst of all this, they are displaying the love of God through His supernatural power, and as a result leading many people to Jesus. The Great Commission is being fulfilled (Matt. 28:18-20; Mark 16:15-18)!

In response to these reports, many believers have been pondering why Bethel has been so successful in tapping into the supernatural power of God and advancing His Kingdom, compared to most other churches. They are asking themselves questions like, "How is Bethel accessing the power of God so strongly and consistently?", "What are they doing that we aren't?", "Can everyone operate in what they have, or is it something special that is only for them?", "If it is for everyone, do we need to go to Redding to get it or can we receive it where we are?", and of course, "How can we receive it?"

These are great questions to be asking, and the purpose of this book is to answer the thrust of such questions, in detailed ways, so that everything is laid bare. I have already hinted strongly at some of the answers, not only in this introduction, but also in the title/subtitle of the book and its preface. For example, it should hopefully already be clear that I am arguing that everyone who loves God can operate in the same power and authority of the Spirit that Bethel people do. This, in turn, means that they can have the same signs and wonders following them, along with the same degree of impact on the world.

There is nothing inherently special about Bethel people, other than the fact that they have been chosen by God to be forerunners and leaders of what He wants to do at this time: manifest His supernatural power on every believer like never before, and collectively use them to advance His Kingdom on Earth to such an extent that we see the greatest harvest of souls ever witnessed. It is to be like the Book of Acts, but on steroids!

I expect that it will also now be apparent that you don't need to actually visit Bethel to access what they have, although it certainly wouldn't hurt to do so! Seeing them in action should shorten your learning curve to moving in God's power, while participating in some of their ministries could be a complete game changer. However, the Spirit of God is everywhere, and equally as powerful where you live, as in Redding, California. There is no difference!

If there is nothing "special" about either them or their physical location then what are the secrets to the unusual supernatural power that they move in, and their incredible impact on the world? And how can you employ these things in your own life and/or ministry to move in the same signs and wonders? These questions are going to form the main focus of this book.

It might actually surprise you to learn that the differences between Bethel and most other churches diligently seeking after God are not that great. For instance, like these other churches, Bethel has a music team that has a passion to praise and worship God, leaders who love their people and want to see them thrive, administrators who work hard behind the scenes to make everything happen, and most importantly, they have a congregation of highly committed Jesus followers who believe that the Gospel is the greatest message in the world. This is all the same.

Nevertheless, there are some key differences that make all the difference, in terms of their notable success over the last two decades. And after much analysis and consideration, I have identified the 10 that appear to be the most significant. These differences fall mainly into the categories of beliefs and strategies (along with associated mindsets and tactics), and together form the core of what I call the "Bethel Signs and Wonders Culture"[15]. It is this culture that is ultimately responsible for the consistent flow of signs and wonders seen at Bethel. When new people with no background in supernatural ministry are inserted into it, they are able to quickly start replicating the results of those who are already there doing great works.

The reassuring thing is that each of these key components (or "secrets") of the Bethel signs and wonders culture can be implemented by any church or group of believers, in any location in the world, with the expectation of the same sort of results over time. Everything that they have can therefore be yours if you create a similar culture based on these fundamentals, while not neglecting basics of the faith like love, servanthood, and the authority of Scripture – which are already assumed in this book.

The majority of these secrets can also be applied directly in the life of the individual, so that every person can move in more of the power of God. There are, however, some (e.g. "Culture of Revival" and "Culture of Empowerment") that, due to their nature, are technically only applicable to a group, although there are related principles that can certainly be actioned at the individual level.

It must be emphasized, though, that to see the full effect of each of the 10 secrets of the Bethel signs and wonders culture, these secrets need to be applied in a group setting, because what we are trying to do is create a culture – which, by definition, involves more than just one person. And as you will discover in reading this book, the power of community (see Chapter 7: Culture of Revival) is a crucial part of Bethel's culture, in that the talents of everyone are leveraged, and strength in numbers is utilized, for mutual benefit. After all, God designed us to work together rather than as lone wolves trying to do everything ourselves (1 Cor. 12).

However, it is certainly not necessary to begin with a large group to create your own Bethel-like signs and wonder culture. All you require is a few friends who are committed to going on this journey with you (or even just your spouse/family) and you are good to go. But once others start to see the power of what you're creating, some of them will want to jump on board and be part of it as well!

I invite you, therefore, to make use of the secrets of Bethel's signs and wonders culture so that you too can unleash the supernatural power of God in your life, along with every member of your tribe. When you do, I believe that you're going to have some experiences of the kind that you probably never thought possible for yourself!

HOW TO READ THIS BOOK

This is not the sort of book that has been designed to be read cover-to-cover once, and then consigned to the bookshelf forever. I have written it to be a resource, specifically a manual for supernatural ministry and revival that you would consult over and over again.

Due to its sheer size and detail, there is no way that you're going to absorb all of the information in just one quick read. It will take a few times through to digest everything adequately. And you may want to camp in particular places for extended periods of time to mull over some of the material. In this regard, the scriptural references that I have provided should help you to dig much deeper and make your own discoveries. I actually believe that you will get the most out of the book if you treat it like a Bible study and let God speak to you through the material.

In view of all this, I strongly suggest that you read this book through at least two or three times and then refer back to it when you need to - particularly if you are not yet seeing the desired outcomes. This is, after all, a system that needs to be fully implemented and persevered with to see the greatest possible impact of it. I do not believe that any of its components can be neglected without having an effect on results. For example, if you are not yet embracing a culture of risk then you will be missing out on most of the opportunities that God is giving you to see the miraculous take place – especially if you don't normally have people approaching you for prayer ministry.

That said, I am not asking you to imitate everything that Bethel does in order to see their kind of results. Quite the contrary, the secrets of Bethel's signs and wonders culture are all principles broad enough to applied to your unique context, in your own way – with your DNA stamped all over them. There is absolutely no requirement, for example, that your church has to run healing rooms, have prophetic painters on stage during worship, or do "fire tunnels", like Bethel. Nor do you have to adopt their set of core values as your own. The power is in the principles (most of which are rooted strongly in Scripture), not in the specifics of how Bethel applies them – which I describe in detail merely as examples, to help you understand the ideas and stimulate your thinking.

Of course, you are more than welcome to steal anything of theirs that you think might work for you. Beware, though, that if you try to copy everything they do verbatim, you might end up being disappointed with the results, as not all things will translate well to your setting. For example, a supernatural ministry school like Bethel's will probably not be appropriate for every church (or even the majority of churches). Theirs has been so incredibly successful because of mandate that God has placed on them – to be a global resource center for revival.

Finally, I would like to point out that the ideas in the book are for the most part presented in a logical order and build on one another. My recommendation, therefore, is that the first time you go through the book, you read it in the order presented, otherwise some of the context may be lost. But on subsequent reads, please feel free to jump around more to the stuff that is of most interest to you.

DISCLAIMER

In this book, I not only identify and explain the key components of Bethel's signs and wonders culture, I also reflect on them with my own thoughts and experiences. What I need to point out, therefore, is that although I believe these reflections are for the most part harmonious with the views of Bethel, the emphasis may on occasion be slightly different from theirs on the matters in question. As a result, some of the conclusions reached may not be 100 percent reflective of their thinking in that area. That said, I believe that these conclusions are generally in strong alignment with their views.

1. GOD IS GOOD

There is one non-negotiable, foundational truth to the Bethel movement that is absolutely key to creating a culture of signs and wonders. This is that God is good, a belief which Bethel senior leader Bill Johnson identifies as the cornerstone of all theology[16] and calls the backbone of his faith[17]. It has become both the first cornerstone[18] and first core value of Bethel Church[19]. What "God is good" means to Bethel people is that He is for us (i.e. all of humanity, not just believers) rather than against us, and it is His desire to prosper each of us in every area of our lives. An important part of this is that He wants to save and heal everyone, rather than just a few.[20]

While the overwhelming majority of Christians in the West today would probably claim to agree with the statement "God is good", it has to be questioned whether many of them really do believe this in practice. This is because, among other things, they attribute all of the devastating natural disasters occurring around the world to God's judgment on the ungodly. They argue that He either allows or places sickness, poverty, and other troubles on people, in order to refine their character, by teaching them lessons like patience, humility, and dependence on Him. A not insignificant number believe that He predestines people – apparently most people – to everlasting torment in Hell.[21] Some also suppose that God hates sinners, and that He even has a simmering anger toward believers, such that He is ready and waiting to punish them for their slightest misstep.[22]

It is difficult, though, to fathom how anyone could see such things as being compatible with a loving and good God. As Bill Johnson points out:

> If I were to do to my children what many people think God does to His children, I'd be arrested for child abuse.[23]

Clearly, those who have beliefs along these lines are very confused and just do not understand how loving and good God really is. Yes, it is true that most of them would recognize how amazing and wonderful it is that through faith in Jesus we get to go to Heaven when we die, instead of the Hell we deserve for all of our sins. But God has so, so much more for us than just this. His will is not only to bring us from Earth to Heaven, but to bring Heaven to Earth for us and through us (Matt. 6:10). When Heaven (i.e. the Kingdom of God) comes in its fullest extent, everything that it touches functions exactly as it was designed to, free from all brokenness, dysfunction, and insufficiency - whether that be someone's physical body, their spiritual condition, the economy of nation, or the level of social harmony in a society, for example. What we therefore need to comprehend is that God wants to bless all of humanity in this life - not just the next one. And the amount of blessing that He desires to release on us is extravagant. He is that good!

However, there is another kingdom, the kingdom of darkness, which violently opposes this agenda and this places us in a battle - one that we often feel we're losing. This is why, for example, it is still the case that "bad things happen to good people", many walk in spiritual darkness, there are recurring problems in the world, and not everyone receives instant healing as a result of prayer.

The error that these people make is that they look at what is still wrong with the world (e.g. disasters, terrorism, poverty, crime, pollution, and sickness) and everything desirable that is not happening (e.g. healing not occurring, unanswered prayer in general, and most people rejecting the Gospel message), and conclude that these things must be God's will – which is most definitely not the case. Just as it is not His will for there to be any sickness in Heaven, He does not want any sickness on Earth. Likewise regarding there being any poverty, crime, and people unsaved – none of which is remotely His will, either in Heaven or on Earth.

It is actually our job as believers to work with God to enforce His will, such that we make these desirable things a reality. But this often requires a lot of hard work and persistence. Remember, for example, that Jesus had to pray for a man twice to get him fully healed (Mark 8:22-25). So could this possibly mean that we too might have to sometimes keep praying and praying to get a desired result (cf. 1 Kings 18:41-45; James 5:14-18)? It certainly appears to be the case, but I am getting well ahead of myself here. We will leave much fuller discussions of these issues until later in the book, particularly Chapter 5: Optimistic and Victorious Eschatology.

What I want to say now, however, is that sadly these people with seriously mistaken beliefs about God and His character are unwittingly portraying Him as some kind of petty, capricious tyrant who requires absolute mindless obedience and frequent fawning adoration in order to be appeased. Furthermore, they give the distinct impression that He is someone who will fly into an uncontrollable violent rage against anyone refuses to comply with His "onerous" demands, marking them out for utter destruction. Not surprisingly, therefore, most non-believers want nothing to do with this kind of "religion", and who can blame them?

These beliefs, therefore, make it extremely difficult for anyone who holds them to witness for their faith effectively. For when the inevitable objections about God's character are raised by their listeners, they are forced to reply along the lines of: "Sorry, but that is just how it is. In this life, God is going to subject us to a lot of trials and tribulations in order to discipline us and refine our character. But the good news is that if we follow Jesus and endure these things patiently then we will be allowed to go to Heaven when we die, instead of suffering God's awful judgment in Hell. This is something to be incredibly grateful for!" And then when they're told to "get lost" in response, they might walk away thinking to themselves, "This person's obviously not one of the elect chosen by God to receive eternal life."

Their message, however, was not rejected because God did not want that person to get saved and have eternal life. It was because they portrayed Him in such a false and unappealing way. The unfortunate consequence of this is that those with accurate beliefs about God, who try to share their faith the "right" way, have to overcome the great damage to His reputation that these people have caused through their misinformation. Therefore, evangelism is a lot harder for everyone else and, as a result, many end up shying away from it.

But the great news is that God is more than able to deal with this public relations challenge. He has equipped all of us with His supernatural power to demonstrate His incredible love and goodness to people, rather than just talk to them about these qualities. This will often take the form of healing their bodies and/or giving them prophetic words to encourage them in their lives – both of which tend to make people more open to the Gospel salvation message. But these things are not just for evangelistic situations, they are for all occasions, covering non-believers and believers alike. As I indicated earlier, God wants to bless everyone – no exceptions!

Why Believing that God is Good is Vital for a Culture of Signs and Wonders

The reason why believing that God is good is so vital to having a culture of signs and wonders is that what you believe about God determines how you expect Him to behave, how you respond to this expectation, and what you'll receive as a result of your response. If you don't think, for example, that He is interested in healing people of sickness then it's unlikely that you're ever going to pray for anyone's healing[24] and therefore you won't see any healing. And even if you do believe that He sometimes does desire to heal, you won't ever be able to pray in faith for healing, because you can't be sure on any given occasion that it is His will.

If you desire to see healing occur on a regular basis then you need to first be absolutely convinced that it is God's will to heal, and heal through you, on each and every occasion. No exceptions. After all, there is no specific record of Jesus ever failing to heal anyone who came to Him in faith seeking healing.

This, of course, does not guarantee that healing will actually occur every single time when holding this belief, or that you've never see any healing if you pray without such a belief. Neither does it eliminate the process of failure and disappointment that many people (including healing greats like John Wimber) have to go through to eventually see the kind of results that they're expecting. But what it does do is set you up to see God heal a lot more consistently through you than without that belief.

As Bill Johnson says, "Faith is the currency of heaven."[25] God's Kingdom operates by faith[26], not simply according to human need or want. For without faith it is impossible to please God (Heb. 11:6). Our expectation of how God is going to respond to our prayers plays a large part in what we will actually receive from Him.

As I write this, my mind goes back to the time of the Asian tsunami of December 26, 2004, which caused the deaths of over 200,000 people. Every night over the following few weeks, heartbreaking images of death and destruction were splashed across the six o'clock news, making it quite difficult to watch. Shortly after this, the speaker at an Alpha Course dinner held at my then church told a story about how, on one occasion, his little daughter really wanted butterflies and asked God for some. Moments later, a bunch of beautiful butterflies suddenly appeared and she was delighted. This girl obviously had a very simple faith that she could just ask God for anything she wanted and He would give it to her – because He loved her. [Note: this is a big lesson to all of us, in terms of receiving from God!]

For quite a few years, however, I was offended by what this speaker had said. I thought that he was very insensitive in telling a story like this (particularly to an audience that included a number of non-Christians) right after so many people had tragically lost their lives, and no doubt many more their homes and livelihoods. For why would God give his daughter butterflies but not rescue all those poor souls from death and destruction, many of whom would have desperately cried out to Him for help? It simply didn't make any sense to me and I remember thinking something along the lines of, "If this story is actually true, then what sort of God is He that I believe in and serve?"[27]

What I didn't understand at the time, though, was that human need, no matter how great, is not in and of itself enough to access the resources of Heaven needed to fill it. While I am now certain that God does care deeply about every person who is in a desperate situation, and longs to help them out much more than they desire to be helped, the fact is that Heaven is moved primarily by faith. This seems to be a spiritual principle that even God cannot violate. It is true of healing and every other aspect of the Kingdom, including salvation. Great faith, though, is not always a requirement (Mark 9:20-27; Luke 17:6).

Faith is Multidimensional

One thing that I would also like to point out is that faith is multidimensional. By this, I mean that there is a separate type of faith for each specific area of our lives. There is a faith for salvation, one for healing[28], another for financial provision, a different faith for hearing God's voice, for finding a marriage partner, for miracles over nature (e.g. changing the weather), etc. Every person has different levels of faith over the various areas of their life, which each must be exercised in order to be strengthened, just as with individual muscle groups at the gym.[29] These different levels of faith are a reason why some people are consistently able to get breakthroughs in one area, but struggle to in others. There is not one level of faith that applies universally over ever area of our lives.

Furthermore, it is a serious mistake to think that faith and power go hand-in-hand with godly character. Having an abundance of the fruit of the Spirit does not imply a corresponding measure of the gifts of the Spirit, and vice versa. Character and power are two completely separate things that are not necessarily correlated with each other. We should not be surprised, therefore, that some of the most godly people we know move in no discernable power, while others with significant character flaws move in extraordinary power.

Bill Johnson argues, though, that it should not be an "either-or" situation, but a "both-and" one. We need to have both character and power, rather than play one off against the other (2 Cor. 6:4, 6-7). As an observation, I find it interesting that Christlikeness is almost always associated with character traits like love, kindness, compassion, self-control, and humility, but rarely with other important qualities that Jesus also possessed, such as faith[30] and power.

Since faith and power are things that we need to work at strengthening in our lives[31], we should never blame God because we're weak and therefore unable to move in the supernatural. God's power is available to each and every one of us if we are prepared to pay the price to obtain it – through things like risk-taking, persistence, and the endurance of criticism/persecution.

The thing about healing, though, is that only one person needs to have the faith to effect it, unlike salvation which cannot be received directly through anyone else's faith. A person being prayed for can be a complete atheist and still be healed due to the faith of the person praying for them. So we should never limit God because of who we're praying for. Their acceptance of our offer to pray for them is enough, even if they're at best only curious as to what might happen. God can even use their desire to prove us wrong!

What Happens When Healing Doesn't Occur?

Despite having an atmosphere of faith, just as at the Bethel Healing Rooms, healing doesn't always occur and it can often be difficult to understand why, when we've been full of expectancy and done everything that we know to do. But in these situations, it is vital that we continue holding to the standard of Scripture, that all who came to Jesus in faith were healed (cf. Psalm 103:3). Jesus set the benchmark for us and it is our responsibility to keep going until our experience matches up to that standard.

What we should never do, though, is bring that standard down to the level of our experience, by creating false theologies out of our disappointment (e.g. God doesn't always want to heal; He sometimes has higher purposes; or, the timing has to be right). This is something that Bill Johnson is absolutely adamant about. Equally, we should not beat ourselves up or, even worse, blame the person we're praying for, by questioning their faith or suggesting that they have sin/unforgiveness in their life.

Instead, when we fail to see full and complete healing, we keep pushing on toward that goal. In the moment, this will often mean offering to pray for the person a second, third, fourth, and even fifth time (cf. Jesus' two-stage healing of the blind man in Mark 8:22-25). In practice, healing is often not a binary event (i.e. either total healing or no healing); many times it occurs progressively.

At Bethel, ministry team members and Healing Rooms prayer servants are trained with this in mind. They are taught to keep praying and then testing out the condition, in the expectation that total healing will eventually be reached. For example, before prayer, they will ask the person to rate their level of pain, on a scale of 0-10. Then after prayer, they will request an update on this: e.g. "What is your pain level now?"

But if you don't go through such a process and just ask the person in pain how they're feeling after prayer, they will frequently say, "The pain is still there", when it has actually gone down a few notches e.g.

from an '8' to a '5'. This is because many people are locked into a mindset of what God is not doing, rather than what He is doing. Reframing this towards what God is doing and has done can be enough to change the focus and move progressively toward full healing – which, in my experience, often happens.

However, even if full healing does not occur during a session of prayer, we need to still celebrate what God has done and thank Him for it, while expecting the rest to manifest in the near future (cf. John 6:5-11, 23). But the idea that a partial healing was all God actually wanted to do in such a situation is incomprehensible to everyone who does healing ministry at Bethel. They are trained to always celebrate the small, while expecting and moving toward the big. This is because they believe that God is a good God who always wants to bless us. When you get to know Him and become active in ministering to people, you can't help but recognize His overwhelming love and goodness toward all humanity. He cares deeply about everyone and everything that is important to them – even the little things.

As I write this, I am reminded of a middle-aged lady whom I ministered to in the Bethel Healing Rooms, one Saturday morning. She had very large varicose veins on one of her calves, which she was apparently quite self-conscious about. Although I never actually saw what they looked like (since she had jeans on), I could feel the size of them as I placed my hands on her leg to pray. However, after a relatively short amount of time, her leg strangely started to feel smooth as I moved my hands around the affected area. I then asked her to roll up her trouser leg and discovered that the varicose veins had almost totally disappeared. She was astounded and obviously extremely happy. This is the sort of God that we serve. He is just as willing and able to remove any disfigurements that we're self-conscious about, as He is to heal pain in our bodies and save us from life-threatening conditions like cancer. If it matters to us, it matters to God!

Nevertheless, some people make the case that when a person doesn't get healed, it obviously wasn't God's timing (or even His will at all!). Apparently, whatever happens when they pray must be the will of God (i.e. they believe in His absolute sovereignty). It couldn't possibly be anything to do with them.

I will not, however, entertain any such theory that calls into question God's will (or ability to heal), in order to get myself off the hook. Please give me one example in the Bible to back up the theory that one's timing can be wrong. There is no record of Jesus ever sending any person away who came to Him for healing because it wasn't the right time. He healed each and every person who came to Him in faith. And He is my model (John 14:12). End of story!

Any limitation lies at our end, not God's. While we should never beat ourselves up for failure, our response to healing not occurring needs to be one of going back to God and seeking more of His Spirit – which will enable us to move in greater faith and power. Then we must get right back on our horse and have another go. In any case, it is vital that we let go of all the lame explanations that we have concocted in order to excuse our lack of power – which normally have the effect of casting aspersions on God's character (i.e. His goodness).

The unfortunate thing is that when believers hold defective beliefs about God and His goodness toward humanity (as I suggested many do, at the beginning of the chapter), they don't have the confidence to use the spiritual gifts or seek help from others who do (e.g. request prayer for healing). After all, if you weren't sure that it was God's will to heal then you might be opposing His will by trying to either impart or receive healing. I have even heard people say that it is an act of presumption or arrogance to expect God to heal through prayer, because it may or may not be His will in any given instance. But is it presumptuous to expect a doctor to heal? You might equally be opposing His will by seeking healing through him or her! God might have some special spiritual "blessing" for you instead.

In practice, people who are unsure of whether it is God's will to heal will usually not go out of their way to pray for anyone for healing; and if someone does ask them for prayer, they might offer a token prayer, not expecting anything to happen. And not surprisingly, it almost never does. This then vindicates their theology that

God often doesn't want to heal. After all, if He really did want to heal someone, He could just do it sovereignly (i.e. independently of any human intermediary), without anyone praying for the person. Well yes, but God usually chooses to do it through us, rather than all by Himself. That is why He gave us gifts of healing (1 Cor. 12:9). And even when He does act sovereignly (as sometimes happens in the "Encounter Room" at the Bethel Healing Rooms), it almost always occurs in an atmosphere of faith - created by expectant believers who are convinced of God's power, goodness, and desire to bless us through all available means, including the supernatural.

Cessationism and the Theology of Suffering

Cessationism is the logical extreme of this point of view. The basic premise is that the supernatural spiritual gifts of 1 Cor. 12:4-11 ceased to exist when the last New Testament apostle died - meaning that we should not expect God to heal supernaturally anymore (cf. James 5:14-18), or operate through us in any of these other ways (e.g. prophecy, tongues, and miracles).

To be fair, many cessationists do accept that God sometimes moves sovereignly in miraculous ways (e.g. healing and exercising control over nature) and that He, on occasion, also miraculously answers prayers. Some even acknowledge that He can give a believer a temporary ability to heal (most likely in the missionary context of an unreached people group). However, these events are considered to be rare exceptions, as cessationists normally believe that the primary purpose of the supernatural gifts was to authenticate the messiahship of Jesus, and therefore the Gospel message. They argue that the miraculous is no longer needed for this purpose as we now have the Bible, which is infallible and all sufficient for faith and practice, according to the principle of Sola Scriptura.

Regardless, though, of the different cessationist views, from the absolutist position of no supernatural gifts or miracles to the more moderate one described above, all adherents of cessationism at least believe that signs and wonders will not be a normal feature of the Christian life today.

Despite believing by faith that all of the miracles in the Bible actually occurred literally, as written, they refuse to accept that the same miracles performed by Jesus, the apostles, and others can and should be happening regularly through each and every believer today – even though the scriptural evidence in favor of this is quite overwhelming (e.g. John 14:12-14; James 5:14-18; Mark 11:22-24, 16:17-18; 1 Cor. 12:4-11) and there are no direct biblical statements against the continuance of the supernatural gifts. Not to mention, the abundant historical evidence of their continuance throughout Church history – from the early Church, right up until the present day, as John Wimber has found[32]. What is more, in the last few years, the prevalence of the miraculous has exploded to levels unprecedented. There has never been a time that God has worked miraculously through as many people as frequently as He is doing today. This includes both the Old and New Testament periods, and all the great revivals of history.

One thing that is important to understand is that a major reason why Jesus performed the miraculous was because of His compassion for those suffering (Matt. 14:14, 20:29-34; Mark 1:40-42, 8:1-8; Luke 7:11-15) (demonstrating the goodness of God (Acts 10:38)). It wasn't just to establish His messiahship as John, in particular, emphasizes (John 2:11, 23, 14:11, 20:30-31).[33] In fact, Jesus, on occasion, flat out refused to prove Himself to others by performing miraculous signs on demand (Matt. 16:1-4; John 2:13-22). However, there is no record of Him ever failing to help any person in need, who approached Him from a position of faith.

Our commission today is similar: we perform the miraculous to help those in need, and in the process we end up authenticating the Gospel message (Mark 16:20; 1 Cor. 2:4-5) as well as demonstrating the goodness of God to others.

Cessationism, though, is really convenient, in that it removes all responsibility to rise to the challenge that Jesus set His followers –

that they would do the same works that He did, and even greater things than these (John 14:12). It therefore gives us an excuse to be weak, and not do anything other than wait helplessly for Him to return and rescue us from all our sufferings - many of which are the result of us not exercising the power God has given us to repulse such things.

Taking a few steps back, we see that cessationism is symptomatic of a much broader issue within certain pockets of the Church in particular. This is that a sizable number of Christians have the view that it is God's will for faithful believers to suffer here on Earth, in order to develop their character and make them more like Jesus.[34] According to this theology of suffering, they expect hardship after hardship and trial after trial, and attempt to endure these things gladly when they come - which they believe indicates faithfulness to God. Despite the New Testament only identifying persecution as a hardship that faithful believers cannot avoid (2 Tim. 3:12; cf. Phil. 1:28-30; Matt. 5:10), such people will add to the mix things like poverty and sickness, along with anything else unpleasant that could potentially happen to them in life.

The implication of this theology is that we should just be grateful that we're going to Heaven when we die and comfort ourselves with that hope, knowing that our earthly sufferings are producing an eternal reward for us. Consequently, those who subscribe to this view generally expect little good to happen to them. Furthermore, they can be extremely suspicious of those who do expect good things from God in life, such as health and success. They tend to be very quick to label any such claims as "prosperity theology".[35]

In their view, He either withholds what is good from them, allows Satan to successfully attack them, or He even afflicts them Himself. But none of this is consistent with the belief that God is good, except in the perverted sense that He makes them suffer for their own good, as a kind of divine discipline. Essentially, God is getting blamed (or in this case, the credit) for the work of the enemy to bring destruction to their lives - which is abhorrent.

The sad consequence of this is that these beliefs can actually deliver a person right into Satan's hands, to do what he loves to do: steal, kill, and destroy (John 10:10a); and then they get what they expect i.e. a lot of suffering. Usually, though, this suffering does not come in the form of persecution, as a result of witnessing for their faith (as happened to the original apostles) or righteous living, but through things like sickness, poverty, and marital breakdown.

If you think that it's God's will for you to suffer in such ways then it is also unlikely that you're going to ask Him to remove the suffering when it actually occurs. For example, if it takes the form of sickness, prayer for healing will be the furthest thing from your mind. After all, it does not make sense that God would want to heal you if it was His will to afflict you.

I choose, however, to believe that God is a good God who gives good gifts to those who ask Him (Matt. 7:11) and rewards those who seek Him (Heb. 11:6). I believe that, just like most earthly parents who want the best for their children, God wants the best for us (John 10:10b) – which includes our current life on Earth. Yes, troubles will come and He will use them for our good (Rom. 8:28), but I happen to believe that their origin is Satan, rather than God. Neither are they His perfect will for us. In fact, it is my view that God has provided the means for us to be victorious in this life over anything that Satan can throw at us.[36] And by being victorious, I am not meaning merely enduring hardships, but defeating them through their elimination. Persecution would be the only exception to this, although God often helps us in this area as well by delivering us from the worst of it (cf. Acts 5:17-19).

Some Questions that Need to be Asked

Going back to the specific case of healing, there are some questions that need to be asked of those who either believe that God only sometimes wants to heal or never does:

Are there going to be any unsaved people in Heaven? If not, is it God's will for anyone to be unsaved on Earth? (cf. 2 Peter 3:9)

Similarly, are there going to be any sick people in Heaven? If not, then why would we believe that it might be God's will for any sickness to remain on the Earth?

Jesus told His disciples to pray, "Your Kingdom come, your will be done, on earth as it is in heaven." (Matt. 6:10) Furthermore, He commanded them to go out proclaiming the coming of this Kingdom and demonstrating it by healing the sick, raising the dead, cleansing lepers, and casting out demons (Matt 10:7-8). Their commission was, and ours is today, to bring the realities of Heaven to Earth. God does not want sickness on Earth any more than He wants anyone to remain unsaved. He is a good Father who wants the very best for the world and all of humanity, whom He made in His image and dearly loves (John 3:16).

Paul's Thorn in the Flesh

One passage that's frequently cited as proof that God's will is not always to heal is 2 Cor. 12:7-10, concerning Paul's "thorn in the flesh" – which the Lord refused to remove. According to these people, the thorn was simply some chronic physical ailment that Paul had been struggling with.

The problem with this position, however, is that it is pure speculation and suffers from a distinct lack of scriptural support. Nowhere in the passage does Paul make any explicit mention of an illness. What he states in v.7 is that the thorn was "a messenger of Satan to harass me" – which indicates that it was metaphorical, just as we use the term "thorn in my side" today for someone who causes us problems.

Interestingly, the word for "messenger" (Greek: *angelos*) is almost always translated as either "angel" or "angels" by Bible translators, when it occurs elsewhere in the New Testament. Therefore, from the text, it is possible that the thorn was an evil spirit, which was causing Paul distress.

It would be unreasonable, though, to assume that Paul was indicating that he had become demonized, as there is no evidence of this in Scripture after he met Jesus. Therefore, we need to look for another, more plausible means by which the messenger of Satan might have been troubling him.

Looking to the rest of Scripture for any references to metaphorical thorns in the flesh, we come up with two direct references to "thorns in your sides" (Num. 33:55; Judges 2:3) and two other mentions of "thorns" that were afflicting the body (Josh. 23:13; Ezek. 28:24). In all four of these instances, the text indicates that the thorns represented opposition to God's people, Israel. Being an expert in the Law, Paul would probably have been alluding to these verses in order to make the point that the messenger of Satan was harassing him by stirring up opposition to his ministry.

It is quite telling that right before the section containing Paul's thorn in the flesh (2 Cor. 12:1-10), we read about his great sufferings as an apostle (2 Cor. 11:23-28). In this long list, he does not mention one sickness arising from natural causes. He does however talk about being imprisoned multiple times (v.23), countless beatings – often almost to death (v.23), being stoned (v.25), shipwrecked three times (v.25), exposed to various dangers (v.26), suffering many sleepless nights (v.27), and enduring hunger, thirst, cold, and nakedness[37] (v.27).

Immediately after this, he says:

> Who is weak, and I am not weak? Who is made to fall, and I am not indignant? If I must boast, I will boast of the things that show my weakness. (2 Cor. 11:29-30)

Furthermore, right after the mention of the thorn in the flesh, he declares:

> Three times I pleaded with the Lord about this, that it should leave me. But he said to me, "My grace is sufficient for you, for my power is made perfect in weakness." Therefore I will boast all the more gladly of my weaknesses, so that the power of Christ may rest upon me. For the sake of Christ, then, I am content with weaknesses, insults, hardships, persecutions, and calamities. For when I am weak, then I am strong. (2 Cor. 12:8-10)

The link between these two passages is unmistakable. Both tie his weaknesses to persecutions and hardships etc., but not any natural sickness. It turns out that Paul's list of sufferings and the discussion of his thorn in the flesh form part of a larger section (2 Cor. 11:1-12:13). In this, he argues his standing as a true apostle against that of some false apostles who were apparently leading the Corinthians believers astray. It is quite unfortunate, therefore, that chapter 12 has been assigned to start where it does, basically in the middle of a section of highly related material. This causes people to lose sight of the big picture and assume that Paul is talking about different subject matter either side of the chapter division.

Since the sufferings described in 2 Cor. 11:23-28 are summarized in 2 Cor. 12:10 as Paul's weakness, we must conclude that the thorn in the flesh is not sickness but Satanic opposition to his ministry, in the form of persecutions and hardships. Therefore, this metaphorical thorn cannot be used as justification for the argument that God's will is not always to heal.

Job and Jesus

Another major portion of Scripture used to argue against the position that it is always God's will to heal, is the Book of Job. In this, God allowed Satan to afflict a faithful believer (Job) in order for his faith to be tested (Job 1:6-2:8). As a result, Job suffered the loss of property, all his children died, and nasty sores broke out over his entire body.

However, when people point to the example of Job in the Old Testament, Bill Johnson directs them instead to the one of Jesus in the New Testament: "Job was the question, and Jesus is the answer."[38]

God revealed His true loving intentions toward humanity through the life of Jesus, whom He sent to rescue us from all the oppression of the devil (Acts 10:38). Jesus came with a mandate from God to bring healing, deliverance, and freedom to everyone experiencing any kind of suffering or bondage[39] (Luke 4:18-19). Furthermore, He commissioned His disciples, and all future believers, to continue this assignment. And to enable them to be successful in this, He endowed them with the same supernatural gifts and abilities that He had, which would allow them to perform miracles of healing and deliverance etc. Therefore, it is completely erroneous to suggest that it is God's will to either inflict suffering on people or withhold healing.

In view of all this, it is clear to see that the tribulations of Job do not reveal the character of God, but instead what Satan is really like – how depraved he is, and the great lengths that he will go to in order to inflict suffering on humanity.

But then, why does God allow Satan to afflict people in the first place? After all, in Job's case, He could have just refused the devil's requests to afflict him.

Yes, in a perfect world God would have prevented all of Job's sufferings. However, Job didn't live in a perfect world (and neither do we today); the shadow of the Fall hung over it (and still does today). When Adam and Eve disobeyed God, by eating from the tree of the knowledge of good and evil, they partnered with Satan against God, and this gave the devil certain legal rights over humanity – including the power of death (Heb. 2:14; cf. Gen 2:17, 3:19) and the ability to inflict different kinds of suffering on them (but with certain limits). In other words, God's hands became tied, making Him unable to prevent all evil in the world.

My strong suspicion, therefore, is that when Satan made those requests to harm Job, it was in the context of a court hearing, in which God was the judge and Satan the prosecutor (cf. Rev. 12:10). Satan was merely making legal demands to the judge, who was obliged by law to grant them – even though He was clearly reluctant to do so (Job 1:12, 2:6).

However, we should not lose sight of Job's eventual fate – that he was apparently healed and received twice as much as he had before (Job 42:10, 12-17). That is how good God actually is! His will is always to bless rather than curse and afflict, and this prevailed in the end – even though Job most likely lived before the time of any divine covenant containing healing (which would mitigate the effects of the Fall).[40]

There is certainly no indication in this story that God's intention was ever for Job to suffer in any way, such as for the purposes of spiritual and/or character development – as people today try to apply it. Therefore, this book of Scripture cannot legitimately be used to support the argument that God's will is not always to heal. Even more so, when viewed from the perspective of the New Covenant enacted on the blood of Jesus – who came to set us free (Gal. 5:1) by destroying the works of the devil (1 John 3:8; cf. Acts 10:38), and give us abundant life (John 10:10b). The devil (Satan) is the thief who comes only to steal, kill, and destroy (John 10:10a). The implications of this are that we need to stop attributing Satan's destructiveness to God and His will. God only wants the best for us, as any good Father does.

Why Does God Send Anyone to Hell?

One question that people (non-believers especially) sometimes come up with, in relation to the goodness of God, is that if God is actually so good then why does He send anyone to Hell?

The answer to this is that He has done everything in His power to prevent people from going to Hell, and can do no more. He gave His one and only Son, Jesus, to be brutally tortured and murdered for the sake of each and every one of us, so that we wouldn't have to endure the punishment due for our rebellion against Him (i.e. ultimately eternal death in Hell). God is a holy and righteous judge, and in our natural states we are all sinners, in need of mercy and grace in order to come into His presence. It is impossible for Him to allow anyone into Heaven who is not as perfectly holy and righteous as He is. But this sacrifice of Jesus allowed His righteous judgment against sin to be satisfied, without having to send any person to Hell.

It therefore grieves Him so much that many are not taking up His free gift of salvation, by rejecting Jesus, and thereby dooming themselves to an eternity without Him, in the lake of fire. But He gives every person a free choice whether to come to Him and accept His gift of salvation, or not. And as people who have chosen to accept this amazing offer, by repenting of our sins and following Jesus, it is our responsibility to in turn communicate it to others, so that they too can be saved.

Supernatural Gifts and Evangelism

It is in this commission to communicate the Gospel salvation message that we discover one of the key reasons why God has given us the supernatural gifts: they enable us to communicate this message in the most effective way. The Gospel was never meant to be conveyed only through words; demonstrations of miraculous power are also required (1 Cor. 2:4-5; cf. 4:20) – ones that bless people (e.g. heal their bodies).

Jesus commissioned His followers to proclaim the Gospel to every person, accompanied by miraculous signs (Mark 16:15-18). This was the pattern from the beginning, as seen in the Book of Acts. The apostles preached the word, and God authenticated their message with signs and wonders (Acts 4:29-30). These signs and wonders authenticate the message by revealing the God who is behind it – both His power and goodness (love).

Occasionally, however, I hear people raise the following type of objection: "Why do you run around all the time trying to do miracles? It is about getting people saved, not performing party tricks for them."

Well, I mostly agree with this sentiment. Leading people into relationship with God is extremely important for us as believers. The thing is, though, that the supernatural gifts (especially those of 1 Cor. 12:4-10) are often the only way to reach a lost and dying world that is sick to death of religion. How hard is it to get people to come to God by just telling them that they are sinners who need to repent and be saved? Most adults in the Western world have probably heard this a number of times before and don't need to be reminded of it.

One thing that Bill Johnson likes to emphasize is that the goodness of God leads people to repentance (Rom. 2:4, NKJV). And how does God show His goodness to those who don't know Him? Well, it is usually through us. While acts of mercy and kindness, such as helping the poor and needy, are important in this regard, many of the other major religions also have people who do these things. This, therefore, is ultimately not something that will distinguish us and our message from others and what they have to offer. However, nothing can compare to the power of God as a means of demonstrating His reality and goodness to those who don't know Him. An encounter with the Living God can melt the heart of the most hardened atheist and sinner.

I saw a great example of this a few years ago. After the end of my second year at BSSM, the night before I was going to move out of my apartment, I found one of my neighbors in a state of distress. Mike, which I will call him for the purposes of confidentiality, was a man in his 50s, who lived with his mother, a woman in her 80s, who was suffering from age-related memory issues. Due to these memory issues, his mother could not go out alone - even for a short walk - otherwise she would quickly get lost and eventually have to be rescued by someone. However, she refused to go into full-time care and wanted to continue living at home. Unfortunately, in this living situation the two of them argued a lot, and he found it very difficult to know what to do. He wanted his mother to be happy, but living with her was seriously affecting his mental health.

On the night in question, Mike had been drinking heavily and was sitting on the steps outside. When I, and one of my other neighbors from the same apartment block (who had just completed BSSM First Year), saw him in that distressed state, we offered to pray for him. But he told us that he didn't believe in God and thought that Bethel people were "weird". I didn't let that offend me and responded by saying that this was fine and that I would just like to bless him – which he agreed to. He allowed my neighbor and I to place our hands on his body and pray for him. This resulted in him having a dramatic encounter with God (and His love), and then, even more dramatically shouting out, "So THIS is what it's all about!!!" A little later, he spontaneously fell to his knees on the lawn in front of the apartment block, and we eventually led him in a prayer of salvation – after he had talked about his encounters with aliens!

At this point, I knew that we needed to give Mike a Bible, to get him started on reading Scripture; but neither my neighbor or I had one to spare. However, I remembered that I'd been given a Gospel of John booklet at the massive *Azusa Now* event that I had recently participated in with BSSM, at the LA Coliseum. So, I went back to my room, found it, and gave it to him.

Being full of the love of God, Mike then had a revelation of love for his mother and wanted her to feel what he was experiencing. He insisted that she receive prayer from us as well, which she agreed to. When we prayed for her, she too had an encounter with God (but not as dramatic as his) and we also led her to the Lord. After this, there was a lot of reconciliation between mother and son. On a later occasion, when I followed up with Mike, he told me that she often read that little Gospel of John booklet that we had given to them.

This story is a great example of how the goodness of God, manifested through His power and tangible love, can lead people to receiving Jesus through our ministry. If we had just preached at Mike, tried to get him to come along to church, or suggested that he get counseling, then most likely nothing would have happened other than him getting angry (in the state that he was in he might have even taken a swing at one of us - probably me, as I was doing most of the talking!). People need an encounter with God to come to a place of repentance - which he did, despite his lack of belief in God.

Prophecy

Prophecy, which we haven't looked at in any detail so far, is another very effective method through which we can demonstrate God's goodness to others. At Bethel, all BSSM students are trained to be able to give encouraging prophetic words (according to 1 Cor. 14:3) to people on demand. Sometimes when students serve at Bethel conferences and events, the speaker on stage will tell members of the audience to find a BSSM student and ask them for a prophetic word. Likewise, many students offer prophetic words to people on the streets while evangelizing or in ordinary everyday life, such as to a cashier at the grocery store. More often that not, those receiving prophetic words outside of the church are non-Christians, who have little or no knowledge of the things of God. Nevertheless, God still very much wants to bless and encourage them in their lives.

However, before going to Bethel I always believed that there was little point in prophesying to those who don't know Him, as I supposed that the only thing He would want to tell them is that they are sinners who need to repent and follow Jesus. But how wrong I was! God wants to celebrate people for who they are and demonstrate His great love for them, through encouraging prophetic words - about how He sees them and the good things that He has for them in life. Often, non-Christians are already operating in the gifts and talents that He has placed on their lives. Therefore, if they were to get saved right now, He would in many cases still want them to continue with what they're doing. (cf. 1 Cor. 7:17-24).

One reason that the prophetic is so powerful is that, unlike healing, it doesn't require a context (e.g. a sickness to pray for). You can offer a prophetic word to anyone, anytime, and as long as you don't come across as too weird they will often receive it gladly. People today are fascinated by the supernatural, as evidenced by the many movies and television series on this theme that have been made in recent years. Fortunetelling, in particular, is something that has grown greatly in popularity. Unfortunately, Christians have been slow to pick up on these trends and have continued doing what they've always done, largely oblivious to what is going on around them. Furthermore, they haven't realized what they hold in their hands (e.g. the revelatory gifts such as prophecy and the word of knowledge), which is far greater than all the counterfeits of the world.

The prophetic, therefore, opens up enormous possibilities to minister the love of God to many people, from all walks of life - without "evangelizing". It can be a powerful way to connect with any type of person, right from the homeless to those who own multiple homes. For when someone hears information about their past, present, and future from another person who couldn't possibly know these things, it will often blow them away and open them up to receiving more of God. All we need to do is go in with the right mindset, which is having a heart to love, serve, and encourage others - with no strings attached. This requires us to let go of any aggressive agenda that we might have to convert them on the spot.[41] After all, we are often just sowing seeds in people's lives that others will eventually harvest the fruit of.

God desires all His people, both great and small, to be "prophetic people" in their circles of influence. When we use our gifts to serve people in this way, they can't help but realize that there is a God who loves them. We don't need to go around Bible bashing anyone, or waving "Turn or Burn" signs. God wants those who don't know Him to "taste and see that the Lord is good" (Psalm 34:8) through our supernatural ministry - which gives Him the chance to reveal Himself to them.

As the subtitle of Bill Johnson's book, *God is Good*, reads: "He's better than you think!" The Father is so incredibly loving, merciful, and gracious. Just like the father of the prodigal son in one of Jesus' parables (Luke 15:11-32), He is eagerly waiting for His lost sons and daughters to come back home, and ready to shower blessings on them at the first sign of their return. Unlike the parable, though, He sends out search parties to find those who are lost (cf. Luke 15:4) and even bless them before they actually show any desire to return.

Equally, He seeks to bless those who have been faithful to Him over many years (cf. Heb. 11:6). But like the older brother in the parable of the prodigal son (mentioned above), everything is available to us now and yet many of us haven't taken advantage of most of what is on offer (Luke 15:29-31). When we believe that God is always in a good mood and wanting to bless us, we are able to access all of His provision for every area of our lives. Just as He has wonderful things waiting for us in Heaven, He has great things available to us on Earth – which we can access by bringing Heaven to Earth, through our faith in Him. Remember, faith is the currency of Heaven!

2. FOCUSED ON HIS PRESENCE

The second secret of Bethel's signs and wonders culture to seeing the power of God move so strongly, in the life of both the church and the individual, is to be focused on His presence. This is another one of their 13 core values.

The presence of God is a special manifestation of the Divine that we normally associate with the Holy Spirit. It is over and above what is meant by saying that God is omnipresent.

Personally, I find it difficult to recall being in any place where the presence has been as highly valued and sought after as it is at Bethel – other than a Benny Hinn meeting. It is therefore no surprise that these two ministries are known around the world for outpourings of the miraculous – which is what happens in the presence of God.

The presence comes when we seek God with all of our heart, and value Him above everything else. This requires us to be in a place of hunger for more of Him. But if you are not hungry for more of His presence then it will be difficult to move in more of His power, because that is its source.

The presence can come upon a person or object (e.g. a prayer cloth), and reside in certain geographical locations, such as church auditoriums and prayer rooms. It includes, but is not limited to, the normal indwelling of the Holy Spirit inside every true believer (Rom.

8:9). This reflects the fact that while every believer has the Holy Spirit, not all of them are filled with the Spirit (cf. Eph. 5:18).

But even those filled with the Spirit can still experience the Spirit moving upon them in a special way, normally for a particular purpose. An example of this would be "the anointing", which comes upon Benny Hinn during his meetings. In this state, people become overwhelmed by the presence of God when he touches them – to the point where they often shake violently and/or fall over. And this also illustrates another principle, that the presence can be transferred from one person to another.

When we are in God's presence or His presence is on us in a special way, we are actually encountering the Living God. Through such an encounter, He reveals His love to us, and at the same time He often brings healing, transformation, and empowerment.

At Bethel Church, extremely high value is placed on people having personal encounters with God, although absolutely no pressure is put on anyone to do so. Nor is there any expectation that such encounters will be dramatic; often they aren't. For example, people frequently experience special senses of peace and joy while at Bethel services. These are just as valid as someone being "slain in the Spirit" or having an open vision of Jesus.

Once we have given our lives to Jesus, it is important that we place high priority on seeking God's presence. This should not just be for the purpose of getting stuff from Him, such as greater power to perform signs and wonders. If that is the only reason we seek after God's presence then we will miss the primary purpose of our existence – which is to love God and be in intimate relationship with Him. After all, when we die and go to Heaven, the supernatural gifts of the Spirit on us will cease to operate, since they will no longer be necessary (1 Cor. 13:8-12). Therefore, we will be spending a lot of time enjoying God's presence!

Nevertheless, we cannot be in the presence of God without being incredibly blessed, especially through being changed to become more like Him. At the Fall, when Adam and Eve disobeyed God by eating from the tree of the knowledge of good and evil, the image of God in humanity was tarnished by sin, although it still exists to some degree in every human being – whether they know God or not (Gen. 9:6; cf. James 3:9). However, the image of God becomes more and more restored in us when we spend time in His presence. Like Moses, we shine when we have been with Him (Exod. 34:29-35; 2 Cor. 3:7-18), and our character becomes more like His. Furthermore, His power becomes our power, enabling us to perform signs and wonders in His name. And His wisdom, knowledge, and insight become available to us in the form of revelation.

To be clear, I am not suggesting that we will ever become gods or the equal of God. We can only operate in His power, wisdom, knowledge, and insight etc. through dependence on Him (John 15:5), because it does not originate from us – which is why faith is necessary.

In addition to this process of being changed and empowered, God's presence brings the immediate benefits of peace, joy, and freedom to our lives, because these things are part of His nature and are contained within His presence.

John 14:27:

> Peace I leave with you; my peace I give to you. Not as the world gives do I give to you. Let not your hearts be troubled, neither let them be afraid.

Psalm 16:11b:

> ... in your presence there is fullness of joy;

Rom. 14:17:

> For the kingdom of God is not a matter of eating and drinking but of righteousness and peace and joy in the Holy Spirit.

Rom. 15:13:

> May the God of hope fill you with all joy and peace in believing, so that by the power of the Holy Spirit you may abound in hope.

2 Cor. 3:17:

> Now the Lord is the Spirit, and where the Spirit of the Lord is, there is freedom.

Peace is the antithesis of fear. Joy is the antithesis of depression. And freedom is the antithesis of oppression and bondage. The presence of God therefore protects us against some of the major ways that Satan tries to attack us. This, of course, does not mean that we will never have problems and issues arise in our lives. It is just that the peace, joy, and freedom of God (which are not dependent on circumstance) allow us to navigate through these things, without partnering with the enemy e.g. by fearing (cf. Phil. 1:28). Bill Johnson puts it beautifully when he says: "Like Jesus, we have authority over any storm we can sleep in."[42]

Whenever we are not full of the peace, joy, and freedom of God, this is a very strong sign that we are not full of the Spirit and are in need of refilling[43]. There is no reason to be ashamed of this, as it can happen to the best of us at certain times. It is important, though, that we take heed of these signs and respond by seeking after His presence in an intentional way, to become filled again.

Unfortunately, a lack of the peace, joy, and freedom of God is the normal experience of a lot of Christians who feel dry and walk around with blank, beaten up expressions on their faces, constantly troubled by what the devil is doing to them. This comes from frequently partnering with the fear and oppression that the enemy tries to put on us – through believing his lies, not facing our fears in life, and not being in God's presence enough. Contrast this with other Christians, such as many of the people that I met at Bethel who glow with the presence of God. It is not that these people have it easy in life. They deal with the same sort of stuff that everyone else does, but don't allow it to rob them of the peace, joy, and freedom that God gives them.

It is Our Responsibility to Seek His Presence

It is our responsibility to seek His presence, rather than wait for it to come to us (Luke 11:9-13; James 4:8a; cf. Jer. 29:12-14). Many people suppose that if God is interested in coming to them (and their church) in a powerful way then He will, because He is God and does whatever pleases Him (Psalm 115:3, 135:6). Such people might also cite the example of Saul of Tarsus being encountered by Jesus Christ on the road to Damascus (Acts 9:1-6) as evidence of their position. But in that case, God was just taking the initiative to invite Saul into seeking Him (as He does with all of us in some way, whether dramatically or otherwise (John 6:44)). Saul still had to accept this invitation and then begin pursuing Him passionately, to build a relationship with the Lord - which would lead to him becoming the world changer that he was called to be.

Similarly, we need to continue seeking God's presence if we want a closer relationship with God and be powerfully used by Him. I once heard a preacher say something to the effect of, "We are always as close to God as we choose to be", and I think there's a lot of truth in this statement. It is not about earning His love, but passionately pursing the One who loves us and has given everything for us. Being focused on His presence and seeking Him therefore leads to powerful encounters with God, which change us for good and empower us to turn the world upside down for Him (cf. Acts 17:6). As Bill Johnson explains:

> This present move of God is all about retraining us to lock into His manifest presence and live for nothing else.[44]

How to Seek God's Presence

Seeking God's presence is not an especially difficult task, although we have to be very intentional and disciplined about doing so – which most are not. The important thing is giving God quality time in which our attention is devoted to Him and Him only. This involves turning off our smart phones and eliminating any other avoidable distractions!

Some of the key ways to seek God's presence are praise and worship, thanksgiving, and prayer (all both corporate and individual). Each of these is emphasized strongly at Bethel. Other possibilities include, meditating on the Scriptures (especially verses specific to the Holy Spirit and encountering God), journaling with God, speaking in our heavenly languages (tongues), prayer and fasting, receiving impartation from people full of the Spirit (through the laying on of hands), and attending the services/conferences of churches known to experience God's presence in great measure. You can probably also think of others in addition to these.

On the topic of worship, Bethel, as you may be aware, is now known all around the world not only for its signs and wonders ministry, but also for its music. Thousands of churches use its songs as part of their corporate praise and worship times. I believe that an important reason why Bethel Music has been this popular is that the music is birthed from the presence of God, through great lovers and worshippers of God connecting with Him. The words are inspired by the Holy Spirit and there is therefore a special anointing on them, to draw people into the very throne room of God. Heaven comes when people sing these songs in spirit and in truth (or even just listen to them!). They represent prophetic declarations that announce the Kingdom of God, as both present and coming in greater measure. They call believers to their destiny of intimate fellowship with God, and extending His Kingdom – through the power of His presence. I can therefore highly recommend Bethel Music as an aid to facilitating more of the presence of God in one's life.

Stewarding the Presence

Despite the importance, though, of these intentional times that we seek after God and His presence, we also need to learn to steward the presence of God so that we can host Him continually. It is not enough to only seek Him during certain times of the day and week, and then forget about Him the rest of the time. To the degree we that do this, we will leak His presence and need to be filled again at some point. And if we don't get refilled, we will begin to become very dry as we are exposed to things that drain us spiritually. This includes anything that causes us to experience negative emotions such as fear, worry, anxiety, depression, overwhelm, frustration, stress, loneliness, anger, sadness, grief, and self-pity etc. When we steward these emotions rather than the presence of God, we are unwittingly aligning ourselves with the kingdom of darkness, instead of God's Kingdom. The result is that it will be hard to trust God, and we might instead be drawn into relying on our own strength. But even worse, we could become enslaved to harmful and/or sinful addictions (e.g. pornography, drugs, alcohol, and food etc.), in an attempt to numb the pain.

When we are able to steward God's presence well, it becomes very easy to abound in all the fruit of the Spirit (Gal. 5:22-23) and avoid sin. Two of these fruits, peace and joy, are automatic since they come directly through the presence, as we discussed above. And where the presence of God is, the powers of darkness are forced to flee. They are unable to stay in such an atmosphere for very long, since it is completely against their nature and causes them torment (cf. Mark 5:7-8). Therefore, the presence of God is a spiritual weapon that has the potential to change atmospheres when it is stewarded well. The obvious example of this is at church services like Bethel's, where there are invariably atmospheres of peace, joy, and freedom. But also as individuals, when we steward God's presence well, we have the power to change atmospheres wherever we go – sometimes without even having to do anything.

It is, of course, imperative that we do change atmospheres for God, otherwise atmospheres will change us by draining the presence of God from our lives (which prevents others from experiencing it through us). For there is no neutral territory; any place occupied by people comes under the influence of either God's Kingdom or the kingdom of darkness, to varying degrees – depending on which one people are partnering with and how effectively they are doing so.

Make no mistake, though, this is not a titanic struggle between two equal forces. The presence of God that we are able to bring completely dominates any oppressive atmosphere that the kingdom of darkness causes. It is really just a question of whether we will enter enemy territory, and if we do, whether we will bring the presence. We therefore have the great responsibility and privilege to wage war on behalf of God – to win enemy territory for Him and to bring even greater degrees of His presence to territory that is already His. I am preaching to myself here as much as everyone else, as I'm slowly learning how I can become a positive influence on any environment, by how I position myself in relation to God.

To illustrate how this can work in practice, I would like to reference one of Bill Johnson's stories. In his book *When Heaven Invades Earth*, Bill describes how he used to frequent a local health food store that was a bit New Agey. This was part of a commitment he had made to bring the light of God to the darkest places in town. He would pray before entering the store for the anointing of God to be on him and move through him. And when inside the store, he would pray quietly in the Spirit. Then one day, the owner told him, "Something is different when you come into the store." This opened up many future ministry opportunities for Bill.[45]

An even more dramatic example of changing atmospheres occurred in 2005, when Bethel revivalist Chad Dedmon was ministering to people affected by Hurricane Katrina, in the Houston Astrodome. A "portal of God's presence", as he called it, formed in the area where he and his friends were ministering. When people entered it, they were touched by God, and some of them were healed.[46]

At Bethel, this idea is implemented in very intentional ways. For instance, in the Bethel Healing Rooms, there is an "Encounter Room" in which a worship band plays continuously, "prophetic dancers" dance on stage, and "prophetic painters" paint pictures inspired by God. People wait here before they are called to receive prayer for healing. In this room, an atmosphere thick with the presence of God is created for people to soak in, preparing them to receive their healing. In fact, some people reportedly receive their healing here, without any prayer - which is the ideal scenario. However, if this doesn't happen, healing prayer is available in the next room - where the principle of changing spiritual atmospheres continues to be applied. Before anyone arrives for prayer, prayer servants often spend a significant amount of time praying for each other and getting re-filled with the Spirit. This enables them to create an atmosphere conducive to healing, and to impart that atmosphere directly to the people they pray for.

One thing that Bethel as a movement has discovered, is that the release of peace is a modality through which people can be healed - especially of emotional conditions like anxiety and depression. When I served in the Healing Rooms, we frequently released peace over people, and more often than not they felt a lot better emotionally (and sometimes even physically), as a result. Of course, we still did a lot of the traditional laying on of hands and commanding conditions to be healed in the name of Jesus - which also utilizes the power of the presence.

The presence of God has just so many applications to our lives. In His presence there is no challenge too big for us; He has the answer to every question that we could ever ask and the solution to every problem we will ever face. The more we know Him and abide in His presence, the greater the access we have to His wisdom, revelation, and power to overcome life's obstacles. There can be no legitimate reason to leave the perfect peace, joy, and freedom that He offers. Therefore, any time that we find ourselves moving away from this state, it must be the case that we're believing some particular lie or lies about our situation. What could they be? Identifying these lies and attacking them with truth will be key to moving back into the peace, joy, and freedom of His presence, and living a victorious life.

For instance, if we become worried about how we're going to pay the rent for the following month, we are probably believing the lie that God is either not willing or not able to provide for us. To attack this lie with truth, we could declare Phil. 4:19, personalizing it to ourselves (i.e. change the "yours" to "mine"):

> ... my God will supply every need of mine according to his riches in glory in Christ Jesus.

Following this, we need to ask God how He intends to provide for us in this area[47] – in a renewed state of peace, joy, and freedom. For God is practical, and understands all of our needs and concerns. However, if we partner with the lies of the enemy (i.e. accept them as truth) and even begin to accuse God of not providing for us then we start to cut off our ability to receive provision from Him. In other words, His divine solutions become much more difficult to access, meaning that we will more than likely be left to our own devices to find the money we need. God can, after all, only move in response to faith – not fear (which is actually faith in the devil's ability to harm us).

How to Steward the Presence of God

Now, I would like to discuss how we can steward the presence of God effectively, so that we remain full of the Spirit, abound in both the fruit and gifts of the Spirit, and are able to use the presence as a spiritual weapon to change atmospheres. I have created a list below, which offers some important pointers on this:

1. Seek Him regularly

It should be no surprise that if we want to steward the presence of God well then we need to seek Him regularly, through activities like praise and worship, thanksgiving, and prayer. The more quality time that we spend with God, the more His presence will fill us and remain on our lives. Bill Johnson suggests that the more of Him we experience, the hungrier we get for more.[48] The lesson, therefore, is to start where we're at and build on this, as our desire for more grows.

2. Practice the presence of God

Obviously, though, few of us are able to devote all of our waking hours to seeking after God. We have various responsibilities to fulfill, such as in the areas of work, family, and household chores. But during these times that we are not actively praying or worshiping etc., we can still maintain an awareness of His presence and enjoy communion with Him, by being intentional about it.

Brother Lawrence, a 17th century French monk, called this "the practice of the presence of God". The idea was of having our focus always on Him – loving Him and delighting in His presence. This is probably what Paul was writing about when he instructed believers to pray without ceasing (1 Thess. 5:17).

In a modern context, an example of this would be that we keep singing our favorite worship song over and over again under our breath. We might also have a continual dialogue with Him in our head, as we go about our daily activities.

3. Make Him and His Kingdom our main focus

When we make God and building His Kingdom the main focus of our lives, we attract His attention and presence. This happens when His heart becomes our heart and His priorities become ours. It is just the same as how in the natural, we tend to make friends with those who like us, have similar interests to us, and with whom our beliefs are aligned.

4. Not grieving or quenching the Holy Spirit

Bill Johnson argues in his book *Hosting the Presence* that an important part of stewarding the presence of God is not either grieving

(Eph. 4:30) or quenching the Holy Spirit (1 Thess. 5:19).[49] We grieve Him when we sin – in thought, attitude, or action. This includes partnering with the devil's lies and stewarding the emotions that result from doing so – particularly fear. As Bethel senior associate leader Kris Vallotton says, "Fear is the most socially accepted sin in the Church."[50]

We quench the Holy Spirit when we stop Him flowing in our lives (and those of others), such as by losing passion for God. Another example would be not following His direct leadings, such as failing to pray for someone He has asked us to pray for – preventing Him from moving in their life at that moment. Being obedient to the revealed will of God is therefore a very important part of stewarding His presence.

5. Take every thought captive and make it obedient to Him

This follows on from not grieving the Holy Spirit (mentioned directly above). We need to take every thought captive and make it obedient to Christ, as Paul discussed in 2 Cor. 10:5. We cannot allow ourselves to steward any thoughts opposed to God and His ideas.

Kris Vallotton explains in his book, *Spirit Wars*, that not every thought in our mind is our own.[51] The enemy implants thoughts there and tries to convince us that they are ours. Most people, of course, readily accept such thoughts and dwell on them – which he then uses as a basis to accuse and torment them.

These thoughts are sometimes lies about ourselves (e.g. we're not good enough; we're unlovable), lies about God (e.g. He doesn't answer prayer; He puts sickness on us for our spiritual growth; He doesn't care about us, otherwise xyz wouldn't have happened), sinful thoughts and ideas (e.g. lustful, hateful, and prideful ones), and thoughts that lead to fear, hopelessness, and depression etc.

What we need to do is reject such thoughts and refuse to dwell on them. But if they are strong and persistent, we might need to challenge them with truth (especially that derived from Scripture) and command them to leave in Jesus' name. Furthermore, we may need to first repent of entertaining these thoughts, to give ourselves a legal basis to get rid of any demonic strongholds in our mind that might be causing them.

In my first year at BSSM, when I read *Spirit Wars* (which was part of the assigned reading material), I had been having some persistent sinful thoughts, which I just could not get out of my mind, no matter how hard I tried. I believed that these were my thoughts, and that I had a problem that needed addressing. Well, I did have a problem, but it wasn't what I thought it was. In the book, I read about a woman called Martha, who had been plagued with suicidal thoughts. Kris ministered to this lady by leading her in a prayer of deliverance, which resulted in her instant and complete freedom.[52] So I had an idea: if I modified the prayer to fit my situation then I too could get free of the thoughts that were harassing me. And when I did this, I got exactly the same result as Martha – instant and complete freedom! Obviously, the devil had tricked me too into accepting his thoughts as mine.

I will repeat the prayer here that Kris led Martha in:

> Jesus, forgive me for making a covenant with the devil by inviting <u>death</u> to comfort me. Thank You that You gave me the Holy Spirit, who is my comforter and my friend.
>
> You spirit of <u>suicide</u>, I break my agreement with you. I no longer want you in my life. I command you to leave in Jesus' name![53] (emphasis mine)

If you want to fit this prayer to your situation, all you have to do is modify the two underlined parts, making them relevant to what you're going through. For example, if you were struggling with lustful thoughts, you might change "death" to "lustful thoughts" and "suicide" to "lust".

Finally, to prevent these thoughts from coming into your mind in the first place, it is helpful to follow the advice of Paul:

> ... whatever is true, whatever is honorable, whatever is just, whatever is pure, whatever is lovely, whatever is commendable, if there is any excellence, if there is anything worthy of praise, think about these things. (Phil. 4:8)

Hosting God's Presence Brings Heaven to Earth

It is important to realize that when we steward God's presence well, such that we host Him on a continual basis, Heaven literally comes to Earth, since we are the house of God and gate of Heaven of Gen. 28:10-19 (1 Cor. 3:16, 6:19). Doing so therefore allows people to experience Heaven through our ministry, and by just being around us. This is why we need to be full of the Spirit of God to minister effectively to people. It is no use merely having head knowledge and preaching out of worldly wisdom (1 Cor. 2:4-5) – which most of the Church continues to do. The majority of non-believers in the Western world are not interested in this kind of Christianity, which is largely devoid of power. Our job as Spirit-filled believers is to show the world the real Jesus Christ and Christianity – full of life and power in the Spirit. As Bill Johnson declares:

> We owe the world an encounter with God.

Further to this, he says that a gospel without power is no gospel at all; it is not the one that Jesus preached.

If we are truly serious about reaching those who don't know God then there is no option other than becoming filled with the Spirit, staying filled (by being focused on His presence), and ministering a Gospel of power – through great signs and wonders. But this is not just a nice sounding theory that doesn't really work in practice. Neither is it only for a few special people like Bill Johnson and Benny Hinn. It works well, and is for everyone who desires it. Personally, I know of many, many "ordinary" believers who minister in this sort of power, especially outside of the four walls of the church. Some of them regularly lead people to Jesus through their supernatural ministry. Every single one of us needs to do whatever it takes to move in this sort of power – if not for ourselves, for others who don't yet know God, and probably never will without a supernatural encounter with Him.

I will leave you with a challenge from Bill Johnson:

> Hosting God is filled with honor and pleasure, cost and mystery. He is subtle, and even sometimes silent. He can also be extremely obvious, aggressive, and overtly purposeful. He is a guest with an agenda — Father to Son. Heaven to earth. It is still His world — His purposes will be accomplished. This leaves us with a question that has yet to be answered: What generation will host Him until the kingdom of this world becomes the Kingdom of our Lord and Christ?[54]

3. PARTNERING WITH GOD

The third secret as to why the power of God moves so strongly at Bethel, and through its people wherever they go, is its partnering with God – to a degree that many would doubt is even possible.

Partnering with God is about being led and inspired by the Holy Spirit. It involves agreeing with what God is saying and doing at any given moment, and bringing oneself into alignment with these things. This partnership is necessary for seeing a consistent flow of signs and wonders in one's life and ministry.

Partnering with God is relevant at both the individual and corporate levels. It is for every individual believer and group of believers, in all areas of life. We should never limit it to just those in full-time ministry, and to religious/spiritual contexts. Partnering with God is just as applicable to a business or family, as it is to a church. He wants to work with us wherever we are and in whatever we're doing – to benefit us and help others, both of which end up extending His Kingdom on Earth.

When we partner with God, we typically see supernatural results in what we do; and, at the very least, things generally work out much better than what they would have otherwise. This is because He has access to all wisdom, knowledge, power, and foresight – much of which He is willing to share with us if we will just ask Him. All that

He requires from us is our ears to hear what He wants us to do and our hands to actually do it. He even helps us with the doing. In truth, most of the time all we do is just go along for the ride. What could be simpler?

However, when we fail to partner with God, through not taking the time to listen to Him, or hearing, but not doing what He says to do, results will generally not be as impressive. This is because what we can do on our own is usually far less than what He can achieve - either with or without us.

What we need to understand is that God is willing, ready, and waiting to provide the blueprints for many great ideas and strategies that can literally change the world. Therefore, we might as well take advantage of this special access that we have to the Creator of the universe. There is absolutely no shame in getting help from on high.

This is what happens at Bethel. Everything is birthed in the encounter with God and is inspired by the Holy Spirit. People are trained to "download" ideas and strategies from Heaven, rather than just come up with their own initiatives. The result is supernatural success, increase, and favor in areas as diverse as healing and business, family and government, evangelism and the arts. It is difficult to think of any area of life that Bethel people are not impacting supernaturally through the power of God.

Two Common Mistakes

There are actually two common mistakes that Christians and churches make, which lead to them failing to partner with God, and therefore not reaping the benefits of divine partnership:

Trying to Do It All Ourselves

Firstly, many of us make the mistake of trying to do it all ourselves, based on our own natural strengths and good ideas. God is pretty much left out of the equation, other than our prayers for Him to bless what we're doing and our desperate cries for help when things go wrong. This leaves little room for the miraculous to take place.

In ministry, this applies particularly when a church is run predominantly according to natural-level giftings, especially in a program-heavy and tightly controlled way. Everything depends on their skills and abilities rather than His. The man with the most advanced theological degree becomes the senior pastor and does the majority of the teaching. The best musicians form the worship team. A woman who is great with kids runs the children's program. The admin is carried out by people who are highly organized and skilled at completing tasks. The finances are controlled by accountants and business people, according to standard business principles.

There is, of course, nothing necessarily wrong with recruiting those most qualified for the various roles. But an issue arises when these people depend solely on their natural skills and abilities, rather than on God and what He can do through them – which is much more than the most gifted people can do on their own.

It is important to point out, though, that God frequently chooses those least qualified for particular roles, as He did in the Bible with Gideon, David, and the disciples of Jesus. Furthermore, He often uses people in the areas that they consider themselves to be the weakest in. For example, Kris Vallotton was very poor at writing and God turned him into a bestselling author. In this way, God is able to display His incredible power to the world, and therefore reveal Himself more than when talented people work in their areas of greatest expertise. I love this, as it gives most of us a chance to be used powerfully by God who aren't naturally the best of the best in any area (me included!).

What this means is that leaders need to seek God's direction when appointing people to fill roles, rather than just choosing those who, on paper, have the best credentials. Otherwise, their church is likely to miss out on the full power of God working in their midst – meaning that they, as a group, will operate at a much lower level than what they're capable of.

Individual believers can also make the mistake of trying to do it all themselves. This happens when there is a disconnect between one's faith and the rest of their life. For if we don't see a place for God in our careers, finances, and families/relationships etc. then we will leave Him at church and in our prayer closets, while living the rest of the time like those who doesn't know Him. In other words, as with the church scenario we just looked at, we will lean heavily on our natural talents and what we can do ourselves, rather than what God can do with us and through us.

The outcome of this is that without God's input, we will keep getting us-sized rather than God-sized ones. The miraculous will simply not be a factor, because we're leaving no room for it to occur. We might then begin to wonder whether it is God's will to use us in any significant way. Or alternatively, we might simply be content with being small like vast numbers of Christians and churches are. This is unfortunate, as God has a plan for all of us to be world changers in some sphere or spheres of society (not necessarily religion). But it all hinges on whether or not we will cooperate with Him.

Expecting God to Do It All

There is another group of believers who end up making the opposite mistake to the first group. Instead of trying to do it all themselves, they sit back and wait passively for God to do it all for them – through His sovereign and unilateral action. They may wait for revival and pray faithfully for it to occur, but just won't partner with Him by putting feet to their faith.

Their great hope is that God will release a huge outpouring of His Spirit on them, which will attract a flood of non-believers to their services. But it doesn't dawn on them that they actually have to do something to bring these people in (i.e. evangelism) – which will require divine strategies. Or alternatively, they know in their heart of hearts what they need to do, but fear prevents them from taking the required action.

It is vital to understand that God normally works in partnership with us: we give Him everything we have and stretch beyond what we can do ourselves, leaving Him room to do the rest. In other words, action and risk is needed on our behalf to implement the strategies He gives to us. Perhaps that is why many of us prefer to wait passively for God, rather than stepping out into what He's calling us to do.

Most of the time, He is not going to suddenly strike us with lightning, causing everything to instantly change – from a life of relative obscurity to having an international ministry, bringing revival to the nations. We have to learn to hear God, consistently do what He says, and continually steward the little things until we ever reach the big stage. But for the vast majority of us, there is not going to be any big stage, in terms of preaching to thousands or achieving international acclaim for what we do. We are going to be workers, business people, and parents, who most of the time just do ordinary things in extraordinary ways – using wisdom, creativity, and power drawn from Heaven, through the Holy Spirit abiding in us. God is not looking for superstars, but an army of faithful people to partner with and thereby do amazing things through.

How to Partner With God

As you might expect, partnering with God starts with relationship. In business, you typically wouldn't get into a partnership with someone until you know, like, and trust them. And there is little difference when dealing with our Heavenly Father. Therefore, before we can partner with God in any significant way, we have to know Him and be known by Him. In terms of the language of the last chapter, we need to be focused on His presence, by seeking Him with all our heart. Then when He reveals Himself to us, we need to learn how to steward His presence so that it is always with us (or more to the point, so He is always with us). In this state, we are consistently filled with His Spirit and have available all of His power, wisdom, and revelation. This is the place from which He gives us divine direction and we are able to access ideas and strategies from Heaven.

Remember also, that Jesus said that He only did what He saw His Father doing (John 5:19). This has to be our modus operandi as well, since we are called to walk as Jesus did (1 John 2:6). The Spirit reveals to us what the Father is doing and wants to do in our lives. When we discern this, we can normally assume that He is offering us an invitation to partner with Him in these things, since He always chooses to work with His people.

Some Christians might point to Scripture and say that God reveals His intentions to us in this - which is true in a general sense. For example, we know from the Bible that Jesus taught us to proclaim the Gospel of the Kingdom to the whole world (Matt. 24:14), making disciples of all nations (Matt. 28:19), and that signs and wonders will accompany our message (Mark 16:17-18). The question, though, is how? What should our strategy be in our own unique setting? We can't just use a cookie cutter, one-size-fits-all approach that has worked for someone else but may not work for us. Therefore, we need specific guidance from God, as to how He wants us to partner with Him in fulfilling our part of this Great Commission.

These issues are things that not only need to be grappled with by churches, but also individuals. For Scripture does not tell us specifically what we should do with our lives. And guess what, it is not all about church ministry and evangelism - which most Christians will never be involved in on a full-time paid basis. Yes, these things are important, but not everything. It might be a strange idea to some people that God actually wants to bless us, and those around us, in practical rather than just "spiritual" ways. He wants to transform the world through us, to make it look more and more like Heaven (Matt. 6:10), by bringing prosperity, good government, strong infrastructure, peace, justice, health and wholeness, strong families and relationships etc., etc., etc.

Our part in this might be as a bus driver, computer programmer, teacher, or any number of other occupations. There is really no legitimate job or area of business that God does not want to use His people in to bring Heaven to Earth. He even uses non-Christians for this purpose as well. For example, the inventors and developers of much of the technology we enjoy today (e.g. computers, the Internet, and smart phones) were not Christians. They have made the lives of most people on Earth a lot better through their endeavors. Moreover, this technology has contributed greatly to the advancement of the Gospel.

If secular inventors can change the course of history with their products and services then we as the people of God have absolutely no excuse. We have access to the greatest creative mind in the whole universe – the mind of Christ (1 Cor. 2:16). He desires to give His people ideas and strategies from Heaven, especially in the areas He has placed them. These ideas and strategies can come in many forms – dreams, visions, thoughts, intuitions, and many other modalities.

This book, I believe, is an idea that I downloaded from Heaven. Somewhere around the middle of my second year at BSSM I started receiving ideas for a project of this nature. Fortunately, I had the foresight to jot these things down on paper when they came to me, which sometimes occurred in class, at other times while reading books for school, occasionally when I was in bed, and also at other more random times. I thought that this might be something I'd pursue in a year or two, after doing other things that I had been thinking about. However, shortly before leaving Redding, I sensed that God was telling me to start writing as soon as I returned to New Zealand – not later.

I have to mention, though, that the writing of this book has not been a process of divine dictation, with God giving me the exact words to write. Most of the time, I have been using my own brain and the talents He has given me, with inspiration and guidance from Him on how to apply them through my own perspectives and writing style. It has involved a significant amount of research in terms of reading books by Bethel authors, consulting others sources, reviewing my class notes, and recalling personal experiences. Not to mention, countless hours of editing and proofreading. This has been a partnership with God; what I've come up with is I believe something much greater than I could have ever accomplished on my own. It has involved a lot of God and plenty of me.

God Wants to Partner With Every Believer

I firmly believe that God wants to give each and every believer great ideas, and walk with them through the process of implementation. But the issue for us is whether we have developed a close enough relationship with Him to discern His voice when He speaks to us. If not, it is going to be difficult to partner with Him on anything but the most general basis i.e. through scriptural principles, like evangelizing the lost.

However, once we are able to hear His voice, the question becomes: will we decide to partner with Him when He gives us ideas and asks us to implement them, or will we just play it safe and carry on with what we're already doing?

This is an important point, because to truly partner with God and give Him the opportunity to move through us supernaturally, faith (expressed through risk) is required. For without faith it is impossible to please God (Heb. 11:6). We are fooling ourselves if we think that it is going to be any other way, because His ideas and plans will usually either not make sense or seem way too big for us. Bill Johnson nails this point when he says:

> To honor Him fully, we have to live in such a way that unless God shows up, what we are attempting to do is bound to fail. This kind of abandonment was the nature of Jesus' life on earth and is now the nature of the believing believer.[55]

Partnering with God is where all the magic happens. It enables us to move from normal, earthly results to supernatural ones. When we partner with Him, there should be an excellence on our lives in what we do, just as Daniel and his companions were acknowledged by King

Nebuchadnezzar of Babylon as being ten times better at what they did than all of their colleagues (Dan. 1:20). Such excellence will require much more than just our natural abilities and good old-fashioned hard work. God must be strongly involved in the process.

This partnering with God is why Bethel Church and its affiliated ministries have exploded over the last two decades, to the point where they're now having a serious global impact. Revival was on the heart of God, and Bill Johnson said "yes" to this, at any cost. He was the pastor of a smallish church, in the tiny town of Weaverville, California. Few had heard of him, but he heard the heartbeat of God. And when he partnered with this, God used him to build a revival movement that is now starting to shake the nations. But this is still only the very beginning!

The lesson is that if we seek God, discern His plans for our lives, and use the power of His Spirit to carry them out, then He will use us mightily. This does not mean that we will all become internationally recognized as Bill is now. But whatever we do, if we do it with all our heart and involve Him in the process, we will end up changing the world in some way and become famous in Heaven – even if we're "only" the best janitor in the hotel where we work, and no one knows who we are. God knows and that is all that counts!

Declarations and Prophecy

Often though, our partnering with God will not require the implementation of some elaborate idea or strategy. It will involve simply speaking out what He wants to say in a given situation, sometimes with little or no prior warning. Remember, Jesus said this about the Father:

> ... he who sent me is true, and I declare to the world what I have heard from him. (John 8:26b)

We need to follow His example, by declaring the words of the Father. For sometimes, there are things that God particularly wants to do that He requires us to speak out, in order for them to take place. When we declare these things, great power comes on our words, which can cause the miraculous to occur.

A prime example of this is words of knowledge for healing in church services and revival meetings (see 1 Cor. 12:8b, NKJV). In such a setting, revivalists like Bill Johnson will often sense that God wants to heal people of specific conditions, and when they call these conditions out there is special grace for those afflicted in these ways to be healed – sometimes without them even being prayed for. It is not that God doesn't always want to heal everyone of every condition that they're suffering from. But in some moments, He creates a special focus for particular ailments, which helps people partner with Him through their faith.

These words of knowledge can come through various means, such as by thoughts, impressions, pictures and words in our mind; visions and dreams; and feelings of pain in particular parts of our body that we know is not ours. When we sense these things, we normally need to act quickly and declare them to our audience before the window of opportunity passes.

This type of ministry is not only for those who have speaking ministries and official leadership roles within their churches. God can use anyone, in any setting to work through in this way. I know people who use words of knowledge in street evangelism; they receive supernatural information about people's healing needs and will then ask them whether they have such an issue. If the person says "yes", they will offer to pray for them. Success rates for effecting healing in these situations are often very high.

It is exactly the same for prophecy. Sometimes God will give prophetic words to us for someone else. These come through similar means to the words of knowledge for healing. When we get one, it means that God desires to speak to that person in some way through us, to encourage them. Sometimes also, prophetic words can activate parts of a person's destiny and actually cause these to happen, just as when Ezekiel prophesied life to the dry bones, and life was restored to them (Ezek. 37:1-14).

One thing that is important to point out, though, is that whether it is words of knowledge for healing, prophecy, or anything else that God wants to do, we don't have to passively wait for Him to tap us on the shoulder (which may happen very infrequently for a lot of us - me included!). At any time of our choosing, we can ask Him for information on what He wants to do (or is currently doing), especially in relation to a particular area, such as healing needs or a person's life. For example, we can ask the Lord for a particular condition that He wants to heal right now.

One method that I've used successfully to minister healing in meetings is to imagine a picture of a body in my mind. I then scan over the body until I feel drawn to one particular part, such as the hips. I would then conclude that God wants to heal someone's hips. It is also helpful to try to distinguish between the right and left side, if possible, and any further detail that might be relevant. Another variation on this method is to imagine a red dot moving over the body and then looking to see where it stops - which is the part that you assume He is ready to heal.

I've also had success in just asking God for healing needs and then waiting until thoughts and impressions of certain conditions come to mind. Others often see pictures in their mind or hear words. God speaks to different people in different ways, and therefore we should not try to turn this into a formula that works for every person, every time.

The important thing to realize is that, despite the different ways that God speaks, when He does speak it is essential that we declare what He's saying to our audience (or those around us). For very often, a thing will only happen after it is called out by somebody. God desires to partner with us in the work of the ministry rather than just do it all by Himself, sovereignly. The downside of this is that if we are not attuned to His voice or are not obedient when we do hear Him, we can stop what He wants to do in that moment - which is a form of quenching the Spirit (see 1 Thess. 5:19), as noted in the last chapter.

I encourage you to have a go at some of these methods that we've looked at and see which ones work best for you. If you are at your church and get some words of knowledge for healing, I suggest that you approach your pastor and share these with him or her. They may allow you to announce them to the congregation if there is an appropriate opportunity to do so. But even if your pastor is not open to this, there is nothing stopping you from practicing with people on the street.

The prophetic can be easier to begin with, though, if you do not have any official role within your church. Usually there wouldn't be an issue with asking God for prophetic words for people and sharing these with them one-on-one, either during worship or after the service. I would strongly suggest being quite low-key about it (e.g. "I feel the Lord is saying to you ...") rather than declaring, "Thus saith the Lord ...". We need to allow people the opportunity to evaluate any prophecy that we give them. After all, we can be wrong, especially when we're just starting to learn how to hear God speak. Also try to focus on encouraging words, in line with 1 Cor. 14:3. Stay well clear of exposing people's sins and predicting things like who they'll marry. More about this later in Chapter 10: Culture of Risk.

Making Declarations over Ourselves

Regarding this topic of declarations, one thing that would be easy to overlook is that the principle of declaring what God is doing also applies to ourselves. When the Lord gives us information on our lives concerning what He is doing and wants to do, we need to speak it out and continue to do so periodically until it occurs.

For instance, when He gives us personal words, prophetic words through other people (that we judge to be true), or promises in Scripture jump out at us, we need to write them down and regularly declare them out loud, so that the whole spiritual realm can hear. In this way, we prophesy our future and cause our God-ordained destiny to come to fruition.

Soon after returning to New Zealand from Redding, I had a bit of a surprise when sorting through one of the boxes that I'd placed in storage. I rediscovered some pieces of paper that I had done some journaling with God on, approximately 10 years earlier. One thing caught my attention in a big way, which I have reproduced below, exactly how I wrote it:

I thought God said that I would write many books for him.

When I read this, it was like a lightning bolt from Heaven had just struck me. It came several months into the writing of this book that you're now reading. However, back when I recorded that word, the idea of me writing a book was so far-fetched that it was in the realm of complete fantasy (excuse the pun!).

Finding this old word from the Lord was like receiving a new prophetic word over my life. It was released at the perfect time for it to be quickened in me and serve as a major encouragement going forward in my writing. It also caused me to remember that one of the leaders of my church at the time, who was recognized as having a strong prophetic gift, had given me a prophetic word about writing, approximately one year before I received that word. WOW!

This illustrates an important point with receiving prophetic words. Sometimes people give us words that make absolutely no sense at the time we receive them. In those situations, we need to place them on the shelf until an appropriate time in the future when they might make more sense. In my case, those words about writing now make complete sense and needless to say, I have been declaring these things over my life in a big way!

When we declare what God is saying over our life, it activates our faith and causes the promises to be drawn toward us, since faith is the currency of Heaven (as we discussed back in Chapter 1: God is Good). But we also need to put feet to our faith, by taking practical steps toward these promises when the time is right. In my case, it was full steam ahead with the writing!

Finally, we also need to be careful not to speak out the negative thoughts and feelings that come to us, as a lot people have a habit of doing. By this, we are effectively prophesying the devil's plan for our life into existence, since death and life are in the power of the tongue (Prov. 18:21). We can choose to either speak life over ourselves, by declaring what God is saying about us and our future, or death by voicing the devil's words. Whichever we choose, and to what degree, is empowered in our life and will be drawn to us.

Living a Life Aligned With God

There is another aspect to partnering with God that is really important. This is living in line with His revealed will in the Bible. Our thoughts have to align with how He thinks. Our actions must match His general will. As mentioned in the last chapter, sinful thoughts and actions represent a partnership with the enemy instead of God. The same with unbelief and doubt; God actually requires faith and hope instead of these.

In any given moment, we have the opportunity to partner with either God or Satan, in our thoughts, beliefs, and actions. Unfortunately, many Christians often unwittingly partner with Satan when they believe lies about themselves, lies about God, and allow negative emotions such as fear to hold them captive. Although I discussed this in the last chapter, it is also very relevant to this chapter on partnering with God, and therefore deserves further treatment.

According to Bill Johnson:

> *Every believer has an open Heaven.* For the believer, most closed heavens are between the ears. Living as though the heavens were brass over us actually plays into the devil's hands as it puts us in a defensive posture. This violates what Jesus

accomplished. He put us on offense with His commission, "*Go!*"[56] (emphasis original)

Opens heavens mean that we have divine favor over our lives. The resources and opportunities needed to enjoy success in every area that is important to us are available. We access them through relationship with God, when we partner with Him in faith.

Satan, though, seeks to steal all of this blessing from us, by getting us to partner with him instead – through deception. If he cannot get us to partner with him in outright sin (which is his number one goal), he will try to render us ineffective in every area of our lives. And ultimately, he hopes that if he can discourage us enough, he might then be able to convince us to numb the pain with sin, such as through addictions like alcohol, drugs and pornography. At this point, we become his slaves again.

Since Satan has no power over us, except that which we give him, he needs to convince us to partner with him instead of God. His strategy is a very simple one that has never changed since the Garden of Eden, when he convinced Adam and Eve to make agreement with him against God, through getting them to believe lies (Gen. 3:1-6). Once Adam and Eve did this, they lost access to all of the blessings they enjoyed in the garden, particularly their face-to-face relationship with God. Similarly today, Satan wishes to deceive us out of what we have available in God. What is different, though, is that as Christians we usually don't lose everything forever through one silly mistake, as with Adam and Eve. As long as we are still alive, we have the opportunity to stop believing his lies and to instead partner with God. He is gracious to forgive us and to restore access to everything that He has for us.

As believers, God has given us so much. Few have any idea of the number of blessings that are actually available to us. On the other hand, many think that all being a Christian entitles us to is going to Heaven when we die, instead of the Hell we deserve for the sins we've committed. While I don't want to minimize this in any way, going to

Heaven is just the tip of the iceberg. Salvation is so, so much more than this. We actually get to enjoy Heaven on Earth (before we die!) – having intimate fellowship with God, receiving incredible blessings, and living a life full of purpose, reigning over all the powers of darkness.

What Satan does is tell us that we're not good enough, that God doesn't care about us and our needs (He withholds blessing from us), and that we had better fight hard to protect the little we do have, otherwise we might lose it. Scarcity thinking and limitation are always a big part of his lies. These lies are diametrically opposite to the truth that, in God, we are more than enough (Rom. 8:37) and have more than enough (Psalm 34:9-10; cf. Luke 19:26).

When we entertain ideas of following God with all our heart, according to scriptures like Matt. 6:33, the devil will tell us that those who do so are just irresponsible dreamers who are chasing fantasies. It is better, he will suggest, to let go of such lofty ideals, be more realistic, and just look after ourselves.

Satan actually wants to hold us back so that we don't use the incredible power we have available to us against him and his kingdom of darkness. He is desperate to keep this power hidden from us, as he has from most of the Church since the days of the (original) apostles. His plan is to get us into a mindset in which survival is our main focus. That way, we become preoccupied with ourselves, allowing him to therefore continue to destroy those who are in bondage, without any significant opposition. It is our job to fight for these people. But if we decide not to join the army and fight, due to things like low self-esteem and discouragement, many of them will have no chance.

Tragically, most of the Church is in this place today. It has shocked me to learn that so many of God's people are on antidepressants and other psychological medications – often not because there is anything physically wrong with them, but because they have partnered with the devil in his lies, and as a result have been imprisoned in depression, hopelessness, fear, discouragement, worry, anxiety, ... you name it.

Satan will tell us as many lies as what we are willing to believe, to keep us below where we could be by trusting God and partnering with Him. As Bill Johnson says, "... believing a lie empowers the liar."[57]

The way out of this is simply to learn who we are in Christ, what God says about us, and His plans for our lives – through reading Scripture and being in relationship with Him. Once we learn this, we need to break our partnership with Satan and every one of his lies, and instead partner with God in what He's saying to us. Spiritual warfare, in the form of taking thoughts captive and making them obedient to Christ (2 Cor. 10:5), will be an important part of the process until we have momentum in partnering only with what God says. From this place, we will quickly move toward being the history makers that God has called us to be.

4. SAINTS, NOT SINNERS

Another key component of the signs and wonders culture at Bethel relates to our identity in Christ. While many Christians would describe themselves as "sinners saved by grace", Bethel leaders teach their people that they are actually saints, not sinners, who are sons and daughters of the King, and therefore royalty. Furthermore, they explain that this royalty involves power, for the purpose of being world changers who advance the Kingdom of God on Earth - especially through the supernatural gifts of the Spirit. In this chapter, we will navigate the theology, practice, and implications of this view, contrasting it with the other more widely held one.

Identity and Why it is Important

Identity is one of the major focuses of BSSM, particularly in First Year. The leadership team of the school has recognized that who we think we are as people and believers (i.e. our identity) goes a long way toward determining how we will actually behave in the world. For instance, if we believe that we're a victim because we had a difficult upbringing and/or suffered abuse, then most likely we will continue living as a victim, attracting further bad circumstances into our life. Similarly, if we think that we're a sinner, it is likely that we will live a life struggling with sin, never quite being able to overcome it. But if we see ourselves as a righteous son or daughter of the Living God then we will tend to live a holy and righteous life, free from the bondage of sin.

The school's aim is to so completely immerse students in the message that they're royal sons and daughters of the Living God (John 1:12-13; Gal. 3:26) and members of the royal priesthood of believers (1 Peter 2:9), who are holy and righteous (Eph. 1:4), powerful and significant (Mark 16:17-18; John 14:12; Matt. 5:13-14), that it becomes a core part of their identity. The expectation is that this will lead to royal, saintly, and priestly behavior that literally changes the world. And from what I've seen, it is very often the case, with many people at least making significant steps along the way toward this ideal.

Bethel students, because of this identity, typically stand out as being quite different from other Christians. People often notice that they are very secure individuals, who are confident, powerful, full of faith, and absolutely believe that they're going to change the world for God. But this is not at the expense of humility and servanthood, which are key aspects of the Christian faith that Jesus as the servant king modeled to His disciples. Entitlement has absolutely no place in the character that BSSM leaders are trying to develop in their students.

No Longer Slaves to Sin

At this point, we will begin to explore in depth how our identity in Christ relates to our behavior in terms of sin and righteousness. Sin originally infected the human race when Adam and Eve, the first couple, made the decision to eat from the tree of the knowledge of good and evil in the Garden of Eden (Gen. 3:6) – against God's instructions (Gen. 2:17). Ever since that time, sin has corrupted all of humanity, making each person a slave to it (Rom. 6:16-17) – leaving them spiritually dead (Gen. 2:17; Rom. 6:23a). What is more, this spiritual death turns into eternal death when a person dies physically. In other words, their final destination is the lake of fire (Rev. 20:11-15), being eternally separated from the presence of God (2 Thess. 1:9).

Jesus, however, died on the cross for all the sins of humanity, making it possible for every person on Earth to be freed from the power and corruption of sin (1 Peter 2:24), and its consequences: spiritual and eternal death (Rom. 6:23b). All that is required is that they repent of their sins and then follow Him - which His blood enables them to do. At this point they leave behind their identity as sinners and transgressors of the Law to become saints who are holy and righteous.

Scripture declares that if there is any sin in our life then we are a slave to sin (John 8:34; Rom. 6:16). But saints have been freed from the power of sin and are therefore no longer slaves to it, as the apostle Paul teaches in Rom. 6:6. This means that we no longer have either the compulsion or the tendency to sin, since our sin nature has been removed. Instead, we are slaves to righteousness (Rom. 6:18-19) with the strong predisposition to do what is right in God's eyes.

This, of course, does not imply that we will never sin again, because like Adam and Eve before the Fall, who at that stage had no sin nature, we still have both a free will and the capacity to believe a lie - which Kris Vallotton argues are all that is needed to sin[58]. Kris points out therefore that "... we can still choose to sin. However, as saints it doesn't come easily anymore."[59]

When a believer truly knows their identity as a holy and righteous son or daughter of the King, they understand that such a deed is not part of who they are anymore. Therefore, they have the strong inclination to avoid doing it (and to repent quickly if they fail to do so). This is due to the tendency people have to act according to who they think they are.

Yet, it is common in much of the Christian world today to refer to ourselves as "sinners saved by grace", based primarily on Romans 7. The argument goes that in this chapter Paul admitted his great struggles with sin and his inability to be victorious over it - even as a believer in Jesus. In his mind, he wanted to do what was right, but his flesh was telling him to sin, and he was powerless to stop it from compelling him to do so. Only the blood of Jesus enabled him to be justified by God as a sinner saved by grace, one who would never be free from the power of sin in this life.

Contrary to this, Kris contends that:

> If we read [Romans 7] in light of the preceding and succeeding Scriptures, we find that it is impossible for Paul to have been speaking about his redeemed life. The entire Book of Romans is a letter of contrast between the life lived under the Law and the life that is in Christ.[60]

What Paul is doing in Romans 7 (with the exception of vv.1-4, 6) is talking about his previous life under the Law, before he met Jesus and was saved. The thing that creates a great deal of confusion, though, is his application in Rom. 7:14-25 of the historical present tense (i.e. the use of the present tense to refer to the past[61]) rather than the past tense to describe his situation under the Law (i.e. his bondage to sin and death). The issue is that when people see his inability to do what is right described in the present tense (e.g. v.18), many of them come to the erroneous conclusion that Paul must be portraying his current situation as both a believer in Jesus and a sinner – implying that this is what they can also expect as Christians.

These folks, however, are missing some important clues within the passage as well as neglecting to read the passage in the context of what Paul says elsewhere – both in the rest of Romans and in his other letters. In the analysis that follows, we are going to explore these things in detail.

We will begin with Rom. 7:24, which presents the most direct clue within Romans 7 that Paul is not referring to his current life in Christ when describing himself as a sinner who is incapable of doing what is right. In this verse, he asks about who will deliver him from this desperate situation of being captive to sin, such that he has a body he cannot control. Therefore, it must mean that an answer had, at that time, not yet been found (i.e. he was then a sinner without a deliverer/savior).

Paul reveals the answer to his question in v.25 (Jesus!) and presents it as a later development to what he had just discussed about his bondage to sin etc. But this verse throws up some more confusion, as it reiterates the problem of his bondage to sin after the answer has been stated - which helps to reinforce and confirm people's perceptions from earlier in the passage that being under the law of sin is part of the redeemed Christian experience.

What we need to remember, though, is that while Scripture is inspired, the chapter and verse divisions are not. The subject matter in v.25a belongs with that in v.24, not v.25b. What Paul is doing in vv.24-25a is briefly breaking out into thanksgiving to Jesus for delivering him from the law of sin[62], before summarizing, in v.25b, his main argument that under the Law (of God) he was powerless to prevent himself from sinning (because the Law (of God) gives the law of sin an opportunity (7:11)). Two verses later in 8:2, he says that in Christ Jesus we have been freed from the law of sin and death, which completely contradicts the argument that he is saying that those redeemed by Christ still serve the law of sin (and death) - making them slaves of sin.

What adds further evidence to Rom. 7:14-25 being in the historical present tense (and that it refers to Paul's pre-Christian life) is that in v.25b Paul talks about serving the Law of God with his mind (in the present tense), while in 7:6 he says that we have been released from the Law (past tense) and no longer serve under it.

Moreover, he states that apart from the Law, sin lies dead (7:8b) - which he explains another way in 6:14 by saying that sin will have no dominion over us since we are not under Law but grace. But how could sin be dead and have no dominion over us if we, as Christians, still have a sin nature and are unable to control ourselves?

Some would argue in response to this that sin no longer has total dominion over us, but we are still not completely free from it and have to progressively gain control over it through the process of sanctification (a theological term that refers to us becoming more holy in our conduct). However, this outworking of our freedom from sin that such people are describing is really just a learning to yield our will to God by more frequently choosing to do what is right and resisting the temptation to sin – which we now have the power to do. We will discuss the issue of temptation shortly.

For the moment, though, we move on to Rom. 7:5 where Paul talks about "living in the flesh" in the past, which contrasts with v.14 where he refers to himself being "of the flesh" in the present (NB. We will be examining the "flesh" in detail soon). Clearly, we can only reconcile these two very similar statements if the latter is in the historical present tense (i.e. it refers to the past) along with the rest of that passage. Even more so when we consider what he says in Rom. 8:8-9:

> Those who are in the flesh cannot please God. You, however, are not in the flesh but in the Spirit, if in fact the Spirit of God dwells in you. Anyone who does not have the Spirit of Christ does not belong to him.

Paul also in Rom. 7:14 refers to himself as "sold under sin" in the present tense, which contrasts with his description of us as having been set free from the law of sin and death in Rom. 8:2 (past tense), as we looked at earlier.

Besides all of this, if Paul was arguing that in Christ he was still powerless to stop himself from sinning, it would be strange for him to warn his readers:

> Let not sin therefore reign in your mortal body, to make you obey its passions. Do not present your members to sin as instruments for unrighteousness, but present yourselves to God as those who have been brought from death to life, and your

members to God as instruments for righteousness. For sin will have no dominion over you, since you are not under law but under grace. (Rom. 6:12-14)

Likewise, the following passage makes no sense if Jesus died for us to continue to be slaves to sin, but free of its consequences (i.e. spiritual, and ultimately, eternal death):

So then, brothers, we are debtors, not to the flesh, to live according to the flesh. For if you live according to the flesh you will die, but if by the Spirit you put to death the deeds of the body, you will live. For all who are led by the Spirit of God are sons of God. (Rom. 8:12-14)

To cap it all off, Paul reminds us in Rom. 5:8 that:

... God shows his love for us in that while we <u>were</u> still sinners, Christ died for us. (emphasis mine)

Since "were" invokes the past tense, it clearly indicates that, in Christ, we are no longer sinners. Therefore, we cannot now be accurately described as "sinners saved by grace". It is true, however, to say that "we <u>were</u> sinners who have been saved by grace". The difference is that it is in the past ("were") rather than the present tense ("are").

All of this analysis therefore strongly establishes that Paul is talking in Romans 7 about life lived under the Law before one becomes a believer in Jesus. He was clearly using the literary device of the historical present tense in vv.14-25 to do so.

Paul's Theology of Sin and Righteousness

What Paul is saying regarding sin and righteousness is that when we were under the Law we were slaves to sin (Rom. 6:17, 20), powerless to stop ourselves from continually doing what is wrong (Rom. 7:15, 17-18, 20) because the Law aroused sinful passions in us (Rom. 7:5). But when Jesus died on the cross, He released us from the Law (Rom.

7:4, 6) and thereby freed us from the power of sin (Rom. 6:18, 22; 8:2), since apart from the Law sin is dead (Rom. 7:8b; cf. 6:14). We now live under grace, which enables us to stop sinning (Rom. 6:14), and have become slaves to righteousness (Rom. 6:18) – provided that we have died with Him (Rom. 6:3-11), have the Spirit of God dwelling in us (Rom. 8:9), and allow the Spirit to lead us (Gal. 5:16-18; Rom. 8:5-6).

Since we are slaves to righteousness, our natural inclination is to do what is right rather than what is wrong – which should be reflected in our behavior (2 Tim. 2:19b-22; Eph. 5:8; cf. 1 Peter 1:14-16). Living any other way is a dangerous deception that jeopardizes the continuation of our position in Christ and therefore God's grace (Gal. 5:19-21; cf. Heb. 10:26-31). The apostle John concurs with this in stating that no one born of God keeps on sinning; anyone who does sin is of the devil (1 John 3:4-10).

None of this, however, is "legalism" or constitutes any sort of works-based gospel as some might suggest. We don't obey the Law to earn our salvation; rather, we uphold the Law (Rom. 3:31) because we have been saved from sin and are no longer captive to it (Rom. 6:18, 8:2). It is not a matter of human effort in disciplining ourselves to "be good". We are free from the tendency to sin and therefore doing what is right is the most natural thing for us to do with the help of the Holy Spirit (Rom. 8:13) – who guides us into truth (John 16:13) and convicts us of sin and our need for repentance if we stray from this (John 16:8; Rev. 3:19)[63].

What we are talking about is definitely not just an issue of semantics and playing around with words, but an extremely important distinction that all of us need to fully grasp. This is that, as Christians, we are no longer sinners, but saints; our sin nature has been removed and we are now righteous. This righteousness is not merely declarative in the sense that we have been pronounced innocent, just as though we had never sinned (i.e. the concept of "justification" in theology). It is also reflected in the restoration of our ability to actually do what is right on a continual basis.

However, many Christians are being led to believe, based on Romans 7, that they're still sinners (i.e. slaves to sin (cf. John 8:34)) as Paul supposedly was after he became a believer in Jesus. Such an interpretation of the passage rings true to them as it seems to explain rather well their experiences of being continually tempted to sin and often giving in to these urges. As a result, they associate temptation with having a sin nature (cf. Jesus, and Adam and Eve before the Fall, who we know were all tempted without any sin nature). But temptation to sin is not equivalent to having a sin nature, since we no longer have to give in to it as we did in the past. As Paul explains:

> No temptation has overtaken you that is not common to man. God is faithful, and he will not let you be tempted beyond your ability, but with the temptation he will also provide the way of escape, that you may be able to endure it. (1 Cor. 10:13)

Temptation and the Flesh

What we must understand is that freedom from our former sin nature does not mean that we will never be tempted. In fact, on Earth, temptation is absolutely normal and expected, because there is a devil and one of his main roles is to tempt (Matt. 4:3; 1 Cor. 7:5; 1 Thess. 3:5)[64]. He is able to tempt us because we still live in our earthly bodies which, unlike our spirits, are not immediately redeemed when we become believers (or at any future time in this life – Phil. 3:20-21). That is, they are still subject to decay and physical death. And most importantly for our current discussion, they continue to experience unmet wants and needs, which the devil tries to exploit through the "flesh".

The "flesh" (Greek: *sarx*) is a term, roughly equivalent to the "old self" (Eph. 4:22), which Paul often uses metaphorically to represent the incarnation of sinfulness (i.e. sinfulness as a living, physical entity of its own). This incarnation of sinfulness stirs up desires in people to fulfill the body's unmet wants and needs in inappropriate (i.e. sinful) ways, rather than through the legitimate means endorsed by God (e.g. stealing money instead of earning it). Before one becomes a believer in Jesus, it manifests in the form of a sin nature (i.e. a tendency to sin (Rom. 3:9-18, 7:5)). However, at the point of our conversion we become free from the power of these sinful desires to compel us to do what is wrong (Rom. 6:14). Nevertheless, we can still choose to follow them through our free will (cf. Rom. 6:12).

It is important to be absolutely clear, though, that the "flesh", in this context, does not refer to the human body (Greek: *sōma*). Our bodies are not inherently sinful[65], for Jesus too lived in an ordinary earthly body (Rom. 8:3b) but did not have a sin nature. He was tempted in every way, yet He remained without sin (Heb. 4:15). As believers, our bodies are "members of Christ" (1 Cor. 6:15) and temples of the Holy Spirit (1 Cor. 6:19). It is therefore a personal insult to both Jesus and the Holy Spirit for any believer to even suggest that their body is a source of sin. God does not dwell within anything unholy (cf. Ezek. 5:11) – end of story.

Nevertheless, throughout Church history, people have often confused the flesh with their bodies, leading to them harming themselves physically through various ascetic practices, in an attempt to become more spiritual. This betrays an unbiblical Greek mindset that the body is evil and the spirit good. Paul is adamant, though, that such practices "... are of no value in stopping the indulgence of the flesh." (Col. 2:23).

His solution to the issue of temptation is to crucify the flesh (put off our old self (Eph. 4:22; Col 3:9)) with its passions and desires (Gal. 5:24), and put on the new self (Eph. 4:24). Although the flesh/our old self was crucified with Christ (Rom. 6:6), we need to continue crucifying it (Rom. 8:13; Col. 3:5) so that it does not regain control over us and make us slaves to sin again. We do this through walking by the Spirit (which involves setting our mind on the things of the Spirit instead of those of the flesh (Rom. 8:5)), and the result is that we will not gratify the sinful desires of the flesh (Gal. 5:16; cf. Rom. 8:4).

When we are led by the Spirit, we are children of God (Rom. 8:14) and not under Law (Gal. 5:18; cf. 1 Tim. 1:9-10). The Law becomes redundant because, as I mentioned above, the Spirit leads us into all truth and righteousness (John 16:8, 13), and we naturally do what is right when we follow these leadings.

If, though, there is an area of our life where doing what is right does not feel like the most natural thing to do, this does not necessarily mean that we are a slave to sin and not truly born again. It could just be that we need deliverance from a demonic stronghold in our life; for even though we may be legally free from something, the devil can still try to hold us captive to it, unlawfully. This is no different from the situation of someone stealing our car despite the law forbidding them from doing so. If this is the case then what is required is enforcement of the law, to seize the car from the person and retake possession of it.

Let's say that we have an overwhelming desire to view pornography online, with thoughts to this effect nagging us relentlessly. Assuming that we have repented of any such behavior in the past and have the desire to avoid it in the future, we are legally free of the compulsion to do this. In such a situation, the way to enforce this freedom would be by taking the offending thoughts captive (2 Cor. 10:5), which we touched on back in Chapter 2: Focused on His Presence. This involves verbally rejecting these thoughts and the spirits speaking them, telling them to go, and ideally challenging them with Scripture in the process. For example, "I reject these immoral thoughts and desires; I have the mind of Christ, I have been set free from the power of sin, and am now holy and righteous. I reject you spirits of pornography and lust, and I command you to leave in Jesus' name and never come back." It can also help to invite the Holy Spirit to fill our mind with holy and righteous thoughts in the place of the offending ones after we have done this (cf. Luke 11:24-26).

If nothing changes after trying to take the offending thoughts captive and commanding the spirits speaking them to leave, we may need to seek the help of a Christian who is experienced in deliverance ministry. Such a person can guide us in a process with the Holy Spirit to discern the issue, declare scriptural truth in that area, break any agreements that we may have made with the demonic realm, command the demonic opposition to leave, and identify any open doorways that need to be closed to prevent future attack and help us to close them.

The Consequences of Believing that We're Sinners Saved by Grace

Since we have now established that, as Christians, we are no longer sinners but saints, we need to discuss the consequences of incorrectly accepting as truth the idea that we are instead actually sinners who have been saved by grace. This is important, because although righteous behavior is now natural to us, it is certainly not automatic - which will only be the case in Heaven, where no temptations exist. The devil can and does trick many people into believing that they do have a sin nature through false theology and the experience of temptation - which they have the power to resist. A lot of believers are thereby being conned into needlessly tolerating a certain amount of sin in their lives.

When we tell people that they are sinners saved by grace it therefore has the effect of normalizing, excusing, and even legitimizing failure - including willful disobedience to the Spirit of God as He tries to guide us into truth. The basic premise of repentance is that a change in how we think leads to a change in behavior - righteous behavior instead of sinful behavior. But giving people the identity of being sinners reinforces any struggles against sin that they may be having, by implying that these struggles are normal, will continue, and won't ever be overcome. Sure, temptations are normal, but giving in to them is not and should never be (1 Cor. 10:13). We need to resist the devil and he will flee from us (James 4:7).

This normalization of failure naturally leads to failure (i.e. sin) becoming a habit, since that is what is expected. As Kris says, "The word sinner implies that we are prone to do wrong. If we believe we are sinners, we will sin by faith!"[66], because "... we have put our faith in our ability to fail instead of His work on the Cross!"[67] Remember, people tend to act according to who they believe they are.

John Wimber makes a similar point:

> A key reason why [Christians] give in to sin is because they fail to understand and believe that they are new creations in Christ - forgiven, renewed, empowered for righteousness by the Holy Spirit (Rom 8:9-12).[68]

The thing is, however, that while sin can be normalized, excused, and legitimized through false theology, it still affects us as Christians. If our conscience is working correctly (i.e. it is guided by and aligned with the Holy Spirit (Rom. 9:1)), we should feel conviction every time that we do something wrong. But if this becomes a regular occurrence then condemnation and shame will likely be our normal experience. After all, one can only quote Rom. 8:1, "There is therefore now no condemnation for those in Christ Jesus", so many times before it loses its effect to reassure us of our position in Christ against the accusations of the enemy.

At this point, a person will tend to feel like a second-class citizen who is unworthy to come into God's presence or do anything for Him. Their prayer lives, Bible reading, and church attendance will likely diminish. They will lose interest in witnessing for their faith. Furthermore, moving in signs and wonders just will not be part of their grid, as they'll always be thinking that God is angry at them and therefore would never use them in that kind of way. When you have a church that is full of people who feel this sort of condemnation, shame, and unworthiness, is it then any wonder that there is no passion to change the world for God?

That is not necessarily the end of the story, though. If the person does not start seriously resisting temptation, sin will progressively become a more systemic part of their life to the point where they keep repeating the same misdeeds over and over again, and become drawn into new, more extreme ones. Or, in other words, they become totally enslaved to sin. This process is particularly evident with sexual sins such as fornication, the viewing of pornography, and masturbation, due to the highly addictive nature of these things. Likewise, the abuse of alcohol and drugs. But even seemingly innocuous sins like lying will become habitual if one is not careful. We cannot practice any form of sin without becoming progressively more entangled in it, such that the behavior becomes increasingly difficult to stop.

Eventually, it may reach a position where the person is not able to live with themselves anymore regarding the contradictions in their life (i.e. actions not matching their beliefs), forcing them to change some of their beliefs so that they can sleep at night – damaging their conscience in the process. This change of beliefs will be such that their sins become completely legitimate behaviors, or alternatively, they'll choose to believe that these sins are excusable (e.g. "Nobody's perfect"; "Everyone else is doing it too"; "This is not that bad. I've seen others do much worse"; "God understands"; "I've been very good in other areas so I can afford to indulge a little bit in this one"; "It's not hurting anyone else"; "We love each other and therefore how could it be so wrong?"). If you have ever seen a Christian with a glaring hole in their morality or integrity (e.g. they live with their girlfriend or boyfriend and see no issue with it), then something like this could be what is happening.

Some people may as a result of their sin even change their whole belief system such that they no longer consider themselves a Christian and start to become increasingly cynical about the Church and the things of God. They might then begin classing themselves as "spiritual, but not religious", when in reality they're just a backslider. But this is a very dangerous position to be in, as it sears a person's conscience (cf. 1 Tim. 4:2; Titus 1:15) and cuts them off from the conviction of the Holy Spirit. In this place, a person can sincerely think that the way they're living is perfectly good and right, but be completely wrong. Worse still, they have thrown away their faith, leaving themselves outside of the grace of God.

What these scenarios clearly and realistically illustrate is the great damage to our lives and faith caused by accepting the demonic lie that we, as Christians, still have a sin nature and therefore continue to be sinners. Sin is a slippery slope to destruction; it will progressively destroy everything good that we have until finally taking our very lives (James 1:15b). There is no amount of it that we can partake in without being adversely affected in some way – even if we immediately repent[69].

At the end of the day, it all comes down to what people believe about themselves – are they saints or sinners? If you teach them that they're sinners then they will likely live up to that expectation. Similarly, if you tell them that they're saints and world changers. The latter is what Bethel does with its members and ministry school students. They raise the bar up high, according to the Scriptures, and watch a large number of their people soar like eagles.

However, when some fall below that standard Bethel leaders don't beat them up and try to shame them into acting right – which would be attempting to put them under Law again. This projects a new, negative identity onto them, which is likely to reinforce their failure. Instead, these leaders affirm their true identity by telling them something to the effect of, "You're too amazing to be acting like this" and encouraging them to return back to living as the saint and child of God who they really are. This does not mean that there will never be any consequences arising from making bad choices. It is just that when people make those bad choices, we still believe in them and affirm their value, even though they may not value themselves. The difference is that instead of telling someone they're bad and need to start being good again, we tell them that they're good but need to make some changes in order to live up to this identity. The latter approach is far more likely to lead to their restoration.

To conclude this section, our true identity in Christ is as saints who have the natural tendency to live righteously and not sin. We are no longer sinners, nor are we sinners saved by grace, because no sinner will inherit the Kingdom of God (Gal. 5:19-21). However, if we occasionally sin again in the future (cf. 1 John 2:1), the blood of Jesus cleanses us from all sin and unrighteous to make it just as if we had never sinned – provided that we confess our sins (1 John 1:7, 9) and turn from them (cf. Luke 24:47).

When we understand this identity of ours, we will have the strong tendency to live up to it and be free from any condemnation of the devil. This will also position us to live as the world changers that God has called all of us to be.

Princes and Princesses

Being saintly and acting accordingly is a very important part of Bethel's signs and wonders culture. But another vital thing that Bethel tries to instill in its people is a sense of royalty, and with it significance, worthiness, and power – due to our status as sons and daughters of the King (and therefore princes and princesses) and members of the royal priesthood of believers, who have the Holy Spirit living inside of us.

This is not royalty as in how the world defines it – being above everyone else and having them bow down and serve us. We are talking about the royalty Jesus modeled, as the humble servant king. This does not give us any special rights pertaining to the present world, such as first-class and five-star treatment wherever we go. Nor does it mean that we will all be multi-millionaires who live extravagant lifestyles (cf. 1 Tim. 6:3-10). Instead, there are special responsibilities: to serve everyone else and give up our lives for others, as Jesus did. The greatest among us is the one who is the servant and slave of all (Mark 10:43-44). This kind of royalty is therefore free of any sense of entitlement.

What being members of the royal household does give us, though, is the security that comes from relationship with the most loving and powerful being in the whole universe. We have intimate access to our

Father, the King, and the right to use all of His resources for Kingdom business. And these resources are infinite!

For us personally, we get all of our needs met, many of our wants, and countless other good things that we neither wanted, asked for, or even thought we needed. This is because the Father gives good gifts to His children (cf. Matt. 7:11); He knows what would benefit us far more than we do!

Since everything that we have access to as the children of God is unlimited, there is no limit to the number of people who can enjoy the same privileges as us – unlike worldly royalty, which is restricted to only a very select few. In fact, it is God's will for every single person on Earth to become part of His royal family and enjoy these privileges. He offers them the opportunity to exercise His delegated authority to reign over the earth, extend His Kingdom, and in so doing destroy the kingdom of darkness on His behalf.

There are only two kingdoms (both of which are spiritual) that ultimately reign over everything in the physical realm: God's Kingdom and the kingdom of darkness (Satan's kingdom). If someone is not a prince or princess in God's Kingdom then they are a slave of the kingdom of darkness – regardless of their position and status in this world. There exists no territory outside of the domain of these two kingdoms; you are under the authority of either one or the other, whether you like it or not.

It is therefore the job of every member of God's royal army to free those who are enslaved by the kingdom of darkness and bring them into their true identity as fellow royal children of God. Every resource that our King has available is at our disposal to make this happen, including His power and authority.

Living as Paupers

If, however, some of God's children don't know their royal identity then they will likely live as paupers, who never access most of what their Father has made available to them. Consequently they won't be able to complete their part of the royal assignment to free slaves of the kingdom of darkness and restore every aspect of this world back to the dominion of God. In fact, in many ways, they will actually live like the slaves they're called to rescue.

This pauper identity, the very opposite of royalty, was something that God spoke specifically to Kris Vallotton about. He revealed that Kris was a pauper who had become a king, but in some ways was still acting like the pauper he once was. And if this continued, he would destroy the people he was trying to lead.[70] That began a journey for him which led to being transformed into the royal son he was called to be. He then became a key part of creating a culture of royalty - particularly through the Bethel School of Supernatural Ministry, which he co-founded, oversees, and teaches extensively at.[71]

Being a pauper, which at Bethel is normally referred to as having an "orphan spirit" (cf. Rom 8:15-17), is primarily a way of thinking that arises from not knowing your true identity as a son or daughter of the King. It is marked by the need to work for what has already been freely provided to you as a member of the royal family - particularly significance, worthiness, and the fulfillment of material needs. This sort of thinking causes insecurity and leads to behavior that is undignified, unroyal in nature, which ends up bringing others down, as was the case with Kris.

Paupers, at their core, do not feel significant; nor do they feel worthy of being valued, treated well, or loved unconditionally by others. The belief "I am not enough" always runs in the background for them. They may try to compensate for this by attempting to stand out in certain areas of their lives, such as through achieving high levels of success or practicing attention-seeking behavior - even in a negative sense e.g. offensive, antisocial, or criminal behavior. You know that you're dealing with a pauper when you come across a guy in sports car who has to race everyone else, or you see a girl dressed in very skimpy clothing, particularly when the weather is not especially warm. There are, of course, many other forms that this sort of behavior can take. These are just two very clear examples of it.

Paupers either don't feel sufficient self-love, or if they do, it is highly contingent on their level of performance (which can include things like looking attractive and having a desirable partner/spouse) and, of course, ultimately the approval of others – which they gain from this performance. If they perform well then they will tend to like themselves, while if they perform poorly they will not. Their identity is therefore built on performance (i.e. their levels of success in different areas of life) rather than relationship, in being a son or daughter of the King. This is why they feel the need to strive for significance.

On the other side of the coin, they may have the inclination to be jealous of the achievements of others and put them down. Paupers often feel that the success, recognition, and honor that anyone else receives comes at their expense, rather than there being enough for everyone to enjoy (cf. Luke 15:25-32). For such people, life is a zero-sum game.

When people try to treat paupers well or show interest in them, paupers will sometimes sabotage the relationship so that these people cannot get close enough to them to find out what they're really like – which many paupers are deeply afraid of because of their poor self-image.

Paupers Have a Poverty Mentality

One important key to understanding paupers is that they have a poverty mentality, as Kris identifies. They always feel that their resources are limited[72] owing to the fear-based belief "I don't have enough" that is deeply engrained into them. However, as Kris also explains, this is not limited to those at the bottom end of society. People from all walks of life can have this poverty mentality, no matter how wealthy they are. For instance, someone may have a lot of stuff but still be fearful of one day losing it all.[73]

Since paupers do not know their status as members of the royal household, they have little or no knowledge of what that is available to them – all of God's unlimited resources, which would give them great security and make them extremely powerful in terms of what they can accomplish in life. They therefore tend to constrain themselves to what they can do and achieve on their own. Furthermore, they will often chase after money and do whatever they have to do to make a buck – even to the point of metaphorically prostituting themselves.

One thing that I will always remember Kris saying in a BSSM Second Year session is that he doesn't work for money anymore (although he apparently still enjoys quite a decent income). The difference is that he sees himself as having a calling rather than working a job or running a business in order to make money. And when he operates in his calling, he trusts God to provide for all of his needs, regardless of how the money comes in and its particular source.

As King David wrote:

> Oh, fear the LORD, you his saints,
> for those who fear him have no lack!
> The young lions suffer want and hunger;
> but those who seek the LORD lack no good thing. (Psalm 34:9-10)

Matthew (Matt. 6:33) and Paul (Phil. 4:19) also make similar points regarding God's provision of our earthly needs. This demonstrates that it is not just an Old Testament idea, nor is it anything to do with modern "prosperity theology" – which taps into the selfish desire for earthly wealth (indicative of a poverty mentality because it presupposes lack).

Children who grow up in a loving family know that their needs are provided for, not because they have earned or deserve them, but because they are part of the family. It is the same with the royal family of God of which every true believer is a member; the Father provides for us because we are His children[74].

Paupers, though, unlike royal children, will not trust. They can't because they don't know who their daddy is – especially how loving and powerful that He is. Therefore, fear rules their lives and they feel forced to rely on their own strength and abilities to provide for themselves. They work to attain what has been freely given to them as family members.

Kris, however, rails against this survivalist mentality, which he argues has no place in the hearts and minds of any child of the King. He believes that it prevents us from living as the history makers that God has called each of us to be, and therefore greatly reduces our impact on the world.[75]

Those who are paupers in the Church will not step out into their God-ordained destiny. They will tend to just work hard to earn a decent living, while often doing little more than the minimum of what they think is required to get to Heaven when they die. This is sad because, as legitimate members of the royal family, they were created to do great things and, as a result, change the course of history. God never intended them to be reduced to a state of fighting for their very survival – just like everyone else.

Of course, this poverty mentality that paupers possess is a lot broader than just insecurity over money and finances. It extends to everything else that they may have need of in life, such as a fulfilling career, a loving relationship, good health, and abundant free time. But poverty runs a lot deeper than even the striving after these things, which is really just a symptom of a person not feeling enough – arising from them not knowing their true royal identity as a son or daughter of God.

A Lie that Keeps Many People in a Pauper State

Unfortunately, many people in the Church are being kept in a pauper state by certain lie, cloaked in spiritual language, which Kris explains:

> This lie tells us that any recognition of our strength or goodness is pride, and that the only way to deal with pride is to demean ourselves, which is humility. The truth is that it is neither pride to recognize our strengths nor humility to demean them. This kind of false humility keeps the saints in darkness and results in us never stepping into our destinies.[76]

In addition, the desire for greatness (which God has placed inside of every person) has been associated with selfish ambition, and confidence has been viewed as arrogance. Meanwhile, it has been regarded as "spiritual" to be poor, broken, and weak.

All of this, however, just reinforces the two major pauper beliefs of not being enough and not having enough. In essence, what is happening is that a religious spirit is causing people to keep themselves in a pauper state by thinking of themselves as being less than what God thinks of them. This is because they're afraid that if they do recognize the truth of who they are and the gifts He has placed on their lives, then other Christians will accuse them of being proud and reject them.

This lie is an attempt by the devil to destroy our morale and get us to bury our talents (cf. Matt. 25:18), thus rendering us ineffective as the army of God in our war against his kingdom of darkness. For he knows how powerful that the people of God can be when they know their royal identity, recognize the gifts that God has placed on their lives, and use them effectively. Satan and his forces have no answer to the power of God operating in and through us when we exercise it against them. His desire is to prevent us from accessing this power so that he can continue his reign of oppression unhindered.

To be clear, I am not talking about the battle against sin which, as explained earlier, has already been completely won; we are no longer slaves to sin. For too many Christians have an inward-focused and defensive mindset, instead of the outward-focused and offensive one that we require. I am actually referring to the fight to free people still imprisoned by the devil and create a world in which the Kingdom of God reigns supreme – as evidenced by the elimination of sin, sickness, oppression, war, poverty, crime, corruption, and every idea/philosophy that is antichrist in nature. While on this side of eternity it is unlikely that such a utopia will ever be fully reached (cf. John 12:8) (outside of a literal millennial reign of Christ on Earth, if this eschatological view ends up being correct), this should not stop us from making every effort to move closer and closer to that ideal.

Despite a lot of progress having already been made in most of the areas mentioned above, we obviously have a lot of work to do in bringing Heaven to Earth. And it should be apparent that this work is not only evangelistic in nature (i.e. leading people to salvation in Jesus); it also involves influencing every sphere of society toward alignment with Heaven (see Chapter 5: Optimistic and Victorious Eschatology). Therefore, we as the people of God do not all need to quit our jobs and become full-time evangelists. We must follow our individual callings and collectively bring Kingdom transformation to business, government, academia, education, science and technology, medicine, arts and entertainment, the media, and every other area you can think of. It may not sound as glamorous as preaching to multitudes in Africa and seeing many thousands saved, healed, and delivered, but it is just as necessary. The supernatural gifts of the Spirit are very relevant to this "ministry" in the real world, especially the gifts of supernatural wisdom and knowledge (1 Cor. 12:8).

The enemies of this mission, though, are the apathy and discouragement that come from not knowing our royal identity. When we don't know who we truly are, we will end up just going through the motions of our boring "dead end" jobs, having no vision for how God can use us where we are. Not surprisingly, this attitude causes us to be largely ineffectively at our assignment of advancing the Kingdom.

This is why it is not spiritual to think of ourselves as poor, broken, and weak, but completely demonic. It does so much harm to us as God's people and the work He's called us to do, when we see ourselves in these ways. Not to mention how disrespectful and demeaning this is to Jesus in terms of what He did for us on the cross: freeing us from slavery to the kingdom of darkness, healing us, and turning us into world changers.

It is not prideful to see ourselves as powerful and great, for that is how God views every one of us. As Kris says:

> ... as long as we acknowledge where our greatness comes from we're not in danger of pride. We don't glorify God by saying we're not great, we glorify Him by acknowledging that He is the source of our greatness. Humility is not demeaning ourselves but exalting our God.[77]

We don't steal God's glory by being great, because He has already freely given it to us (John 17:22-23; 2 Cor. 3:18) – for the purpose of bringing Him even more glory through how we represent Him in the world (John 15:8; 1 Peter 4:10-11; 1 Cor. 10:31). How could we possibly bring Him glory by being a bunch of losers and nobodies – even nice ones at that? But this is how a lot of Christians think – that to represent God well we should just be nice people who are insignificant and don't stand out in any way.

As believers, we need to build each other up by calling out the greatness in those around us, while not forgetting to speak rightly about ourselves. The goal is to spur each other on to become everything God has called us to be and to accomplish everything that He has appointed us to do (cf. Prov. 27:17). At Bethel, particularly BSSM, you frequently hear leaders telling people (both corporately and individually) that they're powerful and world changers. Furthermore, the prophetic is used extensively to identity the unique callings that individuals have. As Kris declares:

> We, the church, are commissioned to develop a princely, prophetic culture that causes people's destinies to be revealed. People will then be changed into the people they were designed to be when God conceived them.[78]

According to Paul, the main purpose of prophecy is to strengthen, encourage, and comfort people (1 Cor. 14:3, NIV2011; cf. Acts 15:32) – which Kris simplifies down to finding the gold in others and calling it out, while overlooking the dirt. Most people are painfully aware of what is wrong with them and don't want or need to be reminded of these things. They are often, however, unaware of the greatness that God has placed on their lives[79], which is our job to draw out. We do this by identifying their major strengths and abilities; their identity, calling, and destiny; and, more generally, the things that God really loves about them, in terms of their personality and character – all through revelational information, possibly supplemented by what we can see in the natural.

Since every person is called to royalty, there is no one for whom you cannot come up with an encouraging prophetic word. This includes non-Christians, who are really just lost sons and daughters of the King, by virtue of being descendants of Adam "the son of God" (Luke 3:38) and bearing God's image – which is still present, to at least some degree, in every human being (Gen. 9:6). (Hint: prophecy is therefore VERY useful for evangelism, as few people do not like to hear good things about themselves). See Chapter 10: Culture of Risk ("Case Study: A Safe Prophetic Culture") for more detailed information on how prophecy is practiced at Bethel.

At BSSM, every student is equipped to prophesy on demand. There are classes on prophecy, at least one book to read on the subject, and many opportunities to practice the skill on one another. Each student receives many prophetic words about themselves, which they are strongly encouraged to record and regularly review. This helps them to maintain an accurate picture of how God sees them and to stay on track with where He's leading them. For "where there is no prophetic vision the people cast off restraint" (Prov. 29:18a).

The result of all this training on our royal identity and the prophetic culture which helps to draw this out, is that the BSSM environment grows many people into being outwardly very confident men and women, who know exactly who they are and where they're going. They feel a sense of significance and believe that they're destined to change the world for God in a major way, affecting many lives in the process.

However, a lot of Christians not familiar with these things may mistake BSSM/Bethel people as being proud and arrogant (especially if they're still very young), just as David was accused of being by his older brother Eliab, when he enquired about fighting Goliath (1 Sam. 17:26-28). In reality, though, their confidence is based on their identity as sons and daughters of the King, who are powerful and have been called to a great mission. But as Kris says, "... confidence always looks like arrogance to the insecure."[80]

Only when we fully embrace this true identity of ours can we enjoy a healthy self-esteem that is rooted in our relationship to God, rather than performance. More importantly, though, we position ourselves as armed and dangerous in our war against the kingdom of darkness – which absolutely terrifies Satan and all his minions!

Our Identity and How it Relates to Signs and Wonders Ministry

In case you're wondering what all this has to do with signs and wonders ministry, it actually has everything to do with it. This is because who you believe you are and the way you perceive yourself will play a large part in determining your behavior, as we have already discussed.

The Bethel leadership team desires its people to live like Jesus as world changers (John 14:12; 1 John 2:6), who operate freely in the supernatural of God. However, they do not spend much of their time attempting to motivate people into those sorts of behaviors. Nor do they try to coerce or shame them into acting in these ways. Such strategies are ineffective at causing the desired change in people. They instead concentrate on developing in BSSM students a healthy, biblical identity as royal sons and daughters of God who are holy and righteous, powerful (especially in terms of the supernatural gifts of the Spirit), and have the awesome privilege of partnering with God to bring His Kingdom to Earth. The leaders of the school know that if they achieve this goal then the desired outward behaviors of moving powerfully in signs and wonders and living as world changers will naturally follow – which they consistently do.

The result is that many people discover their true royal identity and leave their old pauper nature behind – which actually belongs back at the cross where it was supposed to have died and been buried. After all, Jesus became poor so that we could become rich (2 Cor. 8:9).

This had led to an army of believers being formed, who each know their true identity in God. They want nothing more than to charge into battle to end the tyrannical reign of the devil on Earth, so that everyone can be free and enjoy the riches available in Christ. The supernatural gifts of the Spirit are key weapons in their armory.

Contrast this with Christians who are still paupers. As I suggested above, they tend to just focus on making a living for themselves because they are fearful and operate according to a survivalist mentality. Moreover, they often feel like second-class citizens in the Kingdom, such that they don't believe God would ever use them in any significant way – especially not supernaturally, through the operation of powerful gifts like healing and prophecy.

Although most paupers won't be involved in signs and wonders ministry because they feel insignificant, unworthy, and powerless, there are still some who will. However, their motives may be far from pure. Since the gifts of the Spirit are just that – gifts, and operate by faith, a person does not need to have a strong identity in Christ or possess good character to actually use them (cf. Matt 7:21-23). Anyone who understands the principles of faith and steps out in them can see some pretty amazing miracles happen. This means that Christians who see the gifts of the Spirit as an opportunity to achieve recognition and significance can and do become involved. Their aim is to gain identity from operating in signs and wonders in a similar way to how many non-Christians try to gain identity from success in their careers. This is a works mentality that echoes the way of the Law: we have to strive to earn by good performance rather than be given what we have through grace, by being members of the family.

At BSSM, it is ground into students that we do things <u>from</u> identity, rather than <u>for</u> identity. We are already royal sons and daughters of God and have nothing to prove to others by healing, prophesying, or casting out demons etc. (cf. Luke 10:17-20). This is just "normal" Kingdom behavior. Unfortunately, it is actually not very normal in practice, in the same way that common sense is often not very common. This explains why some people see an opportunity to rise above the pack by operating in the supernatural.

But we are still God's children and totally loved by Him even if we do not participate in this ministry of signs and wonders. There is absolutely no possibility of being loved more by God due to our performance, as His love cannot be earned – it is freely and unconditionally given. Our identity therefore cannot be improved on – unless it is not in being a child of God but is rooted in how other people evaluate us, according to our levels of performance.

The problem is that if we base our identity (and our self-esteem, which is derived from our identity) on how others see us then it is going to be all over the place and we will be enslaved by the fear of man – always worried about what others think of us. I don't know about you but I would rather base my identity and self-esteem on what God thinks of me (which never changes) than on how other people do (which constantly fluctuates). It is just a far more healthy and stable way to live, especially considering the fact that our ability to perform to the expectations of others diminishes progressively as we age – meaning that we will be unable to keep people happy.

The Qualities of Royalty

Before we conclude this chapter, I would like to briefly discuss the qualities of royalty as they relate to us as sons and daughters of the King:

1. Strong identity as children of God and saints

Those who are royal are strongly rooted in their identity as children of God and saints. They live from this identity, making it their mission to bring Heaven to Earth, acting in such a way as to bring honor and glory to God, rather than gain the approval of man.

2. Full of the Holy Spirit and power

They are full to overflowing with the Holy Spirit and power. This is not a one-time event, but a process in which they're continually seeking more of God and getting refilled. They don't camp at their last encounter with Him, but are hungry for new and more intimate ones.

As a result, they are full of the fruit of the Spirit (especially love, joy, and peace), and the supernatural power of God is on their lives in extraordinary ways. They evangelize and minister to others out of these fruits and in this power. Signs and wonders follow them wherever they go. Consequently, many people are saved, healed, and delivered through their lives. Furthermore, they bring the Kingdom to other spheres of society (e.g. government, business, education), influencing them to operate more like Heaven.

3. Honor

They honor all people because each and every person is made in the image of God (1 Peter 2:17). This includes those who strongly oppose the things of God. Honoring people has nothing to do with agreement. It is about recognizing them for who they are and have been created to be, rather than what they're not. This, of course, does not prevent us from actively disagreeing with them and strongly critiquing their ideas and behavior, in the right context.

4. Integrity

Royals possess unscrupulous integrity, and conduct themselves with the perspective that God and the whole spiritual realm are always watching them. When they give their word to someone, they honor it even when it hurts. They are people who are fully trustworthy and can be relied on.

5. Dignity

They are dignified and maintain their poise, even when attacked unfairly and dishonored by others.

6. Humility

Royal sons and daughters of God possess true humility, instead of the false humility that many other people have. They judge themselves soberly and are able to recognize others as being more significant (Rom. 12:3; Phil. 2:3). In essence, they have an honest and true picture of themselves: they know they're great and freely recognize the greatness in others as well – to the point of calling out that greatness, even when people don't see it in themselves.

7. Confidence

They are people who are confident, trust God, and have a high level of expectancy that good things are going to happen – both to them and through them. This confidence is able to walk hand-in-hand with the humility we just discussed. The two do not need to be in conflict, unless it is an arrogant confidence – which has no place in any son or daughter of God.

8. Courage

This confidence in God and who He has made them to be, along with the expectancy of good things, gives them great courage to face their fears and take what others would call huge risks. As Kris Vallotton says, "The dogs of doom stand at the doors of destiny." The only way that we can fulfill the destiny God has for each of us is by displaying great courage on a regular basis. Often, our greatest triumphs will result from overcoming our biggest fears.

Several years ago, a well-meaning Christian told me that if something is hard then it is not from God, because He makes things easy for us so that we don't have to strive. I responded by saying that I totally disagreed with him on this point. If it is something worthwhile doing then we are going to have opposition. The devil is not going to allow us to have an armchair ride if he can possibly help it.

Unfortunately, fear is often disguised as wisdom and stewardship, in the Church today. For example, many church leaders will not teach on the power and presence of God because they're afraid that some of their people will become offended and leave. Worldly business, financial, and accounting approaches tend to be applied to finances, rather than allowing God to stretch us in faith. And many missionary and evangelistic activities are aborted because it is "too dangerous" to go to a particular country or region.

We must instead heed Moses' charge to the nation of Israel as they were about to enter the promised land and fight its many inhabitants, in order to take possession of it:

> Be strong and courageous. Do not fear or be in dread of them, for it is the LORD your God who goes with you. He will not leave you or forsake you (Deut. 31:6).

9. Determination/perseverance

Royal children of God work hard and have strong determination to achieve their goals. They persevere through challenges that present themselves and don't give up easily.

10. Resilience

They are resilient, not easily thrown off course by failures and setbacks. Instead, these things typically increase their determination to achieve what God has called them to do.

11. Live with divine purpose

They live with divine purpose; the main goals of their lives are to know God more fully and bring His Kingdom to Earth in a greater way. This is in contrast to the vast majority of others who live for making money, pursuing relationships, owning a house, and entertaining themselves. While none of these things is inherently wrong, our life becomes very self-centered and empty when we make them the main focus. God's perspective on this is:

> ... seek first the kingdom of God and his righteousness, and all these things will be added to you. (Matt. 6:33)

12. Love themselves and others well

Those who are royal are great lovers of themselves and others. Having a healthy identity and self-esteem, they appreciate what is unique about themselves and how they have been fearfully and wonderfully made by God (Psalm 139:14). This carries through to how they treat others: they love their neighbors as themselves (Mark 12:31) and try to be a blessing to everyone they meet.

13. Servant minded

These people live to serve both God and others. They fight to bring His Kingdom to Earth and free the world from the tyranny of the devil. This includes being generous with their time and money, helping people, and supporting worthy causes. However, we are definitely not talking about a doormat Christianity that allows everyone to walk over them, using and abusing their generosity.

Final Word

Over the course of this chapter, we have looked at how our identity affects the way that we think and end up behaving in life. My goal has been to convince you how important it is as Christians that we see ourselves as saints and royal children of God, rather than sinners and paupers. So many things flow out of these two competing belief systems. Our decision regarding which one to adopt for ourselves will determine to a large extent whether we will live a life of holiness or be enslaved to sin, whether we will have the peace of God or constantly feel condemned, whether we will feel significant or insignificant, worthy or unworthy, secure or insecure, powerful or weak, whether we will have our material needs freely provided or work to earn them, whether we will have a vision for our life or live with no purpose, whether we will be a history maker or a person who leaves no real mark on the world. This is not about splitting hairs over subtle theological nuances. The differences in real world results are extremely significant and consequential, even to the point of life and death. Choose carefully and wisely what you will believe about yourself!

5. OPTIMISTIC AND VICTORIOUS ESCHATOLOGY

Another important secret to the power of God moving so strongly at Bethel is their optimistic and victorious eschatology (theology of the end times). This gives them a vision for the proclamation of the Gospel of the Kingdom, and the transformation of society - through various means, including the supernatural.

What is important to understand is that Bethel people have no fear of the Antichrist or the Great Tribulation. They are not worried about any of the cataclysmic earthquakes that have been predicted to hit California (where Bethel is located), which some have prophesied as judgments of God for the great sinfulness of the state. Neither are nuclear war, terrorism, or environmental catastrophe major concerns that preoccupy them. They believe in a supremely powerful, benevolent God, who is present and active in the world, and wanting to pour His incredible love out on humanity. In their view, this is a day of His patience, mercy, grace, and favor, not one of judgment.

The prevailing mindset at Bethel is one of optimism, excitement, and victoriousness. Consistent with postmillennialism[81], there is the belief that things are going to continue to get better and better, rather than worse and worse; the Kingdom of God will expand greatly on

Earth, bringing advancement to every sector of society. They see the greatest days of the Christian Church being ahead of us, and believe that the best time to be alive in all of human history (to date) is right now. For we have never walked in such revelation and understanding of the goodness of God, and the power of the ordinary believer filled with the Spirit to change the world for Him. An army of such Kingdom builders is already rising up, which is starting to shake the nations for God. Bethel people therefore feel that we are on the cusp of a great end-times revival like none before, in fulfillment of the global "billion soul harvest" prophesied by Bob Jones in 1975, and the incredible outpourings of God's Spirit that others have received revelation of.

This sort of optimism is fueling the desire of many at Bethel to demonstrate His love to the world by operating in the kind of signs and wonders that we see reported on the pages of Scripture. For this coming move of God will not be based primarily on the ministry of a small number of "big names" as in the past, but the power of God working through regular believers in their everyday lives - resulting in Kingdom transformation to the world and a powerful revelation of God the Father that leads many to faith in Jesus. Everyone will get to play and be a part of the action! As a forerunner of this revival, Bethel models these things well by equipping its people to be revivalists who bring the power of God wherever they go and in whatever they do.

Pessimistic and Escapist Eschatology

This view is in stark contrast to the pessimistic and escapist eschatology of many Christians today, who largely subscribe to premillennial dispensationalist views of the end times. Although there are various premillennial dispensationalist eschatologies, which differ on certain points (particularly regarding when Jesus is returning in relation to the tribulational period), what they all have in common is a doom and gloom outlook on the future - which inspires fear and leads to escapist/survivalist mentalities. These people believe that things will go from bad to worse as the second coming of Jesus approaches. There will be a mass rejection of the Gospel, morality, and truth, with the sinfulness of humanity increasing to unparalleled levels. Satanic forces led by the Antichrist will take over the world and subject anyone who resists their authority, particularly faithful Christians, to severe persecution. In response, God is going to bring many judgments on the Earth that will inflict terrible suffering on those who have given their allegiance to the Antichrist and persecuted His people.

An interesting feature of this eschatology is that current world events such as natural disasters, wars, terrorism, nuclear standoffs, the rise and fall of governments/world leaders, and financial crises are constantly correlated with prophecies in the Bible pointing to end times. Everything bad that happens in the world is a sign to adherents that the end is imminent and will be utterly terrifying.

Often lacking in premillennial dispensationalist views is any perspective of a loving God empowering a victorious Church to bring Kingdom transformation to every aspect of the world – culminating in a great end-times harvest of souls before the return of Jesus and the conclusion of the period of grace. What we see instead is an absent and angry God, who sits by idly allowing evil to get out of control, so that He then has an excuse to reenter the scene and pour out the full force of His wrath on sinful humanity.

Premillennial dispensationalists who do believe that the Church is going to shine brightly right before Jesus returns, in the form of a great, global revival, normally do so in the context of the world getting darker and darker. This is apparently due to them not fully understanding the concept of the Kingdom of God, such that they see it as only representing the number of people who are saved. It is much more than this as we will discuss shortly.

The hope for those who subscribe to premillennial dispensationalism is to remain faithful and hang on long enough for Jesus to return and rescue them from persecution and all the catastrophic judgments of God that will befall everyone who is left behind.

This has led to some people stashing away weapons and even forming private militia groups, in order to oppose the Antichrist's world government. Others have moved to remote locations in the middle of nowhere to escape the attention of enemy forces when they take over the world. The majority, though, are hoping they won't have to live through the rule of this satanic world government, due to it either not occurring in their lifetimes or Jesus returning to rescue them before the persecutions become too intense. All of these reactions reflect attitudes of fear rather than faith, and defeat rather than triumph.

Those who subscribe to this sort of eschatology would probably respond to these criticisms by claiming, "We are only going on what the Bible says." And to be fair, Jesus is coming back at some point in the future for a pure and spotless bride (the faithful Church) (Eph. 5:25-27). God is also going to judge the world, consigning every person whose sins are not covered by the blood of Jesus, to the lake of fire (Rev. 20:11-15). Furthermore, it has to be recognized that there are many passages that appear to support premillennial dispensationalist views.

But the question is: how do you interpret these passages and in what context do you place them? These considerations can make a big difference as to the final result you come up with, although in this book we are not going to dive into such issues. All I will say is that there are other ways of looking at the key passages, which are still faithful to Scripture. However, few Christians have been adequately exposed to alternative views. In the last half-century especially, the large number of books that have been written on end-times prophecy and the hugely popular (fictional) *Left Behind* series have influenced Christians in the direction of premillennial dispensationalism to such a degree, that it has become the default position. And for many it is seen as the only "biblical" one.

This eschatology, which inspires fear and escapism, is extremely problematic for two main reasons:

1. God has called us to live in faith rather than fear

It is made abundantly clear in Scripture that God has called us to live in faith rather than fear (Matt. 6:25-34; 2 Tim. 1:7; Heb. 10:38). Fear is not compatible with faith, and is one of Satan's chief weapons of destruction. Whenever we're in a state of fear, such that it affects our behavior in a negative way (e.g. it causes us to run from our destiny), we are not living in faith. Or, more accurately, we have more faith in Satan's plan for our life (death and destruction) than God's one (abundant life).

Allowing fear to rule us is like declaring Satan to be lord and ascribing to him greater influence over our lives than God (i.e. a big devil/little God scenario). Unfortunately, this is not a state conducive to God empowering us to live victoriously. It actually becomes a self-fulfilling prophecy through which the devil is able to wreak havoc on us - because we let him! He has only as much power over us as we give him, through our thoughts, emotions, beliefs, and actions. Fear is one of the greatest things that empower him, other than sin. Although technically, fear is a form of sin, as it is opposed to God and His plans.

Even if premillennial dispensationalism is correct in that a great global dictator will rise up and try to force every person to give their allegiance to him (e.g. by taking the mark of the beast (Rev. 13:16-18, 20:4)), we should still not allow ourselves to live in fear. Yes, persecution and trouble may come, but we need to be as bold as a lion (Prov. 28:1) and never bow to the intimidations of our enemy. Many believers over the majority of Church history have experienced significant levels of persecution - sometimes to the point of imprisonment, torture, and even death. The Book of Acts highlights the extreme persecution that the original apostles and some of the earliest Christians faced. The records of Church history describe how this continued beyond the New Testament period into each and every century following, right up until the present day. None of this should surprise any of us, given that both Jesus and Paul warned us that we should expect to be hated and persecuted for our faith (Matt. 10:16-25; John

15:18-21; 2 Tim. 3:12). Furthermore, Paul instructs us to not be afraid of those who oppose us, as this is a sign to them of their destruction and our salvation from God (Phil. 1:28). God will not allow any of His children to be snatched out of His hands (John 10:27-30). Moreover, He will defeat all of His enemies and deliver us from their hands. Not a hair of our heads will perish (Luke 21:18).

As I heard someone once say, "The safest place to be is in the will of God". While there can be no guarantee of physical safety offered, there is a divine protection over your life when you're living one hundred percent for God (Psalm 91). Admittedly, most of the apostles in the Bible were brutally martyred. But we should also not forget how many times these apostles (Acts 5:17-19, 12:3-11), and previous saints such as Noah (Gen. 6:9-8:19), Lot (Gen. 19:1-29), and Daniel (Dan. 6:16-23), were rescued from trouble – often through direct supernatural intervention.

There has, however, been one glaring exception to this rule of persecution: Western Christians over the last couple of centuries. Those of us who live in the West today have gotten so used to the religious freedoms we now enjoy, that we take for granted the ability to go to church freely and own copies of the Bible. Furthermore, we often get upset at just the slurs we are subjected to e.g. "bigot", "intolerant", and "anti-science".

However, a fair number of us are anxious about the possibility of losing these freedoms and being forced to endure the sort of trials that many of our fellow believers throughout history have had to undergo, in order to maintain their faith.

What we need to realize, though, is that the Church throughout the ages has been victorious, even in the midst of persecution. If it had not been then none of us alive today would be believers in Jesus, as the Christian faith would have died out long ago. I am so thankful that many faithful men and women from the past have stood up bravely to proclaim the Gospel, rather than keeping it to themselves out of fear. This has given us the chance to receive the salvation available in Jesus. So do we now have the option to shrink back in fear? Absolutely not! (Heb. 10:37-39) We have to pay it forward to others.

What Jesus tells us is that we need to take up our cross and follow Him (Matt. 16:24). This involves sacrificing and potentially suffering for His name, as have many others before us. For our commission is still the same regardless of whether or not we are persecuted, and how severe this may be: we must proclaim the Gospel to all creation (Mark 16:15; Matt. 24:14) and make disciples of all nations (Matt. 28:19). Fear is not an option and never will be (cf. Rev. 21:8).

However, if our perspective is not that God is in control and will ultimately prevail then we need to change the way we think (i.e. repent!) and gain a new perspective. This is what happened to Elisha's servant in 2 Kings 6:15-17; he saw in a different way, which moved him from fear to faith. We need to see from the perspective that Jesus delivered us from the fear of death (Heb. 2:14-15) and that He is the King of kings and Lord of lords (Rev. 19:16).

It is interesting how the lenses people see the world through cause them to interpret the same things in very different ways from others. It is therefore important that we put on the lenses with which to see from God's perspective – which is the only true one. When we do, we will operate from a position of faith rather than fear.

2. God expects us to be faithful Kingdom builders

All true believers know that one day Jesus will return at an unexpected hour (Matt. 24:44), and at that time He expects to find us doing the work that He has assigned us.[82] This involves extending His Kingdom on Earth, while living holy and righteous lives that bring glory to God – by being people who love well, seek truth, and are excellent at what they do.

However, when we are fearful of the future, spending a lot of our time and energy preparing for the coming of the Antichrist rather than the return of the King, it is unlikely that we will have much of a focus on extending God's Kingdom here on Earth. Moreover, bringing the Kingdom through the supernatural power of God will be the farthest thing from our minds. More likely, we will associate signs and wonders with deception (Matt. 24:24) and the coming of the Antichrist (2 Thess. 2:9; Rev. 13:13-14), since that is the lens we are viewing the world through.

In fearfully anticipating the coming of the Antichrist and failing to work toward advancing God's Kingdom, we are actually being unfaithful servants who have buried our talents (cf. Matt. 25:18, 24-30). Needless to say, God cannot commend us for such behavior. What we need to understand is that He has not given us license to decide that advancing His Kingdom is no longer important because we feel in danger, and believe that everything is about to be destroyed anyway.

Premillennial dispensationalism, therefore, has the tendency to negatively impact our stewardship of the resources we have been entrusted with. Of course, it does lead some to focus on evangelism more, in an effort to rescue as many souls as possible from eternal destruction before the end – which is commendable. Nevertheless, this demonstrates some significant misunderstanding of what God's Kingdom is and what extending it on Earth actually means. In the next section we will discuss these issues.

The Kingdom of God and the Seven Mountains of Influence

As I mentioned at the beginning of this chapter, Bethel as a movement believes that this is a time of God's patience, mercy, grace, and favor, in which He wants to pour out His love on the world. They see this happening through us partnering with Him in building His Kingdom here on Earth, across every sphere of society.

But what exactly is the Kingdom of God?

The Kingdom of God is a rather abstract concept, which in simple terms refers to the effective rule and reign of God. As Christians, we know that God is the creator of all things and the legitimate ruler over every part of His creation. Furthermore, He has all power and authority to enforce His rule if necessary. There is no entity or force that is able to stand against Him if He decides to exercise this power and authority that He possesses.

Nevertheless, God chooses to restrain His power in order to allow all spiritual beings with a moral capacity (e.g. humans, angels, and demons) to have free will – which involves the ability to choose between good or evil. This opens up the potential for God's legitimate rule to be opposed (which it is) and therefore for evil to exist in the world, even though He is all-loving and all-powerful. Opposition to His rule comes through Satan and his kingdom of darkness, and occurs among humankind when they partner with these forces of evil – particularly through sinful actions that result from believing the devil's lies.

Exploring this in more depth, we see in Genesis that God's original plan was to share His rule with humanity. He desired to work in partnership with those He made in His image, to enforce His rule over the earth and all creation existing on it. He gave them the right to have dominion over these things, under His supervision (Gen. 1:26, 28, 2:15, 19).

Satan, however, exploited the free will of Adam and Eve, the first humans, by tricking them into disobeying God (Gen. 3:1-6) and therefore handing their rightful dominion over the earth to him (cf. Luke 4:5-6). This placed them and all their future descendants under enslavement to him (cf. Heb. 2:14-15). In this act of rebellion, they had partnered with Satan in opposing God's Kingdom, which brought sin and death into the world (Gen. 2:17, 3:19; Rom. 5:12), a situation that continues until the present day. Everything that we recognize as wrong with the world, such as sickness, poverty, oppression, terrorism, war, crime, and even natural disasters, is the result of this. All of these evils are contrary to the rule of God – He did not and does not will them on His creation.

It took Jesus' death on the cross to win back for humanity (specifically those redeemed by the blood of Jesus) the legitimate right to have dominion over all the earth (Matt. 16:18-19), but this has to be enforced progressively (cf. Matt. 28:18-20). Satan still has dominion over every person who refuses to come under God's rule and all the structures of human society that are opposed to God. Not to mention, the operation of Satan's kingdom in terms of the evils we just mentioned above. He will continue to oppose God's rule and reign by stirring up rebellion to it, as long as he is on the scene.

At this time, though, God does not wish to destroy all opposition to His Kingdom, because He loves humanity and wants every person who still opposes His rule to come under it and be saved (1 Tim. 2:4; 2 Peter 3:9). This displays His patience, mercy, and grace, rather than any weakness.

Based on this analysis, we can therefore say that God's rule is effective (i.e. His Kingdom is present) in every place where His legitimate rule is recognized, submitted to, and enforced. Another way of stating this is that the Kingdom of God is present whenever His will is done, and to the degree that it is. This idea is clearly affirmed in part of the prayer that Jesus taught His disciples in Matt. 6:9-13, through the use of synonymous parallelism[83] (which I have underlined):

> Your <u>kingdom come</u>, your <u>will be done</u>, on earth as it is in heaven. (Matt. 6:10; emphasis mine)

Here Jesus also reveals a key distinction, that when God's will is done in our world in some way, Earth reflects a heavenly reality in that area. That is, Heaven effectively comes to Earth because Heaven is a place where God's will is carried out perfectly, all the time.[84] This distinction is of fundamental importance to the Bethel movement, as it is central to their understanding of the mission of the Christian

Church – which is to bring Heaven to Earth (i.e. extend God's Kingdom). For we are not just to pray for God's Kingdom to come; we also need to partner with Him in making it happen.

To give some examples, Heaven comes to Earth when a person receives Jesus as their Savior, someone is healed of an illness/injury (either supernaturally, through the body's natural healing mechanisms, or medical intervention), a woman is freed from sex trafficking, an unemployed man finds a suitable job, a homeless person is housed, a broken marriage is restored, crime reduces, and a community in the developing world gains access to clean drinking water.

God is not a tyrant and His rule is not burdensome. His will is for life, love, purpose, prosperity, freedom, peace, joy, truth, and righteousness to exist in all their fullness on Earth. Every place His Kingdom extends to contains elements of these factors, benefitting every person affected. But wherever His Kingdom does not reach, the opposite of these realities will prevail, such as death, poverty, hopelessness, and oppression. This is why there are only two ultimate realities: Heaven and Hell. These represent places where God's rule is absolute and nonexistent, respectively.

Heaven is the abode of God and eternal home to everyone who chooses to come under His rule, by repenting of their sins, accepting His offer of salvation, and living a holy life. It is a completely blissful place, described in the Bible as paradise (Rev. 2:7). Heaven includes every element of God's will mentioned in the paragraph above, and probably many others that I haven't listed.

Hell (a.k.a. the lake of fire), on the other hand, is simply the eternal home for every spiritual being who chooses to rebel against Him, by disobeying His commandments and refusing His incredibly generous offer of salvation (which is available only to humans – not Satan or any member of his kingdom of darkness cf. Matt. 25:41). It involves complete and permanent separation from God (2 Thess. 1:9) and the life that emanates from Him. In other words, it is a kind of divorce from the Creator of the universe. But make no mistake, there won't be any wild parties or fun there as some people like to joke.

Quite the contrary, Hell is a place of eternal death. It involves continuous, conscious suffering and torment, in a lake of fire from which there is no possibility of escape ... ever. Death reigns there because God is the source of all life, and no life can exist apart from Him.

This life on Earth, therefore, is an opportunity for every person to make the decision of whether or not they want to come under God's rule and live with Him for eternity in Heaven, or partner with Satan and end up suffering with him forever in Hell. Although God knows that everyone needs to be part of His Kingdom of life, He desires that they willingly submit to His kingship and will never try to force anyone to come under it. Those who do not will just fail to receive the benefits of His rule – eternal life.

God's ultimate plan is for the whole world to come under His rule, and to reign over it forever (Rev. 11:15). But this will only happen at the end of time, when all remaining opposition to His authority is removed by force (Rev. 11:17-18; cf. Rev. 12:10).

In the meantime, however, even though His rule is greatly opposed on Earth at the moment, making it a less than perfect place, He still has enough influence to prevent the planet from completely degenerating into the hellish abode that it would become without elements of His rule being in place. In fact, if you analyze the situation, you can see that the natural world generally functions well and fosters life. Furthermore, almost every human society operates in a state of law and order, the vast majority of the time. These things reflect the rule of God to some degree, since God is the source of all life, order, justice, and goodness.

Finally, before we move on to the next subsection, I would like to clear up the common misconception about the Kingdom of God that I alluded to earlier in the chapter. This is that it represents only the sum of all those who are saved (i.e. the true Church) and that building the Kingdom on Earth is simply an exercise in evangelism: preaching the Gospel and leading people to Jesus. To be sure, this is a very important part of building His Kingdom and one that should never be ignored, but certainly not the full extent of it. For God is interested in extending His rule to everything, not just the hearts and minds of people. He created the world, it is rightly His, and He wants every part of it back fully under His control. And this is not just for His sake, but ours, so that we can live fulfilled, prosperous lives, in a nourishing and sustaining environment. This is where our responsibility to proclaim the Gospel of the Kingdom (Matt. 4:23, 24:14; Luke 4:43, 8:1) comes in.

The Gospel of the Kingdom

Bethel is committed to proclaiming the Gospel of the Kingdom, rather than just the Gospel of salvation – which is a part of the Gospel of the Kingdom. They know that God wants to co-labor with us as the Church to bring His rule and reign to Earth, in order to make it look increasingly like Heaven. This includes every aspect of the world, and not just leading people to their Savior Jesus and adding them to the Church.

Bill Johnson explains this broader focus on restoring the whole planet back to God's rule:

> The Gospel of salvation is focused on getting people saved and going to Heaven. The Gospel of the Kingdom is focused on the transformation of lives, cities, and nations through the effect of God's present rule—this is made manifest by bringing the reality of Heaven to earth. We must not confuse our destiny with our assignment. Heaven is my destiny, while bringing the Kingdom is my assignment. The focus of the Kingdom message is the rightful dominion of God over everything. Whatever is inconsistent with Heaven—namely, disease, torment, hatred, division, sin habits, etc.—must come under the authority of the King.[85]

If all we are concerned about is evangelizing people then we won't have much of a value for improving the lives of others, except as a way to get them to accept Jesus as their Savior. But then we end up with a distorted key performance indicator such that we evaluate the time, effort, and money that we devote to helping people solely based on the number of converts they lead to, rather than as an end in itself – sharing God's goodness with the world. This can make us feel like we've failed if we don't see spectacular results in terms of salvations, when we may have actually succeeded to a great extent in fulfilling our true mission – to extend God's Kingdom on Earth (i.e. bring Heaven to Earth).

We cannot lose sight of the fact that the Greek word used in the New Testament for "save" and "saved", *sōzō*, can mean saved, healed, and delivered, and potentially all three at once (cf. Luke 17:17-19)! Similarly, the word normally translated as salvation, *sōtēria*, can also be a lot broader in meaning that just a state of being in right relationship with God, such that we will go to Heaven when we die.

"Being saved" should therefore not be construed solely in terms of forgiveness of sins by God. It is a holistic concept which includes being free from all sin, sickness, poverty, oppression, and anything else that hinders us from enjoying the abundant life that Jesus bought for us (John 10:10). Basically, it is the Hebrew idea of shalom (peace, in every dimension of one's life[86]). It is significant that in the Old Testament Jesus is called the Prince of Peace (Isaiah 9:6), where "Peace" is the translation of the Hebrew word *shalom*.

Also of interest, W.E. Vine notes that in the Septuagint (the Greek Translation of the Old Testament), the word *shalom* is often rendered *sōtēria*[87], which as we have just discussed is the New Testament word that is normally translated as "salvation" in English. This connection of these two words adds further weight to the argument that the New Testament concept of salvation is far broader than just freedom from sin.

Much of the Church has simply failed to grasp this. They have largely thought of salvation in the narrow sense of being forgiven of our sins and in right relationship with God. Therefore, to them, extending God's Kingdom just means getting more people saved. And the signs that they've been successful at this are large, growing churches. However, few churches meet this standard of success and many have been content to just faithfully proclaim the Gospel (of salvation), even though most of the time they're really only preaching to the choir, so to speak.

To see what we should actually be doing, it is helpful to look at the life of Jesus, particularly His teachings and the example He set. He described His commission as the following:

> "The Spirit of the Lord is upon me, because he has anointed me to proclaim good news to the poor. He has sent me to proclaim liberty to the captives and recovering of sight to the blind, to set at liberty those who are oppressed, to proclaim the year of the Lord's favor." (Luke 4:18-19; cf. 4:43)

What many Christians do, though, is over-spiritualize this. Therefore the poor, the captive, the blind, and those who are oppressed are all simply people in bondage to sin, who are in need of spiritual salvation (i.e. the forgiveness of sin).

However, both the Old and New Testaments have much to say about caring for those in need, particularly Luke's Gospel. Jesus, in His ministry, supernaturally fed some of the large crowds that came to hear Him speak by multiplying food (Luke 9:10-17). He healed the sick and infirmed (Matt. 4:23-24), cleansed lepers (Luke 17:11-19), delivered those who were demonized (Mark 5:1-15), rescued a widow from possible destitution by raising her only son from the dead (Luke 7:11-15), and He spoke out against social injustices (e.g. Luke 20:47). He did all these things without measuring His success by the number of people He led to repentance, or the amount of followers He attracted.

Jesus also instructed His disciples to do likewise: heal the sick, raise the dead, cleanse lepers, and cast out demons, while proclaiming that the Kingdom is at hand (Matt. 10:7-8). Here we see how the coming of God's Kingdom is linked to people's physical lives on Earth being improved. This is a strong witness to the goodness of God, whose rule people should choose to come under, for their own benefit.

Furthermore, He made it very clear that how we treat those in need affects our eternal destiny (Matt. 25:31-46; Luke 16:19-31). That is, being under God's rule requires us to care for others rather than just looking after self, or even only helping people with their spiritual needs (cf. James 2:14-17).

In the Christian world, there has existed a large divide between the Social Gospel/Liberation Theology/social justice stream and the evangelistic one. Liberal Christians have focused predominantly on helping those in need, seeing salvation primarily in terms of improving people's earthly circumstances. On the other hand, evangelicals have specialized in preaching the Gospel of salvation, seeing salvation narrowly in terms of "being right with God" and thereby owning a ticket to Heaven – through repenting of one's sins and following Jesus. In reality, both are valid and absolutely necessary means of furthering God's Kingdom on Earth.

In view of all this, we need to make sure that we don't misunderstand Bill Johnson in the quote above. He is definitely not saying that there is no place for evangelism in our Christian witness to the world, or that opportunities to receive Jesus should not be offered at church services. Nothing could not be further from the truth; he sees evangelism as an extremely important part of our mission both as the Church corporately and as individual believers out in the world. At Bethel, a huge focus is put on this and I have never seen any other church produce so many powerful evangelists, who regularly lead people to Jesus. The point Bill is making is that bringing the Kingdom is so much larger than just getting people to accept Jesus as their Savior so they can go to Heaven when they die. It involves the transformation of every aspect of human life and civilization on the planet.

Kris Vallotton agrees with this and makes an important additional point:

> People are preaching Heaven instead of the Kingdom. Preaching the Kingdom is about trying to bring Heaven to Earth rather than people to Heaven when they die. When you bring the Kingdom you get both.[88]

Here he argues that when you preach the Kingdom and bring Heaven to Earth, you not only see the transformation of society (which he usually refers to as "cultural transformation"), but people come to faith in Jesus as well. In other words, it is a two-for-one deal. The transformation that we as Christians bring about helps to create a more favorable atmosphere for the salvation message to prosper when it is delivered. For Jesus told us that we are the light of the world and that when others see our good works they will give glory to our Father in Heaven (Matt. 5:14-16). That is, these good works enable people to taste and see that the Lord is good (Psalm 34:8a), and influence them into choosing to come into relationship with Him as the good Father who gives good gifts to His children (Matt. 7:11).

Jesus and His disciples did this frequently with the miracles in their ministries, particularly in the area of healing, and this is a great example of how we can bring the Kingdom and have it lead to salvation. Words of knowledge/prophecy is another example (e.g. John 1:47-51, 4:16-42). But while using the supernatural gifts of the Holy Spirit is one really good way to bring the Kingdom to people's lives, it is certainly not the only way. Anything we do to make the world a better place is also a legitimate expression of Heaven being brought to Earth, and therefore of the Kingdom of God advancing; it doesn't need to be miraculous.

On this basis, some non-Christians are actually doing a better job of bringing Heaven to Earth than we the Church are. Granted, they are not leading anyone to Jesus, but neither are most of us. What they are doing is making the world a better place through some of their scientific discoveries, business inventions, and philanthropic activities, for example. As Kris notes, few of the pioneers of the Information Age were Christians.[89] Yet, these mainly non-Christian pioneers have changed the world, mostly for good, with the technologies they have introduced. I suspect that not many of us would rather go back to life without computers, the Internet, and our smart phones. But would we associate these technological advances with the furthering of the Kingdom of God on Earth?

Kris suggests that our pessimistic eschatology is a reason why the Church has been neglecting its responsibility to be involved in societal transformation.[90] Premillennial dispensationalism has told us that Jesus will be returning any time now and therefore we should forget about everything other than preaching the Gospel (of salvation) and getting as many people saved as possible. In practice, though, even this has not really been happening, at least not very successfully. My strong suspicion is that the majority of Christians in the West have never led anyone to the Lord, and do not actively witness for their faith on a regular basis.

The Seven Mountains Strategy

With all this is mind, an important strategy has emerged for bringing the Kingdom to Earth, into every sphere of society. This is sometimes called the "Seven Mountains Strategy" and has been receiving a lot of attention lately in some circles – including at Bethel, where it has been strongly embraced.

In 1975, Bill Bright of Campus Crusade for Christ and Loren Cunningham of Youth With a Mission (YWAM) each received a message from God for the other. When they met, they found out that both had the same message, which was about seven mountains of influence that were key to transforming society and reaching the nations for God.[91]

These seven mountains are (in no particular order):

1. Government
2. Business
3. Media
4. Education
5. Family
6. Arts and Entertainment
7. Religion

God has given believers in Jesus the task of establishing influence on each of these key mountains, which largely determine how society operates. It is our job to use this influence to make them expressions of His Kingdom, which is His life-giving rule. The more that a society is run according to Kingdom values and principles, the more that it will look like Heaven, function well, and enable people to flourish. However, the less it is run according to these values and principles, the more that it will resemble Hell and deliver poor outcomes for the vast majority of people.

To see the truth of this, we only need to look at various societies around the world. There is clearly a large correlation between a country's historical level of penetration by the Gospel and how prosperous, healthy, and just that its society is. Those that have been strongly penetrated by it tend to be far richer, have less crime, higher life expectancy, smaller gaps between rich and poor, and experience lower levels of corruption – than those that have been less strongly penetrated.

God therefore wants us, as believers, to have a vision for societal transformation to improve the state of the world, so that it more adequately reflects what Heaven looks like and is a better place for everyone to live. This creates a more favorable atmosphere for people to come to know God as the good Father and receive Jesus as their Savior. For when we display Kingdom realities to people, they will often be interested in knowing the King Himself. The idea, though, is not to become "king of the mountain" and then use these positions to shout the Gospel of salvation as loudly as we can.

Essentially, the Seven Mountains Strategy is a call to disciple the nations for God (Matt. 28:19), in line with God's promise to Abraham that he would be the father of many nations (Gen. 17:5). When we establish influence on each of the key mountains of society, it places us collectively in a leadership position. People come to us for answers to their problems, and when we propose our divinely inspired solutions they will tend to implement them, potentially benefitting many. This results from having servant hearts and establishing track records of excellent service over a period of time, so that people want to have us around. It is not about slipping in secretly, taking control, and then dominating everything as other groups have done, for Jesus gave us the mandate to be servant leaders rather than dictators.

The following proverb illustrates how we rise to positions of influence:

> Do you see a man skillful in his work? He will stand before kings; he will not stand before obscure men. (Prov. 22:29)

Two significant models in Scripture for how we can do this are Joseph and Daniel, who both rose to positions of enormous influence on the mountain of government. They served the rulers of the kingdoms they lived in with divine revelation, wisdom, and abilities, which God had given them, and as a result they were given great authority in the running of these kingdoms. Joseph, by interpreting the dreams of the King of Egypt was made governor over the entire kingdom, and ended up preserving it through a severe famine (Gen. 41, 47:13-25). Daniel was promoted to a similar role after he also interpreted a dream of his king (Nebuchadnezzar, ruler of Babylon) (Dan. 2). Through his influence, this pagan king came to honor God (Dan. 2:47, 4:34-37). Daniel also interpreted the writing on the wall that appeared to King Belshazzar (Dan. 5) and served as one of three presidents under King Darius (Dan. 6), which led to the latter also honoring God (Dan. 6:25-27). In addition to all of this, he apparently served well in a similar position under King Cyrus (Dan. 6:28).

One important thing to emphasize about these case studies, is how the supernatural of God was used to gain influence and serve well. Both Joseph (Gen. 41:38-39) and Daniel (Dan. 1:15, 20, 5:12, 6:3) were recognized as being far superior to anyone else in matters such as wisdom, understanding, and problem solving. However, these were not natural, in-born talents, but God-given supernatural abilities, which operated by faith[92].

As believers today, we also need to tap into God's supernatural power to bring His Kingdom to Earth, on each of the seven mountains of influence. God has divine solutions available to many of the world problems, and He has appointed us to bring them. If we want influence in the key areas of the world then we need to earn it by coming up with creative ideas and solutions that could only come from God. Just being nice people who work hard will unfortunately not cut the mustard in this regard. For if we rely solely on our natural abilities then how many of us will be the best in the world at what we do, let alone by a factor of ten as Daniel and his companions were (Dan. 1:20)? The answer obviously is very few!

However, since every one of us has the mind of Christ (1 Cor. 2:16) we are not limited to the natural, but have access to all of the wisdom and revelation that Jesus had on Earth, not to mention the same supernatural powers to work the miraculous. This can just as easily be applied in our work and everyday lives as in "Christian ministry" (i.e. the mountain of religion) if we're intentional about doing so. God wants to change every aspect of the world and bring it under His glorious rule, not just get people saved (although this an important part of the Gospel message which we should never lose sight of).

In case you're wondering, this is not some fanciful theory that has never been successfully implemented before. Christians are actually doing this sort of stuff right now, in the real world. Bethel, for example, has a group called *Heaven in Business*, which as the name suggests is bringing the supernatural of God to the business world. There have been some amazing success stories coming out of it how people have partnered with God and seen incredible results. Bethel people are also heavily involved in the world of arts and entertainment. Government is another area that they are involved in. Bethel Church works with the City of Redding, California (where the church is located) to bring transformation to the local community, in areas such as reducing poverty and homelessness, controlling crime, keeping the city clean, and even in the running of the Civic Auditorium (the city's conference and events center). In addition to this, there are some, such as Kris Vallotton, who work with governmental and political leaders in the United States and other countries (on a nonpartisan basis), to see governments deliver the best outcomes for their people.

Then, of course, there is the bread and butter of signs and wonders ministry in the marketplace, which Bethel is famous for - offering things like healing for bodies and prophetic words to encourage people and unlock their destinies. These gifts of the Spirit are extremely useful wherever we go and in whatever we do, because they match many of the real world needs of people, which often cannot be filled by others.

Like Jesus, we need to have real answers to the real problems that people face. When we bless society through our divine wisdom, solutions and power, people will be led to recognize our God as the one true God, and come into relationship with Him. However, as Bill Johnson points out, Christians have for too long been trying to answer questions that people simply aren't asking.[93]

In recent decades, Christians have largely departed from most of the mountains, in terms of influencing them for Kingdom purposes, and have focused almost exclusively on the mountain of religion - which the Church occupies. We have been busy doing religious stuff (e.g. church services, home groups, Bible studies, reading Christian books, theological studies, youth groups, prayer meetings, men's and women's ministry, conferences, and preaching the Gospel of salvation etc.), but have lacked a vision for the other six mountains.

While Christians have continued to work and be involved in all of these areas, there is a huge difference between just being there and actually bringing the Kingdom. Instead of using our jobs and businesses to transform society and culture, we have viewed them primarily as means to earn incomes for ourselves. Some of us have also seen them as opportunities to witness for our faith and share the salvation message with those around us.

An unspoken belief has long existed that a calling outside of the Church (i.e. the religion mountain) is a second-class one. The real ministry has been seen as in the Church, and in the absence of role models in other spheres of influence, famous itinerant ministers have become the rock stars of the faith, who everyone aspires to be like.

"Ordinary" Christians have struggled to find meaning in their lives outside of religious activities, both on Sunday and during the rest of the week. Conference attendance has become the pinnacle of life for many, helping them to maintain their motivation for and excitement about their faith. The problem is that these activities tend to be all about the mountain of religion (e.g. how we can become stronger in our faith and reach more people for Jesus) but seldom do they relate to areas like how to advance the Kingdom of God directly in our work and everyday lives.

Christianity is being sold as a one-time decision that you make (to follow Jesus), and then a lot of hard work throughout the rest of your life to maintain this faith – so that you don't lose your ticket to Heaven. This is a defensive mindset, as opposed to the offensive one of already being seated in heavenly places (Eph. 2:6) and changing the world for God, that we see presented in the New Testament. Is it any wonder then that we struggle to convince others to join us for the ride when it sounds so dour and boring?

The living out of our faith can and should be the greatest and most exciting adventure on the planet. We get to explore worlds that most others don't even know exist, and are called to epic missions that make Frodo's one in *The Lord of the Rings* pale in comparison. The creatures that we have to fight are far more vile and intimidating than the ones depicted in Peter Jackson's famous movie trilogy. But we have the advantage of divine spiritual protection (Isaiah 54:17), so we might as well just charge into battle and rout every army that stands in our way!

However, due to Christians failing to embark on these great adventures and losing their value for influence in the world, other groups have come in and claimed the neglected mountains for their own agendas, almost unopposed. The result of this is that the government passes immoral and unjust laws. Business funds powerful lobby groups that influence government in the direction of these laws. The media put a liberal spin on the news and current affairs. The education system teaches our children ungodly, humanistic ideas, and blocks everything to do with faith. The arts and entertainment promote extreme violence and immorality. Meanwhile, family is constantly being redefined. Same-sex relationships, for example, are now seen by many as being equal to heterosexual ones, and divorce has become a normal part of the lifecycle of a marriage. The devil, therefore, has not had a very difficult job in corrupting society and opposing the Gospel salvation message when he has exerted such a large amount of influence on six of the seven key mountains, with much of the Church effectively sidelined.

Furthermore, he is not even content with this situation. Currently, the devil is executing a strong offensive on the mountain of religion (which the Church in the West has traditionally occupied, almost exclusively) with the proliferation of other religions, spiritualities, and philosophies. Some of these are now gaining significant traction in the West and have overtaken Christianity in terms of their degree of influence on society. We as the Church have failed miserably at offering the world a spirituality that provides real answers to people's most pressing concerns in life. Consequently, they are going to those who do. For example, Eastern meditation and yoga practices offer people mental and physical well-being. Clairvoyants present insights into the future. Reiki provides physical healing, and New Thought self-help gurus teach their metaphysical secrets to financial and relationship success – sometimes even justifying their teachings by quoting Jesus from the Bible passages e.g. Mark 11:22-24![94]

As Christians, all we've offered people for the things they're concerned about is a ticket to Heaven when they die, telling them that in this life things often just don't work out and that they should therefore focus instead on eternity, when everything will be put right. I'm sorry, but this is simply not good enough. It does not pay the rent and put food on the table; nor does it relieve physical pain, take away stress, or make people feel good emotionally. These are the sorts of things that people are actually interested in. Have you ever wondered why surveys have apparently revealed that the fear of public speaking tops the fear of death as people's greatest fear? I believe it is because the fear of public speaking is a far more immediate concern for most people.

But it gets much, much worse than this. Bible colleges and seminaries are not only teaching students (many of whom are our current and future Christian leaders) that there are no solutions to a number of our biggest issues in this life (e.g. certain types of physical, mental, and emotional suffering), some are also telling them that it is actually more blessed to suffer – not necessarily for Christ, but to in general experience a difficult, painful life. No wonder a lot of churches are empty when they preach this sort of nonsense instead of the true Gospel of the Kingdom – which offers us great hope for both this life and the one to come. The truth is that God has answers to all of our concerns, even though many try to limit Him in order to accommodate their own lack of faith and power.

The result of all of this is that, in addition to surrendering six of the seven mountains, we're now starting to lose the one mountain that we have always prided ourselves on owning – religion. I believe that much of this can be traced back to our failure to embrace an eschatology of hope, and our adoption instead of a very pessimistic and disempowering one, in which we expect bad things to happen now, forcing us to passively wait for all the good things that we believe are reserved for the next life.[95] Consequently, we have not accessed the blessings that God has available for us now and therefore we have been in no position to offer them to the world – through the Gospel of the Kingdom.

Essentially, we have become out of touch with and irrelevant to most of society, leaving us baffled as to why no one in interested in hearing what we have to say – which we believe is the greatest message in the world. This has enabled the devil to have a field day in deceiving the world through his "gospel" of "do whatever you want and everything that makes you feel good", echoing the way he deceived Adam and Eve in the Garden of Eden (Gen. 3:1-6). Such a message appeals strongly to our "buy now, pay later", instant gratification culture.

The deterioration of society that we've witnessed has confirmed to many Christians that the world is going to Hell in a hand basket. This has therefore led them to speculate that the appearing of the Antichrist is near. In reality, we as the Church have failed to do our job, which is to be salt and light to the world (Matt. 5:13-16), and this is why many things have deteriorated. Darkness flees when we shine our light, while the significance of salt is that in biblical times it was used as a preservative to stop foods, such as meat, from going bad. Therefore, when we are salty, we help to prevent the world from becoming as corrupt as it would without our influence.

A lot of us think, however, that all Jesus was meaning in this instruction was for us to share our faith about Him with people. Yes, that is part of it, but we also need to establish influence on each of the seven mountains. And in order for that to happen, we need to be prepared to roll up our sleeves and serve our communities so that they thrive – not just for our own religious agenda of winning converts.

To give an example, Bethel recently offered the City of Redding $500,000 to help prevent the layoff of some police officers who were needed to keep the community safe through crime prevention. Many Christians, though, would say that giving such a large amount of money to this cause is a complete waste, as it could be a lot better spent in other areas much more core to the mission of the Church (i.e. "spiritual" ones). But Bethel argues that being a blessing to the local community, in this and other ways, is an important part of the mission of the Church. For one, it promotes law and order, which advances the Kingdom directly. And secondly, it is a great witness to the love of God that Christians and the Church have for their community.

We must get rid of this false dichotomy of sacred and secular. God does not want to be restricted to only church and "ministry". He desires to be fully involved in each and every area of our lives, and on each and every mountain of society – through our collective efforts (individually, though, we will normally specialize in one, or a few, of the seven mountains). He is the rightful ruler of all, and it is His intention that this rule be established over everything He has created so that Earth becomes like Heaven. Obviously, this will not be completed until Jesus returns and removes all opposition to the Kingdom, but this should not prevent us from faithfully working toward this objective. God wants to partner with us in the task; He has delegated authority to us and supplied the necessary power for us to be successful at our assignment. As Bill Johnson puts it, referencing the original mandate of God for humankind to rule with Him:

> We were born to rule—rule over creation, over darkness—to plunder hell, to rescue those headed there, and to establish the rule of Jesus wherever we go by preaching the Gospel of the Kingdom.[96]

As Christians, it is essential for us to reclaim our vision for God moving through us in our everyday lives to transform the world, as greats like William Wilberforce and Mother Theresa have done spectacularly in the past. We all need to view ourselves as being in full-time ministry, regardless of where we are and how we earn our living.

Working outside of the Church should not be boring and just a necessary evil, enabling us to pay our bills. And we must not reduce this vision down to witnessing for our faith, even though this activity is both right and necessary.

It is important, therefore, that we understand how God can use us in our work, to bring His Kingdom into the very structures of society and influence them for good, bringing life and prosperity to many – especially through the supernatural power of God that we have access to through the Holy Spirit. This will then create the platform for the Church to be successful at converting souls to Jesus on a mass scale, as people see the goodness of God displayed ubiquitously.

Fundamental to all of this is an optimistic and victorious eschatology, which empowers us to change the world for God and is conducive to moving in signs and wonders, as Jesus and the original apostles did. Fear will then no longer prevent us from being the history makers that God intended us to be. We are called to arise and shine in this day (Isaiah 60)!

6. COMPLETE FIVE-FOLD MINISTRY

The sixth key ingredient in the Bethel signs and wonders culture is the complete five-fold ministry being in place, with every element of this functioning as part of the leadership structure and ministry of the church. This is something I had not seen modeled well in any church environment before, at least not to the degree demonstrated at Bethel.

The "five-fold ministry" is described by Paul, in his letter to the Ephesians:

> So Christ himself gave the apostles, the prophets, the evangelists, the pastors and teachers, to equip his people for works of service, so that the body of Christ may be built up until we all reach unity in the faith and in the knowledge of the Son of God and become mature, attaining to the whole measure of the fullness of Christ. (Eph. 4:11-13, NIV2011)

According to this passage, these five types of ministers are given by Jesus to the Church, for the purposes of equipping believers for works of service ("the work of ministry", ESV) and maturing them to become like Him[97]. Many, if not most, churches however seem to only have two of the five elements of this ministry in place (pastors and teachers), with the other three (apostles, prophets, and evangelists) notably absent. While it is true that these neglected roles are sometimes filled without being named as such, people with these callings are most often not positioned in places of leadership where they can teach and equip the body on a regular basis – as they are at Bethel and were intended to be by God.

Apostles and Pastors

One thing which is very unfortunate is that nearly all churches today, for various reasons, seem to have in practice given up on the apostle as an official role within the Church, in the same way that a pastor is. For example, many people believe that only the original 12 disciples of Jesus (who he named apostles (Luke 6:13)), plus Matthias (Judas' replacement (Acts 1:26)), Paul, and possibly a few others mentioned in the NT, count as legitimate apostles. After this, the role ceased to exist and had no ongoing expression, according to their view. However, the Ephesians passage quoted above gives no indication that any of five-fold ministry roles would not continue for the duration of Church, until the return of Jesus. Furthermore, neither does any other passage in Scripture.

Among those who still (at least, in theory) believe in the continuing role of the apostle within the Church, there is much debate as to what it actually involves. The predominant view seems to be that it refers to someone who plants churches. Other people believe that it is a missionary[98] – especially to developing nations that haven't been strongly penetrated by the Gospel. Sometimes also, a business analogy is used to describe the apostle as an entrepreneur figure who innovates and builds, while the pastor is seen as a manager who maintains what this entrepreneur has built. Another popular view is that the apostolic represents a level of success in ministry, such that when the church you're leading achieves a certain amount of growth then people will start to recognize you as an "apostolic leader". Of course, others have come up with variations on these ideas, combinations of them, and even different ones entirely.

To this point, however, no strong consensus on this subject of apostolic identity has emerged, leaving the vast majority of believers (including many church leaders) in a state of utter confusion regarding it. The sad consequence of this is that the definition of the apostle has largely been consigned to the "too hard basket", with people tending to just give up and move on. But this has resulted in the role of the apostle itself also being relegated to a similar basket – which has meant that the God-appointed apostles in the Church have either been sidelined without appropriate places to discharge their ministries, or they have been placed in positions not fully appropriate for their commission (e.g. pastor[99]). And the implication of this, according to the Eph. 4:11-13 passage cited above, would be that the Body of Christ has not been fully equipped for its mission. Could this be part of the reason why, in recent times, the Church as a whole has been so ineffective at fulfilling the Great Commission (Matt. 28:18-20; Mark 16:15-18)?

In any case, though, this situation is a catastrophe that we cannot allow to continue; God appoints apostles for a reason, and without them we are missing out on something extremely important that they offer. It is therefore vital that we rediscover what apostles actually are and grant them their rightful place within the structure of the Church.

My intention here, however, is not to critically analyze the various views of what an apostle was and the potential contemporary expressions of this role. That would probably require a whole book or dissertation on its own. Instead, I will first trace its historical origins and New Testament usage. Following this, I will outline Bethel's view of the apostle and the way that the role operates within their movement. Much of their thinking in this area comes from senior associate leader Kris Vallotton, a five-fold prophet, who received a word from the Lord on church government. I will draw heavily from him in this section.

The Historical and New Testament Contexts of Apostle

The word "apostle" (Greek: *apostolos* – which is the noun form of the verb *apostellō* "send"/"sent") is a term that literally means "one sent forth"[100] (or more simply, a "sent one"). It originated hundreds of years prior to the New Testament period and normally referred to seafaring expeditions (especially military ones)[101]. Most often, *apostolos* carried an impersonal reference, such as to a ship or fleet of ships sent out.[102] Occasionally, though, it referred to the commander of the expedition[103] and the group of men who were part of this expedition (e.g. an army)[104]. It was sometimes also used in a non-military sense for a group of colonists and their settlement.[105]

The central idea of "apostle", under this original usage, was of being sent out for a particular purpose. But it is important to note the predominantly passive character of the apostle; there is no suggestion of either any initiative or authorization on their part.[106]

The use of *apostolos* in Greek literature, however, was relatively uncommon outside of the NT and its sphere of influence (even though its root word *apostellō* was actually common).[107] This contrasts strongly with its frequent use in the NT (80 times in total), particularly in the writings of Luke and Paul, which probably provides some indication of the importance placed on the apostolic by the earliest Christians.

Of even greater significance, though, is the fact that the NT writers adjusted the meaning of *apostolos* to fit the entirely new context of the Church. This adjustment was so substantial that their application of the word bore little resemblance to its normal usage up to that time (outside of the broad meaning of being sent out for a purpose – which remained unchanged). Gone was the strong association with seafaring expeditions and the usual impersonal and collective references. It now referred exclusively to one individual person. In addition, the idea of being explicitly commissioned by someone was prominent (Luke 11:49; 1 Cor. 1:1, 12:28), as was the concept of being a messenger or envoy (Rom. 11:13; 2 Cor. 8:23; 2 Peter 3:2), which was previously rare (the Greeks had many other words that could be used for this sort of purpose instead[108]). Furthermore, the idea of delegated authority came to the fore (Acts 2:43; 8:18; 1 Thess. 2:6) and, in conjunction with this, leadership was often conveyed (Acts 2:42, 4:35; Eph. 4:11) – neither of which had previously been significant aspects of *apostolos*. Finally, the working of the miraculous was strongly associated with this word (Acts 5:12-16; 1 Cor. 2:4-5; 2 Cor. 12:12).

This almost total departure by the NT writers from the way *apostolos* had previously been used, and the lack of explicit information they provide about their usage of the term[109] (i.e. they never define exactly what an *apostolos* is or the unique responsibilities of the role), makes the task of precisely pinning down the concept of biblical apostleship quite demanding. After all, most of what we know about it relates to the documented commissions (e.g. Rom. 1:1-6, 11:13), characteristics (e.g. Acts 1:20b-26; 1 Cor. 4:15; 2 Cor. 11:22-28), and activities (e.g. Acts 5:12; 2 Tim. 4:1-2) of those named apostles in the NT – the bulk of which relates to Paul. And for most of these things, we have no conclusive way of determining whether they are either definitional of an apostle or incidental to this role.

One great example of this is that Paul frequently identified himself as a father in the faith (1 Cor. 4:14-15, 17; Phil. 2:22; 1 Tim. 1:2, 18; 2 Tim. 1:2, 2:1; Titus 1:4; Philemon 10).[110] But does his apostleship and fatherhood in the faith mean that spiritual fatherhood is a defining quality of the biblical apostle? Or alternatively, was fatherhood just something specific to Paul's individual calling? Put another way, was Paul an apostle <u>because</u> he was a father (along with some other key qualities) or was he an apostle <u>and</u> a father – meaning the spiritual fatherhood is separate from apostleship? Unfortunately, though, the biblical data that exists is insufficient to come to any definitive conclusion on the matter.

Because there rarely exist unambiguous answers to issues like this concerning apostolic identity, the necessity arises for judgment calls to be made. And these judgment calls are the reason why there are so many different ideas about this concept floating around today – particularly when people typically zero in on one specific quality of the NT apostles and make apostleship all about that, without adequately taking into consideration the bigger picture. For instance, as we discussed earlier, some see apostles in the limited sense of only being the original ones named in Scripture (particularly the 12 disciples of Jesus, Judas' replacement Matthias, and Paul), based on the fact that only they were taught by Jesus and/or encountered the risen Christ and were appointed by Him to be apostles (Luke 6:13; Acts 1:21-26; Gal. 1:1).[111] Others notice that those identified as apostles were often planters of churches (at least that is implied in the NT) (Acts 14:21-23; cf. Rom. 15:20), and thus this is their definition of the term. Still others observe that the NT apostles were typically preachers, particularly to those of different cultures (Acts 14:8-14; Gal. 2:7-8). Therefore, they conclude that an apostle is a missionary preacher of the Gospel.

Bethel's View of the Apostle

Instead of trying to reverse engineer one's definition of the apostle from the documented commissions, characteristics, and activities of those named apostles in the NT, as many others have done, Bethel takes quite a different approach. It anchors its understanding of the apostle primarily in Eph. 4:11-13, where some foundational characteristics of this role are clearly laid out. These are that the apostle is an important leadership position within the Church (alongside the prophet, evangelist, pastor, and teacher), whose purpose is to both equip believers for the work of ministry and build up the Body of Christ to maturity in the faith, so that they're like Jesus.

Bethel sees the apostle as the overall leader of a church[112] (or movement/group of churches) based on the apostle's primary position in the Eph. 4:11 list of five-fold ministry elements – which is consistent with the list in 1 Cor. 12:28, where the order of each of the three common components (i.e. apostles, prophets, and teachers) is identical. Paul also affirms this hierarchy in Eph. 2:20, where he states that the Church is built on the foundation of the apostles and prophets[113] – which comes with the clear implication that these two roles take precedence over all others in the five-fold ministry (and the Church as a whole). Today however, based on current practice, you could be forgiven for instead thinking that the Church is built on the foundation of the pastors and teachers – the final two elements of the Eph. 4:11 list!

Now therefore, putting together what we have determined so far about the apostle, they are a person who has been sent by Jesus (God) to be the overall leader of a church, for the purpose of equipping their people for ministry and building them up to maturity in Christ. And if they are the overall leader, it would then be reasonable to assume that an important part of their job description is to be a leader of leaders, guiding the other five-fold ministers under their authority to fulfill their individual responsibilities in equipping the people for ministry and building them up to maturity (cf. 1 & 2 Tim., and Titus). Naturally also, the apostle would take a prominent direct role in these two key areas of equipping and building up, especially in communicating the mandate of God for all believers to be active in extending His Kingdom, and advocating particular strategies/tactics for doing so most effectively.

Ultimately, therefore, if the apostle is successful in carrying out these responsibilities (i.e. their people reach maturity in Christ and become powerful Kingdom builders) then their church will be fulfilling its mission to extend the Kingdom (i.e. bring Heaven to Earth) in the areas God has assigned to them as a group – both corporately and individually. Thus, we understand that through their people the apostle's job is about bringing the Kingdom of God to environments where it is not currently (or fully) present, and effecting positive change in those places for the benefit of all. Where His Kingdom is, there exists no poverty, sickness, crime, injustice, sin, or any other kind of evil (cf. Luke 4:18-19). Neither is there any fear, hopelessness, depression, loneliness, or self-hatred etc., since love, joy, hope, and peace reign instead (cf. Rom. 14:17; Gal. 5:22). Kris Vallotton refers to this process as "culturizing" Earth so that it looks like Heaven.

He contrasts apostles with evangelists by saying that evangelists bring the Kingdom to individuals, while apostles bring it to environments.[114] An example of this difference would be preaching the Gospel to villagers in a developing nation versus providing their community with access to clean drinking water. Of course, these things work well together so that when we improve environments in the name of Jesus (Col. 3:17) and take our opportunities to testify about Him, people see our good works and give glory to God (Matt. 5:16). There is therefore naturally a strong harmony between the work of apostles and evangelists. The apostle just has a much broader focus that looks beyond merely how many people make decisions to follow Jesus.[115]

In view of what we've just discussed about apostles extending the Kingdom through the collective efforts of their people, Kris sees the concept of the apostle as being larger than just the basic idea of a "sent one". To him, it can more accurately be described as a "sent one who sends" (cf. Acts 8:14; 15:22-27; 2 Cor. 12:17). Just as Jesus was called an apostle (Heb. 3:1), He sent others out to bring the Kingdom to various places, and ultimately, the whole earth. For example:

> ... he called the twelve together and gave them power and authority over all demons and to cure diseases, and he <u>sent</u> them out to proclaim the kingdom of God and to heal. (Luke 9:1-2; emphasis mine)

But it was not just the twelve who Jesus called apostles (Luke 6:13) that He sent out:

> After this the Lord appointed seventy-two others and <u>sent</u> them on ahead of him, two by two, into every town and place where he himself was about to go. (Luke 10:1; emphasis mine)

Paul, also an apostle of Jesus (2 Cor. 1:1) sent others out as well:

> Tychicus I have <u>sent</u> to Ephesus. (2 Tim. 4:12; emphasis mine)

> Did I take advantage of you through any of those whom I <u>sent</u> to you? (2 Cor. 12:17; emphasis mine)

In each of the above verses, "sent" (which is underlined) is the Greek word *apostellō*, the root word for "apostle". These verses clearly illustrate how important empowering and sending out others as laborers to do the work of extending the Kingdom, is to an apostle (cf. Luke 10:2).

Therefore, in summary, Bethel's view of the apostle is that they are a person sent by Jesus (God) to be the overall leader of a church for the purpose of equipping their people for ministry, building them up to maturity in Christ, and then sending them out to extend the Kingdom of God to environments where it is not currently present (or fully present). As a result, these environments change for the better and many people come to faith in Jesus.

The New Era of Apostleships

When God spoke to Kris on this subject of church government, what He apparently wanted to highlight to him was the governmental structure[116], particularly the difference between a pastorate and an apostleship, and how the Church was moving into a new era of apostleships – churches led by apostles, rather than pastors (pastorates).[117] The new emphasis would be on sending (the role of the apostle) rather than gathering (the role of the pastor). Kris explains that in a pastorate:

> The leader is a pastor, which is essentially a shepherd. Like a shepherd gathering his sheep, the pastor has a God-given anointing to gather people and tend to their needs. The people who follow the shepherd are obviously sheep—people whose primary job is to stay together and stay healthy. Pastorates thrive when people perceive the season to be one in which these goals of staying together and staying healthy define their primary purpose.[118]

Kris points out that the pastorate form of governance emphasizes coming to church in order to get various needs met, such as salvation, healing, deliverance, counseling, and teaching.[119] Apostleships, however, are very different in nature:

> The leader is an apostle, one sent to establish the culture of heaven on earth. Those who follow an apostle are those who seek to have heaven manifest in their lives, and to be sent out to release heaven wherever they go. Apostleships thrive in a season when people perceive that their primary purpose is to transform the culture of earth with the culture of heaven.[120]
>
> Apostleships ... are developed around the principle of training, equipping and deploying the saints to radically alter society. The primary message of apostleships is that the kingdom of God is at hand, and their main strategy is to demonstrate the raw power of God in the darkest places on the planet.[121]

This last point about apostles demonstrating the raw power of God as their main strategy (cf. 2 Cor. 12:12), leads to signs and wonders being more prevalent in apostleships (e.g. Bethel) than churches governed under a pastorate structure. Kris acknowledges that miracles still do happen in pastorates, but claims that they are infrequent and inconsistent.[122]

Reasons Why Miracles are More Common in Apostleships

One reason for this disparity in the level of miraculous activity is that the emphasis of pastors is different. The pastoral process of caring for people is typically a longer term one, often with few available short cuts. For instance, one prayer is usually not going to fix all of a couple's relationship issues or cause someone to immediately recover from a devastating divorce. Most likely, they will require counseling, love, and support over an extended period of time. Pastors, therefore, tend to be focused on longer term solutions rather than miraculous and instantaneous ones.

However, apostles, who are tasked with equipping believers for ministry[123] and do not have the same responsibilities to care for people, will tend to emphasize the power of God, often in the form of signs and wonders (2 Cor. 12:12). There is thus a philosophical difference in motivation between these two types of ministers and how they will typically lead a church – often resulting in very different outcomes.

A second reason why miracles are more prevalent in an apostleship than a pastorate, is that apostles as senior leaders equip and empower their people in signs and wonders ministry, whereas pastors tend to see the miraculous as solely their responsibility (possibly along with a small team of elders/leaders in support) when they are in charge. This arises from the primary motivation of pastors, which is to care for people rather than equip them (as apostles do). Naturally, more is going to happen when many people are operating in signs and wonders ministry rather than just one or a few.

There is also a third reason for the greater level of the miraculous occurring under an apostleship structure. This is something that Kris identifies through the use of two analogies derived from Scripture. A pastorate is like the pool of Bethesda (John 5:2-9), where people gather hoping for a supernatural encounter with God. On the other hand, an apostleship is like Ezekiel's river (Ezek. 47:1-12), which becomes deeper, the further it flows from the Temple. According to Kris, the river represents the grace of God and:

> ... depicts a *movement* in which God's presence grows more powerful as the *people of God* take His presence into the world—businesses, homes, schools, and so forth—with them. The further the saints get from the sanctuary, the deeper the grace of God penetrates the darkness. In other words, the greatest miracles, the most powerful expressions of the

> Kingdom, are destined to happen in the worst places on the planet, not inside the walls of a building.[124] (emphasis original)

This echoes a question that is sometimes asked about why the miraculous often happens when people go overseas (especially to places like Africa and South America), but hardly ever at home. Along the same lines, why do the most impressive miracles always seem to take place somewhere else? Is there something special about leaving the safety of our churches/familiar environments, and ministering in completely different locations - especially those far away?

Based on my own experience I would say that quite possibly there is, but this needs to be qualified very carefully. Firstly, I want to dispute the very idea that miracles (including the most astonishing ones) don't happen at home. In terms of praying for healing, I tend to see good results wherever I minister, and I know of many others who do as well. Some of the craziest miracles that I've ever seen have actually occurred in what I would regard as being home environments.

Nevertheless, it has to be acknowledged that most people are not seeing much happen at home, in the area of healing. Two key reasons why I believe this is the case are that they are not offering prayer to those who are sick/injured and the sick/injured are not seeking out or responding to opportunities for prayer.[125] Regarding the latter, many Christians seem to be quite ambivalent about receiving healing ministry, unless it is from some big-name visiting speaker who has a strong reputation for signs and wonders. They tend to see little value in being prayed for by the person sitting next to them in church (or even their pastor and church elders), who has (have) got the very same Spirit of God living inside of them as the superstar speaker. The fact is that healing prayer is generally not perceived as being effective and as a result is not highly appreciated and sought after. It should therefore not be surprising that this prayer is seldom ever offered or requested in many churches - including a large number of Charismatic and Pentecostal ones, which in theory believe in supernatural healing.

It appears that what we are dealing with here is a "familiarity breeds contempt" type of scenario, similar to the one Jesus faced in His hometown, where He could perform no miracles other than healing a few sick people (Mark 6:1-6). I for one, though, do not believe that Jesus went running around praying for a lot of people with little success. What I think actually took place was that the people just weren't open to receiving from Him because of offense (which led to unbelief) and therefore he didn't get many ministry opportunities. Evidently, they had become insecure about His growing reputation as a prophet/teacher and the messianic speculation surrounding Him (cf. Matt. 11:2-3). They were unable to see past the ordinary Jesus who they used to know and were comfortable with (i.e. the carpenter's son and brother of James, Joses, Judas, and Simon).

I too find that people can get locked into a static view of me that was formed years ago, despite the fact that I am now a very different person to what I was back then. In addition to this, many seem to frame me in terms of everything I'm not (e.g. my personal faults, natural limitations, and lack of conformity to certain norms) rather than the fact that I have the Spirit of the Living God inside of me – which enables me to do everything that Jesus did ... and more (John 14:12)! I would hazard a guess that these things are strong contributors to people being less interested in receiving ministry from me at home than elsewhere. But when they do, healing often occurs!

Having said this, however, I must acknowledge that my level of success in healing ministry (as a percentage of those I pray for) tends to be far greater with those I don't know versus the ones I do know well – which is, in principle, consistent with Kris' Ezekiel's river analogy, given that the vast majority of those outside of our home church will be strangers to us, unlike inside this environment.

Another thing consistent with Kris' analogy is that my results in evangelistic contexts (i.e. ministering to non-Christians outside of church environments) are often significantly greater than those in church settings (both at home and away). To give an example, over the last decade some friends and I have run healing stalls at a New

Age festival in our city that is held twice a year. Typically during these events, the vast majority of people that we pray for regarding areas of physical need receive some degree of healing (although not always total). This has included healing from conditions like arthritis, fibromyalgia, partial deafness, and even cancer.

In terms of raw geographical distance from my home city, Christchurch, New Zealand, I have to say that my results have in general been fairly consistent wherever I have gone. Certainly there has been little difference in healing success between New Zealand and the USA (including at Bethel), two countries where I have done a significant amount of healing and evangelistic ministry.

One exception to this, though, has been Mexico City, where I traveled to for my BSSM First Year mission trip in March 2015, with Kris Kildosher. A large part of what our team did on that trip was healing ministry, and the demand for this was often so great that lines of people would form in front of each of us, to receive prayer. Often it took the best part of an hour to get through everyone, although on at least one occasion we ran out of time to do so. My guess is that more than 90 percent of those I prayed for in these healing lines (whether inside or outside of a church) received some degree of healing, and this included a number of people who had some quite serious conditions.

For instance, one day some of our hosts took me, and about three others members of our Bethel team, to a working class area of the city, to heal and evangelize (that day, our Bethel team was sent out in small groups to different locations, to minister). They set up a PA system with large speakers on a basketball court outside, and then used this to invite people in the vicinity to come and get healed through our ministry. Soon, we each had a line of about three or four people waiting in front of us for prayer, which continued to grow. Most of the people who came to me had serious eye issues (those with such conditions seemed to gravitate toward me following a word of knowledge I had given for eye problems at a church service I ministered at earlier on the trip). From memory, every single one of them received some level of healing. This included an older man with cataracts in his eyes, who could hardly see at all. After prayer, he claimed through an interpreter that he could see perfectly. Also, a lady who had been totally blind for seven years was able to see shadows after I prayed for her. Although it was far from a complete restoration of her sight, she was very happy with the level of improvement, and I believe in faith that God continued the healing process over time.

In another healing line, on a different day and at a church service this time, I prayed for a girl who was cross-eyed, and her vision straightened out. And at an open-air meeting, I prayed for a lady who wanted healing for hearing issues but her eyesight improved instead – something that she didn't ask for. As a result, she claimed that she no longer needed glasses. I'm not sure whether to call this a success or failure! I guess it was an accidental healing!

To sum up this trip to Mexico, I have to say that I've never seen such a great outpouring of the supernatural anywhere else in the world. It was incredibly easy to minister there: the local people were so open to receiving ministry and normally got healed when we prayed for them. This was not only my experience, but that of everyone else on our team with whom I compared notes. And in case you're wondering, it definitely couldn't have all been due to a "Bethel effect"[126], since many of the people we ministered to (i.e. those outside of the church meetings) would have had no idea about who we were, other than that we came from a church in California. There is a possibility, though, that they may have seen the excitement and belief of our team, and grabbed onto this.

However, it is notable that when I prayed for other people on our team (from either Bethel or our host church) absolutely no one got healed of anything![127] This is consistent with my experience of seeing a higher percentage of those I don't know get healed when I pray for them, than with those I do know.

Based on all of this, therefore, I would like to suggest that the truth of Kris' Ezekiel's river analogy, regarding how strongly the power of God moves, relates to the familiarity (specifically the lack thereof) of those we are ministering to instead of the physical distance from our home church (or even just a church). In addition, it appears that these effects are amplified the more people differ from us (and we from them). To give some examples of the latter, the difference between a New Zealand New Ager and myself (a New Zealander) would probably be much greater than the difference between an American Christian from a similar socio-economic group to myself and me. Furthermore, the difference between a non-Christian working-class Mexican, who doesn't speak English, and me would likely be far greater still. Such differences might explain why my success at healing was greater in Mexico and with New Agers in New Zealand, than with Americans in the USA who are quite similar to myself.

Why would this be the case? It is the "familiarity breeds contempt" scenario again. The more people view us as unfamiliar and different to themselves, the more they may see us as someone who could possess something that they don't have, such as the power to work miracles (i.e. it may create a higher level of expectation). And as we know, expectation is a major factor in the miraculous manifesting (Mark 11:22-24).[128]

This could account for why some people report incredible things happening in places like Africa and South America (where the locals are so different to most Westerners), but not so much in Western countries like New Zealand and the USA. And on the other side of the coin, it (along with the two reasons I presented earlier) might provide some explanation for why many people, who minister only inside their home church environments, see very little of the miraculous manifest.

Let me be clear, though, that this is neither Bethel's official view, nor is it something that I've ever heard any of their leaders teach or discuss. It is only a personal theory of mine, which may or may not be true. I offer it as food for thought, and leave it to you, to make up your own mind on. Better still, get out there and experiment; prove me right or wrong for yourself! I therefore strongly encourage you to venture outside of the safety of your church and have a go at ministering to people you don't know, particularly those who are very different to yourself. I think you'll see some amazing things happen if you do, especially with poor and disadvantaged people, who I've found to be the most open to receiving. They'll usually give anything a try if you just treat them with a bit of respect and dignity – which most people fail to do.

The Ultimate Goal is Sending, Not Gathering

Going back to the church governance issue in general, Kris Vallotton is not trying to eliminate the need for pastors and pastorates, or devalue their ministry. Quite the contrary, he views them as vital to the health of the sheep who are gathered. For without pastors, unhealthy sheep would be sent out into the world to represent God and bring His Kingdom. He therefore argues that each apostleship must build and empower a pastorate (or multiple pastorates) within its structure, for the purpose of gathering and developing healthy and happy sheep.[129] Yet, the ultimate goal of this is not gathering a large flock of sheep, but sending out an army to change the world.[130] The success of an apostle therefore cannot be determined by the size of their church. It should instead be measured by the impact those they have sent out are having for the Kingdom, in terms of bringing Heaven to Earth and training others to do likewise.

The Bethel School of Supernatural Ministry (BSSM) is a great example of this idea of having a pastorate (or pastorates) contained within an apostleship. Every year, over 2,000 students, from the majority of US states and many countries around the world, gather together to grow their identity in Christ and become leaders who have the ability to change the culture of any environment God places them in. The structure of the school is heavily pastoral, in that every First and Second Year student is assigned both a pastor (approximately 65 students per pastor) and a personal mentor (usually a Third Year student, but sometimes a volunteer). Every Third Year student also has a personal mentor who is mutually chosen and would normally perform some pastoral role in the life of the student. Whatever the year, though, the emphasis of the school is on growing healthy and powerful men and women, with a view to sending them out after they graduate to effect change in the world – by bringing Heaven wherever they go.

Likewise, Bethel Church (which BSSM operates under) views itself as an "apostleship" (under the apostle, Bill Johnson), and has a number of pastorates contained within it. It serves as a training and resource center for revivalists, who will collectively advance God's Kingdom all around the world, in a multitude of different ways and across every sector of society.

When a church is governed as an apostleship (with a pastorate or multiple pastorates contained inside of it) rather than a pastorate, people gather together for a period of time to get strengthened and equipped. They are then sent out to change the world for God. And to be clear, this sending out is not a dictatorial one, such that people are commanded to leave, directed where to go, and told what to do. Instead, they are empowered to leave when they feel called to do so. At Bethel, for example, no one gets asked to leave because they've been there for too long. Some, of course, will stay and be sent out into the Redding community, where Bethel is based. Being sent does not necessarily mean going to a developing nation; most often it won't.

Furthermore, the majority of people sent out will not be full-time missionaries, evangelists, pastors, or any other kind of professional church worker. They will work ordinary, everyday jobs and be involved in business, the arts, government, and their communities etc. They will be mothers and fathers who bring up amazing Holy Spirit-filled children who end up doing the same sorts of things that they do (and greater!), but at younger ages. Whatever these sent ones do, they bring the Kingdom of God to their environments, which effects transformation and ultimately makes the world a better place.

However, when a church is governed as a pastorate, this is not always the case. Kris argues that:

> ... a pastorate form of government is not designed to transform cities. It is developed to attract people, to create a culture where flocks gather to get healthy and happy. Pastorates are, to some degree, irrelevant to their city's culture because their governmental structures are built to congregate, not to deploy.[131]

Since pastorates emphasize safety rather risk, an issue arises under this form of church government that when people become healthy, they will eventually come to a place where they feel that something is lacking in their lives. They may get bored with the "same-old, same-old" of church every week and complain that they're no longer getting fed. As a result, they might start to "church hop" in an attempt to find something new and more exciting. In reality, people like this are probably ready to step out into their "mission", but have never been adequately prompted, empowered, and equipped to do so.

Pastorates, by their very nature, are good at gathering and creating whole people, but not at sending out an army to culturize Earth with the culture of Heaven. Hence, it is necessary for pastorates to be contained within apostleships. As Kris points out, a church should have a hospital, not be a hospital.[132]

Therefore, in summary, for Earth to be transformed to be more like Heaven in the most effective way, churches need to be governed as apostleships rather than pastorates. In this way, people are gathered for the purposes of becoming healthy and being equipped as cultural transformers. They are then sent out to change the world for God through bringing Heaven to Earth.

Prophets

Moving on to prophets now, I have never witnessed a church culture that is as prophetic as Bethel's. Many people who know about Bethel, but have not visited the church, would probably see it in three main ways: a place of miraculous healing, incredibly anointed worship music, and a world-famous ministry school. While these are not incorrect characterizations of the church and movement, I don't believe that many outsiders actually realize how great the focus is on the prophetic (including the revelational realm in general) – especially in the ministry school. Every BSSM student gets trained in the art of hearing God's voice and being able to give prophetic words to others on demand. These words are often very specific and accurate. Furthermore, a culture has developed such that people are always ready to get out their phones and hit "record" when they're about to receive a prophecy – which is very often. It would probably not be an exaggeration to say that hardly a week would go by in the school without receiving at least one prophetic word from someone.

How did this prophetic culture come into existence and grow into what it is today? Well, it has simply been a case of the five-fold prophets on staff (particularly Kris Vallotton) training people to operate in the prophetic, and giving them permission to practice on each other in the environment. While not everyone is a "prophet" according to Eph. 4:11, every Christian has access to the gift of prophecy and is able to prophesy (1 Cor. 12:10, 14:1, 5). It is the prophet's job to draw this out of their people, for their purpose (as with all five-fold ministers) is to train the saints up for the work of the ministry, according to Eph. 4:11-13. But if this, or any other element of the five-fold ministry is missing then believers are not going to be fully equipped for what God has called them to do. The absence of prophetic ministry in the lives of believers naturally means that they will find it harder to hear God's voice and therefore to move in His revelation. (Don't forget that this revelational realm includes dreams and visions (Acts 2:17).)

What this means is that we will either get fewer "God ideas" (ideas supernaturally inspired from Heaven) or we'll fail to recognize them as such, and therefore instead have to work more in the natural realm, along with everyone else. But just like Daniel and his companions, when we know the Living God we are able to operate on an entirely different level (see Dan. 1:20) – far above the natural realm. The purpose of this is not so that we can make ourselves rich and successful while feeling superior to others, but to serve the world to a far greater extent than we could have with just our own "good" ideas (There is nothing wrong with good ideas, by the way. It is just that God ideas are always a lot better). The prophetic is therefore an important element of what is needed to change the culture of Earth to be more like that of Heaven.

Furthermore, the prophetic enhances other gifts and areas of ministry. For instance, it is an invaluable tool for evangelism, as I mentioned back in Chapter 4: Saints, Not Sinners. The offer of a prophetic word is an easy way to open a conversation with someone and pique their interest in the things of God. No one wants to just be told point-blank that they're a sinner, who needs to repent and follow Jesus. But if you give them something which they perceive to be valuable (e.g. a prophecy about some good things that God wants to do in their lives - especially ones that aren't "religious" in nature), you will develop some rapport with them. And this rapport will often open up a door to talk about God with them in a more direct way.

Evangelists

Speaking of evangelism, the evangelist is another element of the five-fold ministry that has, for the most part, been missing from the Church over the last few decades. Often, true five-fold evangelists don't even feature on senior leadership teams, and the evangelistic activity of many churches has reduced down to a solely event-centered approach. Under this scenario, events and activities (usually entertainment-related) are put on for church members to invite their non-Christian family, friends, and acquaintances along to (e.g. youth concerts, Christmas plays, and men's/women's ministry events), in the hope that these people can somehow be persuaded to keep coming back, and will eventually make decisions to follow Jesus.

Sure, this approach may work occasionally and is preferable to doing nothing. However, it's unlikely to lead to the next great awakening, as it is very difficult to entertain people into the Kingdom (and keep them there through such means), given the fact that the world usually does entertainment a lot better than the Church and there are so many different options available today. Trying to compete with the world in this area, as our primary means of doing evangelism, is therefore a terrible mistake, one that a lot of churches seem determined to keep repeating, in the absence of any better ideas. If we are going to be successful at evangelism on a mass scale then we need to offer something very different from the world.

Fortunately, we do have such a thing to present: the supernatural God of the Bible, who seeks relationship with each of us, and wants to bless us all in so many amazing ways – both in this life and the next. When people are introduced to Him and discover His incredible love and goodness and power, they will often be interested in getting to know Him more. He is just so relevant to every one of our lives!

The most effective way to introduce people to God is the direct approach of going to them and giving them a tangible experience of Him, one that they cannot deny. However, the indirect, "middle man" approach of bribing them with entertainment to get them to come to us (e.g. at church), so that we can hopefully preach them into relationship with Him, is generally quite ineffective. What we need to understand is that God is highly sociable and more than willing to meet people where they're at. There is therefore no need to rely on any middle man like entertainment.[133]

This "bribe them to church with entertainment"- type approach to evangelism, which is predominant in much of Christianity today, appears to be a consequence of church leaders (who, in practice, are usually either five-fold pastors or teachers) having decided that personal evangelism outside of the Church through ordinary believers, doesn't really work anymore (or is not important).[134] We can only assume this given the usual absence of genuine five-fold evangelists on church staffs, combined with the fact that not a lot of time, effort, and money is being invested into the training of believers in this most vital ministry – which significantly, was the last recorded subject that

Jesus spoke to His disciples about while on Earth in three of the four Gospels, along with Acts (Matt. 28:18-20; Mark 16:15-18; Luke 24:47-49; Acts 1:8). As the fictional movie character Jerry Maguire once said, "Show me the money!!!" When we see real resources being devoted to personal evangelism, we will know that it has become something that leaders believe in again and view as being important.

In the absence of any real focus on this ministry from within the Church, personal evangelism has largely been left to individual believers to figure out for themselves and take the initiative in practicing. The result has been that some occasionally share their faith with those they're close to. Others just make the people around them aware that they're a Christian, which they may later use as a bridge to promote the events that their church puts on. Then there are the few brave souls who hit the streets and share very direct Gospel messages with strangers – often with a strong focus on Heaven and Hell. However, only seldom do these three types of approaches end up bearing any tangible fruit, in terms of people making decisions to follow Jesus.

Before I went to Bethel, I had never really come across any model of personal evangelism that I could verify actually works consistently in practice, for regular believers like you and me. I had tried all three of the approaches described above, with pretty much zero success overall. People just didn't seem to be interested in what I thought, and still do think, is the greatest message in the world: the Gospel of Jesus Christ our Savior, who freed us from slavery to the kingdom of darkness and brought us into His Kingdom of light – allowing us to reign on Earth (Rom. 5:17) and have a glorious inheritance in eternity, free of all death and decay, in the presence of the One who is love and truth personified.

Fortunately, at Bethel I had a big "aha" in this area. Personal evangelism can and does actually work well if you do it a very different way, one that I had heard about but never really seen modeled effectively before. Bethel's approach is to give people an experience of God through the use of signs and wonders, such as healing miracles, prophetic words, and even just the raw presence of God imparted through the laying on of hands. In doing so, we cut out the middle man of entertainment, by introducing them directly to Him – which, incidentally, is the only way that they are going to make genuine decisions to become followers of Jesus anyway, regardless of which type of approach is used. This is often enough to pique the interest of people for more of God. Shortly, we will discuss Bethel's approach to evangelism in more detail.

Practical Training and Mentorship in Evangelism is Vital

For a church to be empowered in (personal) evangelism, it is vital that regular training is conducted to equip people to get out there and share the Gospel effectively. Ideally, this training will be run by five-fold evangelists, who have a burning passion to see the Gospel preached to the lost and a track record of success in doing so personally. It is their job to train and inspire the people to share their faith effectively with those who do not yet know Jesus.

What is also very important is that there are opportunities for people to be mentored in evangelism, and programs put in place so that they can learn "on the job" with others. It is not enough to just train people in the theory and then expect them to go out and have a go on their own – which most will never do. Remember that Jesus gave His disciples the opportunity to watch Him first, and then He sent them out two by two on small evangelistic trips, to put in practice what they had learned (Mark 6:7). Following these trips, He gave them further instruction along the way regarding areas that needed attention (Mark 9:28-29; Luke 9:51-56 cf. Luke 10:17-20). Then eventually, right before His ascension to Heaven, Jesus graduated them from His mentorship program to evangelize full time on their own, without any more direct input from Him (Luke 24:46-49). But even then, they usually still did ministry in groups (Acts 3, cf. 13:1-3).

As with Jesus' disciples, when there is safety in numbers and positive peer-pressure, people are often encouraged to step out and share their faith with others – regardless of whether they are the most gregarious extrovert or extremely shy introvert. Furthermore, everyone, with a bit of training and a willingness to have a go, can become a powerful and effective witness for Jesus, who regularly leads people to Him. At Bethel, I saw some of the most unlikely people step out in this way and be used greatly by God. It is such a lie for anyone to say, "I can't evangelize because I'm an introvert/shy". That is just an excuse for giving in to fear. Personally, I was quite afraid of talking to people about my faith when I first started doing it. But I did not let that stop me, and over time I progressively conquered my fears to such a degree, that I now actually enjoy getting out there and talking to people – despite all the 'no's and some occasional abuse. More importantly, however, I have become effective to the point where I can lead people to Jesus on a regular basis, although there is still much room for improvement.

A major reason why Bethel has been so successful at empowering evangelists is that the evangelism part of the ministry of the church is led by a powerful five-fold evangelist – Chris Overstreet. He is very active in raising up other evangelists, especially within the BSSM environment. Ben Fitzgerald, who has now left Bethel to run evangelistic events in Europe, also had a very prominent role in training and mentoring evangelists when I was there. Furthermore, there are a number of other lesser-known, but still very effective evangelists, who regularly take teams on the road to preach the Gospel and train others in doing so. My friend Levi Hug, a man of great power and humility, is one such unsung hero who I would like to honor here. He is tireless in his commitment to equipping believers for ministry and spreading the Gospel, both across America and around the world.

In addition to this, Bethel has established various evangelistic outreaches which ordinary members of the congregation and even visitors to the church can be involved in. An example of this would be the "Treasure Hunts" that many people are now familiar with. There are also opportunities to go on mission trips focused on evangelism. And within BSSM, there are a large number of additional opportunities to get involved in evangelism. All of these things work to develop people as evangelists, so that sharing their faith with others comes naturally to them.

The Bethel Approach to Evangelism

As outlined above, Bethel does evangelism quite differently to most other groups. I would describe it as a Spirit-led signs and wonders approach that demonstrates the Kingdom, with a strong emphasis on the goodness of God. All of these elements are so fundamental to everything Bethel does, especially the goodness of God, which according to Rom. 2:4 (NKJV) leads us to repentance.

Instead of starting with the call to repentance, the Bethel approach is that we must first acquaint people with the One they need to turn to. It is important that they taste and see that the Lord is good (Psalm 34:8a) before they give their lives to Him. Just as marketers often give out free product samples to prospects in the hope that they will like their products and buy them, we need to give people a sample of God in terms of who He is and what He's like, first. As Bill Johnson says, "We owe the world an encounter with God." This is where the signs and wonders approach comes in.

Bethel-trained evangelists typically have a toolbox containing various supernatural gifts, which they use to display the reality of God, particularly His power and goodness. They get words of knowledge about people to demonstrate that God is real, that He knows every detail about their lives, and cares about them. They give them prophetic words about their futures and destinies to encourage them. And they pray for their physical and emotional needs, bringing God's healing to them.

The thing is that today, in Western nations that have strong Christian roots like the United States, people are seldom interested in hearing direct presentations of the Gospel, using only words and Bible quotations. But relatively few will say "no" to a prophetic word up front, even if most of the interest is only due to curiosity. We need to get back to the New Testament approach to evangelism, that the word was confirmed with signs and wonders accompanying it (Mark 16:20; Acts 4:29-31). How do you think that Jesus managed to get great crowds to follow Him and listen to His sermons? It was largely because of the miracles He performed (John 6:2) and the provision that resulted from them (Mark 1:32-34; John 6:26), not because He was a great orator – which He may or may not have been. The Kingdom of God is, after all, not a matter of talk but of power (1 Cor. 4:20).

These days, when there is such a plurality of different religions, faiths, and philosophies on the market, we as Christians need to distinguish ourselves from everyone else by demonstrating the reality and goodness of God, through the power of signs and wonders. It is no longer sufficient to only present the Gospel in words – no matter how accurate and eloquent we are in doing so. People are just going to tell us that they are either not interested or have different beliefs – which causes the conversation to end right there. And this makes whole sections of society essentially unreachable to us, with the notable exception of the young, who are normally searching for identity and therefore more open to different ideas like ours.

If we want to be truly effective, it is essential that we emulate Paul's approach:

> ... my message and my preaching were not in persuasive words of wisdom, but in demonstration of the Spirit and of power, so that your faith would not rest on the wisdom of men, but on the power of God. (1 Cor. 2:4-5, NASB)

Contrast this approach with the evangelists who just go around telling people that they need to repent of their sins and accept Jesus as their Lord and Savior, otherwise God will send them to Hell when they die. In this, they not only fail to demonstrate the reality of God, but also unwittingly portray Him as an evil tyrant instead of the loving Father that He is, who is desperately calling His lost children back.

However, once people have received a taste of God's goodness we can talk to them about repenting of their sins and receiving Jesus – the One who sacrificed His very life to save them. People tend to be much more open to such a discussion when they have experienced the love of God in some way, even if it is only us telling them that they're special and loved greatly by God.

Bethel people are taught to go in with no agenda, other than to love, honor, and bless the people they meet. Some Christians will argue that it is a waste of time doing anything unless you end up telling people of their need to repent and turn to God; but that wasn't Jesus' approach (cf. Luke 19:1-10). He told His disciples to announce the Kingdom and demonstrate it by healing the sick, raising the dead, cleansing lepers, and casting out demons (Matt. 10:7-8; Luke 10:9). What He was talking about was serving people according to their earthly needs: "Freely you have received; freely give." (Matt. 10:8b, NIV2011).

With Bethel, serving people is not practiced only through signs and wonders, though. It also includes helping them in practical ways. For example, it might involve giving a homeless person some items of clothing they need or mowing a single mother's lawns for her. When people see that we really care about them, they will often open up to hearing more about what we believe. Evangelism through serving people, whether by supernatural or practical means, is a great representation of the goodness of God.

Now finally, one important element of the Bethel evangelistic approach that I cannot neglect to mention, is being Spirit-led. This relates to how we decide which people we're going to talk to and how we will engage with them. Our evangelistic efforts tend to be far more successful when we follow the Spirit's leadings and partner with what God's actually doing in the moment. Yes, everyone does need Jesus, but not everyone has the same level of openness to Him right now (and to us, particularly in how we present Him). Therefore, if we allow the Holy Spirit to lead us to those who are open and ready (cf. Matt. 9:2; Acts 14:9), we can lead many more people to Jesus.

The "Treasure Hunt" method is great way of doing this. Here, we ask God to give us words of knowledge about the people He wants us to talk/minister to - regarding specific things like their location, name, appearance, and what they might need prayer for etc. (these are called "clues"). Once we have used this process to construct our "treasure map", we go out looking for the "treasure" - the people who our clues point to! When we find these people, we approach them and offer to pray for their healing needs (especially those identified in the clues), give them prophetic words, and possibly anything else that we feel is appropriate (e.g. encourage them). After this, if things are going well, we may share the Gospel (of salvation) and offer them the chance to give their lives to Jesus.

Another Spirit-led method of evangelism that Bethel people often use is "highlighting". In this, we approach those who we perceive the Holy Spirit is highlighting to us, in that we feel drawn to them in some way, but not due to any natural attraction. He will highlight people to us in different ways, often through subtle impressions, which take practice to recognize on a consistent basis, just as with words of knowledge and prophecy.

In 2016, right before leaving Redding to return to New Zealand, I found myself in such a situation when I was not even in "evangelism mode". I was on my bike riding to the storage unit I had at my old apartment complex, where I lived during BSSM First Year. As I was about to turn into the driveway of the complex, I saw a Hispanic couple - a man with a woman in a wheelchair. At that point, the thought flashed into my mind that I should stop and offer to pray for the woman, so that she could be healed. But then, I had another thought enter my mind - that praying for her could turn into a long, drawn-out episode and end up wasting a significant part of my afternoon. Given that I was very busy with selling stuff and preparing to return home, I'm sorry to say that I actually listened to this second thought and just rode past them toward the storage unit.

However, after finishing my business there (which took maybe 15 minutes), I saw the couple again. They were now across the road and down the street a bit from where I'd seen them before. And again, I felt that I should go over and offer to pray for the lady. My reaction was something like, "Arrggghhh ... okay Lord, okay!", and this time I was obedient and rode over there. I greeted them, and then asked the woman why she was in the wheelchair. She told me that both her and her husband (the man who was with her) had been in a car accident, which she had been badly injured in, with pain over much of her body from broken bones and internal injuries etc. She also mentioned that she had died on the operating table and been resuscitated.

I then offered her prayer for healing – which she accepted. After praying for her two or three separate times, all the pain had apparently left her body. However, she didn't feel confident enough to get out of her wheelchair and have a go at walking. But that was okay.

Following this, I asked the man if he had also incurred any injuries from the accident, and he informed me that there was some pain in his legs, which he then allowed me to pray for. The pain quickly left, and after this, I asked if he needed healing from anything else. In response, he told me that he was experiencing a bad headache, which the two of them were on the way to the store to buy some pain medication for. I offered to pray for this too, and when I did so, his headache disappeared as well.

At this point, I thought that since I had demonstrated the Kingdom of God through these miraculous healings, I should now try to determine whether they were saved. So, I asked them whether they went to church, and they told me that they used to go to a church when they lived in the (San Francisco) Bay Area, but were not currently part of any church. My next question was, "Are you born again?" (NB. Just because someone goes to church or has gone to church, this does not necessarily mean that they are born again.) The woman replied, "No, but I'd like to be." In my mind now, I was doing some huge fist pumps and thinking to myself, "Evangelism does not any easier than this!" But on the outside, I maintained my composure and announced to her, "Well, I can definitely help you with that!" I then asked her husband whether he would also like to become born again, and he said "yes". So, I stood between them, held their hands, and led them in a prayer of salvation to receive Jesus. After this, I released the peace of God over them through a prayer of impartation.

Right before I left them, they said that they were both feeling much better than before. It actually turned out that they were my neighbors from the same apartment block, the previous year. I had never really talked to them before, other than saying "hi" in passing. While I probably should have made more of an effort to get to know them earlier, I couldn't complain about what God had done through me that day. I was so glad that I had responded to His promptings (albeit belatedly) even though I didn't really have a lot of time to spare.

***

In discussing this signs and wonders approach to evangelism and stories like the one I just shared, I realize that there is a risk that most of this might seem unattainable to many people, who don't consider themselves to be "miracle workers", "super evangelists", or "prophetic" etc. What I would say to this is that it is true that when you're new to Spirit-led, signs and wonders evangelism, you may not initially see a whole lot happen. But like everything in life, there is a learning curve involved, and if you submit to the process then you will eventually reap the rewards – which I have seen a number of people do.

Of course, this doesn't mean that everyone is going to be equally good at every aspect of this approach to evangelism, given the same amount of time learning and practicing. During my second year at the school, I co-led two BSSM Treasure Hunt teams and I'm fairly sure that I never found even one person on any of my treasure maps. Others did though, and some had success finding their treasure with very detailed clues.

I did, however, see a significant number of people healed during those treasure hunts through my own hands (NB. You definitely do not need to get a word of knowledge first in order to effect healing). And while I was in Mexico City on my first year mission trip, in

March 2015, I did have one success in finding some treasure. When were treasure hunting with some young people from a local supernatural ministry school, I had a clue regarding someone with hearing problems. We soon found an older, Jewish lady in a wheelchair, who was very deaf. And when I prayed for her, her hearing improved (I am not certain to what degree because of language issues). We also prayed for her back (which was the reason why she was in the wheelchair) and apparently there was a bit of improvement there also.

I believe that everyone who is born again has some level of giftedness in supernatural ministry. And even if it is only small at the moment, it can be grown over time by being faithful in what you do have, stepping out and having a go in the areas you want to grow in, getting continually filled and refilled with the Holy Spirit, and receiving impartation from people who are already operating in the gifts you desire.

Furthermore, if you go out with groups of other people, you can benefit from each other's gifts to help one another see results. Some people may be better at getting specific clues (i.e. words of knowledge) and finding the treasure, while others might be more gifted at talking to people, healing, or prophecy. A helpful acronym is TEAM:

Together

Everyone

Achieves

More

My advice, therefore, is to start by working with what you do have, contribute it to a team, and relentlessly pursue the more of God, in terms of the gifts you want to operate in (1 Cor. 14:1). If you do these things on a consistent basis over time, I challenge you to come back and tell me that nothing has happened, for I simply don't believe that this is possible.

The Reemergence of the Evangelist

One important thing that I observed at Bethel was the reemergence of the evangelist: both the five-fold evangelist and those trained up by them, who become powerful preachers of the Gospel on the streets and in the marketplace. It is so amazing to see that even in the so-called "post-Christian" societies of North America and Western Europe, the preaching of the Gospel absolutely works today, and works very well – if you do it the right way. While many people have absolutely zero interest in "religion", they are still open to an authentic relationship with their Creator if we can introduce Him to them, which is the evangelist's core objective. When non-believers encounter God's presence, love, and power through His people, they will often want to know more. Kris Vallotton makes a similar point:

> I don't understand people who think that Americans aren't hungry for God. Everywhere I go I see folks who are famished and longing for a spiritual awakening, and we have the ability to demonstrate a gospel of power.[135]

Even in countries that are dominated by other religions, when we go in with a view to serve people and give them an encounter with God, many will be eager to receive from us. The reason for this is that what we have is attractive and unique, in that it is something that no other religion or philosophy can offer – an authentic, loving relationship with the one true God.

It is therefore an exciting time to be an evangelist at the moment. Those who go out with this mindset to serve people and offer them an encounter with God, will have the privilege to lead many to Jesus and see some of the craziest and most extreme signs and wonders ever witnessed take place (cf. John 14:12). It will be like the Book of Acts all over again, or "Acts 29", as some people say. How could the Christian life be more exciting than this?

While Bethel has been great at equipping and sending out evangelists to bring in the harvest in many diverse places, there is another dimension to this ministry of personal evangelism: that of the witness in everyday life, spreading the Kingdom wherever we go. The best evangelism doesn't always happen on the street, or amongst the poor in developing nations. God frequently creates situations where we have opportunities to share our faith with those around us, as we go about our daily activities.

You can actually do most of the things that "evangelists" (of the signs and wonders variety) do out on the streets, at your workplace, gym, or while buying your groceries, for example. You just need to have a bit of extra awareness and sometimes be a little more low-key about it. People want to feel assured that you are not going to make a big scene and embarrass them in front of others. They also need you to respect their time by being brief, especially when they are "on the clock" at work.

Personally, I can vouch for the fact that marketplace ministry works in practice, and often very well. I've prayed for a number of people in different locations in my everyday life, and have frequently seen healing occur. For instance, I've had quite a bit of success at various gyms while working out. Weights rooms, in particular, are great because you get to stand around chatting to people when resting between sets. And often they will tell you what's wrong with them, such as their gym and sporting injuries. When they do this, I will frequently offer to pray for them, and you would be surprised at the number of non-Christians who accept prayer in these sorts of situations.

Early in 2016, at my gym in Redding, I met a bodybuilder who was visiting from another city and had served in the marines. He was suffering from hearing loss in both ears (one more than the other) due to loud weapons firing around him. When he mentioned his hearing loss, I told him that I do Christian healing prayer and would like to pray for the restoration of his hearing, as I believed that God would heal him. He accepted my offer, and after maybe 30 seconds to a minute with my hands over his ears commanding his hearing to be restored in Jesus' name, he told me that he felt something happening inside his ears and that his hearing had improved. I asked him if it was now 100 percent, but he wasn't sure, so I prayed again. This time, he felt more happening inside his ears and was blown away by how much his hearing had now improved. After praying with him, we connected on Facebook, and I later messaged him to check on his condition. He told me that his hearing was still good and that he had been telling a lot of people about what had happened!

Stories like this are not isolated events, or limited to a small group of "elites", who have powerful gifts of healing. There are probably many hundreds of people at Bethel (and who have been to Bethel) who could claim these sorts of testimonies. Bringing God's Kingdom wherever we go is just something that is part of the Bethel culture. There is to be no distinction between the sacred and secular worlds. As with Ezekiel's river, the flow of God's blessing seems to actually increase, the further we get from the religious center (e.g. a church building).

The fact is that God wants to use each and every one of us in these sorts of spectacular ways. We may never become a big-name evangelist or itinerant speaker, but that is completely irrelevant. The days of the superstar preachers and evangelists are over. In this day, God desires to use the whole Body of Christ to extend His Kingdom, through preaching the good news in both word and deed. Bethel has been great in recognizing this and utilizing the five-fold evangelists in its midst to train and equip its people for these works of ministry.

Teachers

The teacher is the final element of the five-fold ministry of the Church, and probably the one least neglected in practice, alongside the role of the pastor. It is their job to teach people the key lessons contained in Scripture, equip them to understand the Bible for themselves, and to inspire them to study it on their own.

As Christians, it is vital that each of us possess a good working knowledge and understanding of the Bible, to enable us to have a solid foundation for the living out of our faith. Although the Holy Spirit guides us into all truth (John 16:13), we cannot rely on extra-biblical revelation as a substitute for the Bible. For the Spirit normally speaks to us much more through Scripture than probably all the other modalities combined.

God-appointed teachers are therefore an important part of the process of us understanding the Bible and hearing from God. We should expect that they will be gifted in interpreting the biblical text, extracting the lessons from it for today, and communicating these things effectively to us as the people of God. Ideally, they will also be Holy Spirit inspired and skilled in discerning the things that God wants them to teach at particular times, so that they are always imparting the "now" words of God.

One significant issue, however, with teachers in much of the Church today is their tendency to teach purely from theory, being grounded solely on an intellectual understanding of the Bible, that is largely divorced from real-world experience – particularly in encountering the presence of God and moving in His supernatural power. Such teachers have filled people with a lot of head knowledge, while disregarding the supernatural and experiential dimensions of the faith, which the Scriptures keep pointing to. As a result, they have turned the Christian faith into little more than another philosophy and moral code, and the local church into a glorified social club. This has contributed greatly to the powerless and watered-down Christianity that we are so used to seeing today.

In addition to simply shying away from the supernatural in the Bible, some theoretically-minded teachers have adopted unbiblical theologies to justify their lack of power and experience in this key dimension of the faith, and to maintain their intellectual credibility[136]. For instance, as we have already discussed, they teach things such as that it isn't always God's will to heal a person[137] and that He sometimes allows people to be sick in order to develop their character, through lessons like humility and patience. Or worse, they declare that the supernatural gifts of the Holy Spirit (e.g. healing and prophecy) are not for today. And they argue that anyone claiming to practice these gifts is guilty of living an experience-based Christianity and falling into dangerous spiritual deception.

But if anyone is guilty of living an experience-based Christianity and falling into spiritual deception, it is these "teachers". They are rejecting a set of very normal biblical practices, based largely on their own experiences of not seeing anything happen in these areas e.g. no one getting healed through prayer.

Bill Johnson, though, is highly critical of any approach to Scripture that doesn't lead to people experiencing God and operating in His supernatural power, particularly a purely intellectual one. He points to Jesus as the model that all Bible teachers should seek to emulate:

> JESUS, THE MODEL TEACHER, never separated teaching from doing. He is the pattern for this gift. God's revealed Word, declared through the lips of an anointed teacher, ought to lead to demonstrations of power.[138] (emphasis original)

The Bethel movement strongly believes that the teaching of Scripture should ultimately lead us into greater encounters (though not necessarily more dramatic) and intimacy with God, resulting in us ultimately pulling more of Heaven down to Earth. This involves accessing everything that Scripture says is available to us today, such as the power of prayer and all the supernatural gifts of the Holy Spirit.

Further to this, they believe that teaching should also open us up to receiving everything else God has for us that is not explicitly mentioned in the Bible, such as the limitless ways that we can encounter Him. We need to come to the place where we have the same open-minded and believing attitude that Mary had when told by an angel that she would have some completely unprecedented experiences, including miraculously conceiving and giving birth to the Son of God. Her response was, "Behold, I am the servant of the Lord; let it be to me according to your word." (Luke 1:38). The ability of Bethel leaders to inspire their people to never accept the status quo, to take everything that is offered, and to always chase after more of God, is a major factor in the church and its various ministries seeing such a massive outbreak of signs and wonders.

While Scripture must always be our starting point, we cannot divorce Scripture and theology from experience. Having a theology requires an experience, and will ideally lead to an encounter with the Living God. We should never just stop at the level of theory, or use our theology to put God in a box, in terms of what He can and cannot do, for He is God and does whatever He pleases (Psalm 115:3). This is, after all, the mistake that the Jewish religious leaders of Jesus' day made regarding Him. Although they were earnestly awaiting the coming of the Messiah, they were unable to recognize Him when He did appear, because He wasn't the figure they were expecting.

There are many Christians today, including some prominent leaders, who are putting God in a box by strongly criticizing Bethel (and other similar churches) for reports of strange supernatural manifestations in their services, such as gold dust materializing on people's faces, "angel feathers" falling, people becoming "slain in the Spirit", and appearances of a "glory cloud" (clips of which are available on YouTube). They question where these claimed signs and wonders are in the Bible, with the clear implication that such occurrences, if they are actually genuine, are unbiblical and therefore probably of the devil instead of God.

What these critics, who require specific biblical references to justify each and every thing that happens, have to realize, though, is that Scripture doesn't contain all knowledge and truth, otherwise why would Jesus have told His disciples that the Holy Spirit would teach them (and by implication every future believer) all things, and guide them into all the truth (John 14:26; 16:13)? Furthermore, if these people looked to their own churches then they would discover that much of what they do cannot be found in Scripture either. But that doesn't necessarily make any of it wrong. They need to learn the distinction between what is non-biblical (not in the Bible) and that which is un-biblical (contrary to what is in the Bible) (cf. John 21:25).

One thing that I must not neglect to mention, however, is that Bethel and likeminded churches do not "make" any of these strange signs and wonders happen. Nor is it normal for anyone to pursue them specifically (e.g. pray for gold dust to appear). When such signs occur, they usually do so spontaneously as people passionately worship God, and cannot just be turned off at will.

Bill Johnson says that while we don't seek after these signs, we shouldn't ignore them either. He likes to refer to them as "signs that make you wonder". If we view them in the right way, they will naturally expand our awareness of what is possible with God, and in the process leave us with more of a sense of His greatness and glory.

In general, therefore, when we encounter God, we must be prepared to have our theologies challenged and possibly even completely messed up, since He is God and not us. As Bill points out, He will never contradict the Bible, but He may violate our understanding of it. Because of this, we need to approach Scripture with a degree of humility, and recognize that our understanding of it is at best incomplete, no matter how impressive our theological credentials.

This is not to say that there is nothing absolute and set in stone, such as the death and resurrection of Jesus. I am convinced that there are a number of such truths that can be established from the Bible. However, many other things are wide open to interpretation, especially when the Bible makes little or no specific reference to anything resembling them. We should therefore avoid running around condemning everything that does not fit into our very limited models of how things are supposed to work. If we do, we will most likely find ourselves opposing God Himself (cf. Acts 5:33-39).

To give a personal example, several years ago (this was before I went to Bethel), I found myself in a situation where my theology was greatly challenged by what I was experiencing. It happened when I went with my friend Andy to pray for the healing of one of his neighbors (a woman in her 50s), who I understood to be a non-believer. As I prayed for her, she spontaneously raised her arms in the air (as if praising God) and began speaking in a spiritual language (i.e. "tongues"). She then asked me what was happening to her, as she had no grid for any of this.

I thought to myself that this shouldn't be occurring, because speaking in tongues is something associated with the Baptism of the Holy Spirit, which (supposedly) cannot be obtained before you receive Jesus as your Savior. The only explanations that I could up with were that maybe she already did have some faith in God, or possibly she spontaneously came to faith in the act of receiving prayer. Alternatively, it could be a case similar to the Spirit of God falling on King Saul in the Old Testament, which caused him to prophesy (1 Sam. 19:21-24), even when he was demonized (1 Sam. 16:14) and clearly had murderous intent toward David (1 Sam. 19:1).

This is the kind of messy situation that can sometimes confront us when we are out in the real world doing ministry. What was I to make of the fact that she seemed to have received the Baptism of the Holy Spirit before actually being saved? Well, I just let go of trying to understand everything, I faced what was in front of me without judgment, and then moved toward my desired ministry outcomes (e.g. salvation, healing, and deliverance). This included making sure that she was saved by leading her in a prayer of repentance and salvation – which she was willing to follow.[139]

Of course, this didn't mean that I was now going to come up with a new theology that anyone can receive the Baptism, regardless of whether or not they are a believer. Sometimes we have to let go of our need to have everything figured out and be okay with placing things into the category of "mystery". It is, after all, not essential that we understand everything, but that we trust God completely and submit to Him those things that don't seem to make sense (Prov. 3:5).

Bringing all this back to our topic of teachers in the Church, these leaders have the responsibility to guide their people through a process of discovering truth (with the help of the Holy Spirit) as they pursue everything that God has for them. This is as opposed to just teaching theory and acting as heresy hunters, who reject everything that they either don't understand or are unfamiliar with. While it is not wrong to guard against heresy, there are two scriptural principles that we need to keep in mind regarding this:

Firstly, Jesus said that we will recognize false prophets and deceivers by their fruits (Matt. 7:15-20). This means that we need to evaluate the lives of others (especially leaders) to see what their faith is producing in and through them. Do they demonstrate a love for God as well as other people? And are they living in a godly way that glorifies Him, through the extending of His Kingdom on Earth? The answers to these two questions should be major clues as to what is in their heart regarding their true motives.

Secondly, Jesus also mentioned that Father God will only give us good things in response to our prayers (Matt. 7:7-11). There is therefore little danger that someone with a good and sincere heart will fall into serious deception, to the point of spiritual ruin, by pursuing more of God. In relation to this, Bill Johnson asks a very pertinent question: "What do I trust most: my ability to be deceived or His ability to keep me?"[140] The Holy Spirit, after all, is more than able to correct us if we veer off course.

Being excessively fearful of deception by the devil is one thing that will actually empower the devil to deceive. This is the case with heresy hunters, who throw the baby out with the bathwater in rejecting anything that doesn't fit inside their artificial and very small boxes of how they think God behaves. In doing so, they miss out on much of what God has for them, and discourage many others from accessing these things as well.

Regarding the supernatural, we should certainly have no hesitation in accepting signs and wonders as anything but normal and positive occurrences, in both the life of the Church and individual believers who are passionately following God.[141] There is an abundance of biblical evidence that they are for today, particularly those that originate through the supernatural gifts outlined by Paul in 1 Cor.

12:4-11. But even the more obscure signs and wonders are not without precedent in the New Testament, such as Peter walking on water (Matt. 14:28-29), an earthquake following prayer (Acts 4:31), Philip the Evangelist being supernaturally transported (Acts 8:39-40), and Peter's rescue from prison by an angel (Acts 12:6-11) (NB. I am only including those not directly associated with Jesus). Imagine what the heresy hunters would say if Bethel claimed any miracles like these!

Furthermore, we should not get hung up on whether a particular sign is mentioned in the Bible or not, as those recorded in Scripture are only examples and not an exhaustive list of what is possible (John 20:30-31). But if we do, we will miss out on the greater works, which Jesus promised us (John 14:12). Remember that all things are possible for one who believes (Mark 9:23), and nothing is impossible with God (Luke 1:37)!

All of this therefore underscores the vital importance of five-fold teachers in the Church being careful to never become isolated from the real world and the apparent messiness of it. While the truth of Scripture should always reign supreme, we need to be open to new experiences and having our theology stretched at times, if necessary. Teachers must be comfortable with this process of being challenged, so that they can guide their people into all that God has for them, rather than blocking the way.

Finally, it is essential that teachers (along with all five-fold ministers) explicitly teach their people to expect signs and wonders to follow them in their Christian lives, and serve as examples of this. This is the approach taken at Bethel and it works! When you get in an environment where the supernatural is normal, it quickly becomes normal for you. This is one reason why the ministry school (BSSM) is such a life-changing experience for so many students and that I would highly recommend it to just about everyone who isn't satisfied with their powerless and boring faith. If miracles aren't normal for you at the moment, go to a place where they are, and stay there until you catch it. As Bill says, "Follow signs and wonders until they follow you."[142] There is nothing wrong with this if it is an expression of your ultimate quest for God.

***

In conclusion to this long chapter, having the full five-fold ministry in place, under an apostolic structure, enables Bethel to gather people, get them healthy, train them up as world changers, and then send them out to actually change the world for God. Every five-fold element is ultimately aligned to this end goal of sending, eliminating the need for any tension between the elements that emphasize going out and taking risk (apostles and evangelists), and those that put priority on staying in church, being safe, and becoming whole (pastors and to a lesser extent teachers).[143]

The result is that Bethel (especially BSSM) has become a continuous production line of fully equipped believers, who are healthy and whole, lacking in nothing. The apostolic, prophetic, and evangelistic elements of the five-fold ministry, which are missing from many churches today, are prominent at this church in equipping believers in the supernatural gifts e.g. those listed in 1 Cor. 12:8-10. Should it be any surprise that if these elements are missing, or lack the prominence they deserve in a church, that the power of God is not moving strongly? I think not.

I would therefore encourage senior leaders of churches that don't have the full five-fold leadership structure in place to make a point of recruiting appropriate people to fill the missing slots. It is also important that these people be given adequate opportunity to teach and train the congregation, so that each person is fully equipped as a believer – particularly for the work of the ministry, which involves everyone (Eph. 4:11-12).

Finally, if you are in a church where the complete five-fold ministry is not in place (which would be most believers), I strongly suggest that you access some teaching resources by people who represent the missing elements. Books and video/audio programs can be great for targeting the things that you specifically need to grow in. There is also a lot of good material online, such as on YouTube. Furthermore, I highly recommend Bethel TV (bethel.tv) as a way to get great teaching from outstanding examples of each element of the five-fold ministry. A full subscription does cost money (and is well worth it!), but the free subscription offers access to at least one of the Bethel services each weekend. It is a total no-brainer to sign up for this.

7. CULTURE OF REVIVAL

Many years ago, Bill Johnson promised God that if He would touch him again then he would pursue revival and never change the subject. It would be the purpose of his life to see the outpouring of the Holy Spirit on the Church, with believers being equipped in all the gifts of the Spirit, enabling them to bring Heaven to Earth and totally transform every sphere of society.[144]

To make a long story short, God did touch him and Bill has been faithful to his promise ever since.[145] The focus on revival that he initiated has led to a culture of revival being established at Bethel, which has been a key factor in the explosion of signs and wonders through ordinary, everyday people, as they live supernatural lifestyles. This culture of revival at Bethel therefore plays a crucial role in the overall signs and wonders culture there.

In this chapter, we will be examining some of the key elements of Bethel's culture of revival, to give you a glimpse of what it looks like, and some clues on how you could implement various aspects of it where you are, to create your own revival culture.

Revival is in Bethel's DNA

Revival is in the heartbeat and very DNA of Bethel Church; it is something that is lived and breathed continually. Everything there is geared toward revival, rather than just having good meetings and generally "doing church" well – which happen naturally as a result of focusing on revival. Their mission statement boldly and unashamedly affirms this:

> Bethel's mission is *revival* – the personal, regional, and global expansion of God's Kingdom through His manifest presence.[146] (emphasis original)

In this, it is clear that they see the presence of God as the nucleus of revival, from which everything else emanates. This helps to explain their focus on His presence that we discussed back in Chapter 2, and their desire to partner with Him (Chapter 3) because He is good (Chapter 1) and has good plans for all. When His presence touches individuals, they get free, become empowered to change the world, and their passion to do so is highly infectious.

At Bethel, incredible excitement, energy, and momentum are created through the many "free" people pursuing their destinies in God. If you get involved in the life of the church, it feels like you're actually going somewhere significant, both as an individual and a community. Barriers are being smashed, giants slaughtered, and ground is constantly being taken for the Kingdom. Nothing seems impossible anymore!!! The great end-times revival that has been prophesied appears completely inevitable.

Of course, Bethel is not going to usher in any great worldwide revival on its own. Such a move of God will only happen when many churches play their part, all in unison – which is beginning to happen. Bethel for its part, however, is serving as a training and resource center for revivalists, particularly through its ministry school (BSSM). Their aim is to equip and send out an army of such people throughout the earth, who will spread revival wherever they go and in whatever they do. Ideally, every member of this army will be:

> A believer who is focused, passionate and willing to pay any price to live in community, purity and power because they are loved by God and love Him whose manifest presence transforms lives and cultures.[147]

This culture of revival is therefore founded on principles such as focus, desire, sacrifice, community, purity, power, identity, and love. And as I mentioned above, it all starts with the presence of God. When He touches a person, they will never be the same again; they discover their true royal identity as a son or daughter of the King, who is righteous, powerful, and called to change the world. This ignites in them a passionate desire for even more of God, and to pursue the specific calling that He has placed on their life. A focus is therefore created such that they choose to say "no" to many things in order to say "yes" to God and their calling. This will usually involve a measure of sacrifice, but one that they believe is more than worth paying, just as the man who found the pearl of great value was prepared to sell everything he had to buy that pearl (Matt. 13:45-46).

When all of these elements are in place, which collectively represents having a strong and active faith, such a person will develop an intense desire to live in a community of like-minded people, with whom they will work together to bring Kingdom transformation to the world.

The Power of a Revival Community

The power of the community is a key component of Bethel's revival culture, one that a lot of people who only read books by Bethel authors, watch/listen to recordings of Bethel teachings, and come to Bethel conferences, apparently overlook in their quest for more of God's power on their lives. I would estimate that just by reading one book per month by Bethel leaders like Bill Johnson and Kris

Vallotton, and watching Bethel TV regularly, you could in a year probably access about 60-70 percent of the basic teaching material from Bethel.[148]

What you can't access, though, other than by actually going there, spending time, and becoming involved, is the incredible power of this revival community (or probably more accurately, "revival family"), which makes each person much stronger through the process of synergy (see Chapter 9: Culture of Empowerment). That is, the community as a whole is far greater than the sum of its parts – meaning that everyone needs each other to operate at their highest level.

The presence of God is available everywhere you go, and of course without this nothing happens. But it is simply life changing to be part of a large community of focused, passionate, pure, and powerful people, who both individually and collectively are in the process of changing the world. No more is this the case than in BSSM. Personally, I can think of many individuals I met there who have inspired and empowered me toward becoming a much bigger person in God and believing in a far greater vision for my future. And this is before I even mention the unbelievable impact that the Bethel leadership team has had on my life.[149]

Sadly, a lot of Christians today complain that it is so difficult to find a church community where they feel at home, and this is something that I too have struggled with at various times, so I totally understand. But from the first day I arrived in Redding until the day I left, I felt that I completely belonged in the Bethel community. It was full of dreamers like me, who were not prepared to settle for less in God (and life!) than what is possible, and who fully believed that they were destined to leave their mark on the world. I am 100 percent confident that many of them will; some even are at the moment!

I know of people who are leading many to Christ through signs and wonders evangelism, and regularly seeing the kind of miracles that accompanied the ministries of Jesus and the original apostles. Others have founded and are running revival schools with similar visions to BSSM. Some are also involved in teaching/training ministries, which equip ordinary believers to operate in signs and wonders. Then there are those who are pursuing Holy Spirit-inspired business ideas and careers.

Before my time at Bethel, a few students even organized a "Dead Raising Team" after they graduated from BSSM – which still exists to this day! And no, the name is not metaphorical; they are deadly serious about their goal of raising the dead (pun intended!). According to their website, deadraisingteam.com, they have seen "about 15 resurrections" to date.[150]

Given that this is the caliber of people that the Bethel environment attracts and nurtures through the power of community, who wouldn't want to part of a revival family like this?

What is great about BSSM is that community is almost effortless, and it is nearly impossible to not be involved. When you start school, you are immediately inserted into a large student body. This is divided into smaller groups of about 65 people ("revival groups"), who usually meet together at least once a week for the purposes of connection, spiritual growth, and empowerment. Your revival group, which is led by a pastor who is dedicated to the group, effectively becomes your closest family for the school year. Over the course of the year, you will likely become extremely connected to your group, making for a lot of sad goodbyes after graduation, when everyone disperses to different parts of the planet.

Over a number of years, this revival group structure of the school has been incredibly successful, demonstrating that you can throw together any diverse group of people who have a heart for revival, and they will most likely thrive together. Age, gender, marital status, personality type, interests, and individual callings etc. are for the most part irrelevant. In fact, the differences between individuals are a strength rather than a weakness. There is particular power, for instance, in all the generations being together and running with each other, as we all have something to offer. Younger people often add energy and enthusiasm, while older folks usually offer wisdom and experience, for example. And putting aside differences in age, everyone has different spiritual gifts and perspectives to contribute, which benefit all.

Outside of your revival group, you will of course meet and become close to numerous other people within BSSM through various activities (e.g. outreaches, mission trips, and elective ministry trainings) and as you socialize outside of school. Within the BSSM environment, many people make friendships that will last long after graduation – even a lifetime.

In my opinion, it is the strong vision and common purpose (i.e. global revival) that unites people together and makes the Bethel community so powerful.[151] Here many discover their life calling, find a cause worth dying for, and brothers and sisters to fight alongside. A major lesson which can therefore be drawn from Bethel, is that if a church has a vision that genuinely inspires a lot of people, one which they feel highly empowered to participate in, a great community will develop that continually attracts more like-minded people.

However, a lot of churches are thinking far too small as a result of factoring in only what they can do, rather what God can do with and through them. Consequently, their vision, and how it is actively being pursued in the life of the church, is not compelling enough to ignite a fire in many people.[152] Sometimes this can lead to "community" actually becoming the de facto vision (instead of being the outcome of a powerful vision), through a strong emphasis being placed on social activities and events (e.g. dinners and movie nights), which are designed to get everyone together – but for what ultimate purpose?

We must understand, though, that men and women today, especially Millennials, require much more than just a social club type of experience for them to become (and remain) part of a church. They are looking for a grand and noble cause to give their lives to. If they don't find it in God through the mission of a church then they will give themselves to other things instead, often so-called "gods" like career, money, relationships, and various addictions – none of which truly satisfy. There is simply no substitute for relationship with the one true God, and being part of a powerful community that is on a great mission, following in the footsteps of Jesus.

What is clear, therefore, is that community for community's sake doesn't really work if you desire to have a large, growing ministry that will have a significant impact on the world. If a church community is to be vibrant and successful, it must have a compelling vision that everyone feels part of, which is actively being pursued as a group, such as at Bethel.

Revival Mindsets

A notable feature of the Bethel community as a whole (and BSSM in particular) is their strong offensive mindset, which contrasts strongly with the predominantly defensive one that is common elsewhere. People are constantly looking to take ground (both individually and corporately) from the enemy, rather than just hold onto what they've already got. Furthermore, they expect exponential rather than just additive growth in whatever they do. This involves continually challenging the status quo, thinking and dreaming big, and trying new things – which usually requires risk (we will be discussing this in detail in Chapter 10: Culture of Risk). Bethel people genuinely believe that they can change the world, and they actively pursue opportunities to do so.

Such boldness does not come from them possessing extraordinary natural talents and/or supreme confidence in self. Rather, it arises from knowing that they have a big God, who is willing and able to back them up with His incredible supernatural power, as they work to extend His Kingdom on Earth. When you truly understand that nothing is impossible with God (which is the subject of the next chapter), you will be prepared to set your sights much, much higher, knowing that the risk that you step into creates the space for Him to move on your behalf, to make the impossible actually happen. This process is called faith.

However, it is normal in much of the Christian world today to only go after goals that can be achieved by natural human ability alone, through utilizing the resources that are readily available. Bill Johnson puts it like this:

> ... we are accustomed only to doing things for God that are not impossible. If God doesn't show up and help us, we can still succeed. There must be an aspect of the Christian life that is impossible without divine intervention. That keeps us on the edge and puts us in contact with our true calling.[153]

It is, of course, not wrong to operate in the natural, as God definitely does endorse, anoint, and even require such activity (Matt. 25:31-46; cf. Luke 8:3). In fact, the vast majority of what we do will always be done in this realm. But this needs to be carried out in partnership with Him, such that we cannot ultimately be successful without His support. In other words, we have to prayerfully set goals and objectives with Him that are so big that we have no hope of ever reaching them on our own. Our part is to then move toward them in whatever ways we are able to (or He directs us), while relying on Him to do the rest (cf. Mark 6:35-44).

The issue is that our human strength and ability alone will normally only yield human-sized results, not God-sized ones. Only by partnering with Him will we move mountains, shake nations, and change the course of history. Otherwise, we must be content with being small and having limited impact on the world.

The truth is that we cannot have revival without God. Only His supernatural power is going to bring the Kingdom to Earth in an overwhelming way. We therefore need to give up on human-centered strategies like trying to be "more relevant"[154], stop leaning on our own understanding (cf. Prov. 3:5), and instead do whatever it takes to move in His power, through establishing partnership with Him. This requires seeking after God, asking Him what He wants to work with us to achieve, doing our part, and then leaving Him room to do His. To be clear, I am not talking about trying something completely crazy that He's never told us to do, and then asking Him to bless it. God cannot be manipulated into serving our agenda simply because we pray a prayer and take some bold action.

The story of Elisha and the widow in 2 Kings 4:1-7 is a wonderful illustration of partnering with God, in terms of satisfying personal need. The widow owed money to a creditor, which she was unable to repay, and this man was about take her two sons as slaves, in lieu of payment. When she appealed to Elisha for help (who being a prophet, acted as a mouthpiece for God), he asked her what she had in the house and discovered that there was nothing other than a single jar of oil. In response, he told her to borrow as many empty vessels as she could from her neighbors and then pour oil into these vessels from the jar. When she did so, the oil did not stop flowing until the last empty vessel was filled, allowing her to more than repay her debts by selling the oil.

I believe that this story contains two important Kingdom principles: that God will normally only fill the space we create for Him in faith, and he will only compensate for what we lack in resources and ability (cf. Josh 5:12). After all, why would He help us if we can do it all ourselves?[155] This, of course, does not give us license to be lazy, reckless, and squander what we already have (cf. Matt. 25:14-30). Rather, it highlights the need for us to step out beyond what we can do ourselves, so that no matter how much talent we possess and how great our resources are, they are not enough – forcing us to depend on God.

Another lesson that can be gleaned from this story is how little we need to contribute to our partnership with God for Him to do great things through us and for us. All He really requires from us is our faith (i.e. trust) and obedience (i.e. preparedness to take action based on His leadings).

Bethel people have become used to partnering with God in this sort of way and have an expectation of the supernatural in whatever they do, both as groups and individuals, inside and outside of the church. There is, for example, an absolute assurance that God will encounter people during each and every activity organized by the church, whether it be one of the regular weekend services, the Healing Rooms on Saturday mornings, or even the annual holiday feast for those who are disadvantaged. The anticipation is that He will reveal His love in powerful ways and change many lives for good.

The faith of those at Bethel does not, however, revolve solely around God using Bill Johnson and other powerful leaders in the movement to do great things for Him (which He certainly does). It is actually much more about Him using "me" and those in my immediate proximity for such purposes. In this regard, it is considered normal for ordinary people to move in signs and wonders and to rely on supernatural guidance for life decisions (even everyday ones) - through hearing the voice of God, dreams and visions, prophetic words, and other modalities. For instance, you commonly hear people mention that they did or didn't do something because they "had a peace about it" or "didn't have a peace about it", respectively.

To give a personal example, at the end of my second year of BSSM, I was looking to sublet my apartment over the summer to some other people while I was traveling through Europe, to keep it for the next school year (BSSM Third Year). Apartments in Redding are especially hard to come by around August/September, as there is huge competition from other students and even local people in the city. While I was discussing this plan with my South African friends Steve and Jaco in the apartment clubhouse, a woman (probably in her late 30s or early 40s) sitting on one of the couches overheard us talking and said that she would interested in taking the apartment. On the surface, she seemed like a nice lady from Bethel, who was just after some better accommodation for the summer, until she made some longer term plans. So, I invited her to come over and have a look at the apartment later on, which she did. Steve and Jaco were there when she arrived, and we all talked for a while.

After checking out the place, she decided that she did want to take it and the two of us agreed to meet up again the next day to discuss this further. However, as soon as she left, Steve told me that something didn't feel right about her. And Jaco added that while she was speaking, he saw a picture in his mind of her with a bag over her head and worms crawling over her heart. I had some misgivings about her too, but was trying overlook them in the hope of quickly getting the apartment situation sorted (very bad idea!).

Because I couldn't ignore the feedback that Steve and Jaco had offered, and the little voice inside of me, I did some investigation before meeting up with her again. It turned out that she was a con artist and a convicted criminal, who owed thousands of dollars in unpaid rent to an apartment complex in another state!!! Needless to say, this discovery took the decision completely out of my hands. I was so thankful for my spiritually discerning friends, who helped me avoid making what could potentially have been a totally disastrous decision.[156]

Ultimately, I didn't feel a peace about renting out the apartment to anyone else either, and eventually gave notice on the lease. It turned out that I did not actually end up going back to BSSM for the next school year, so not giving that woman the apartment proved to a great decision from multiples perspectives!

While this story might sound a bit dramatic, it highlights well the degree to which Bethel people involve God in their everyday lives and expect Him to come through for them. After all, we have the mind of Christ (1 Cor. 2:16) so we might as well use it!

***

In conclusion to this section, the revival mindsets that those at Bethel possess contribute greatly toward making the culture of revival there self-perpetuating. The incredible expectation (i.e. faith) that God is going to move supernaturally actually draws Him to move - which further fuels expectation that He will continue to move in this way - which causes Him to move even more (i.e. it is a virtuous cycle). These mindsets also help to generate the great excitement and energy that the people embody as they chase after their dreams and destinies, knowing that nothing is impossible with God. Finally, all of this attracts more people into this culture of revival – meaning that it snowballs in size, as Bethel has been doing for a number of years now. In other words, numerical growth is the natural result of having the right culture.

The Power of the Testimony

Another factor that is important in sustaining/growing the culture of revival at Bethel, and which actually leads to the manifestation of many signs and wonders, is the power of the testimony. As Bill Johnson explains:

> A testimony is the written or spoken record of anything that God has done, and every part of that record becomes your family history the moment you are born again. ... [E]very story of every miracle or sign that God has ever performed is your story because you have become related to the God who made them happen.[157]

The strong emphasis on the testimony at Bethel arose, in large part, because of a revelation Bill received from Scripture regarding this. In Rev. 19:10, the apostle John writes, "... the testimony of Jesus is the spirit of prophecy." The revelation was that when we testify of the things Jesus has done in our lives (and those of others), we are prophesying what He is going to do again for more people – especially those who hear these accounts and receive them by faith. However, as Bill points out:

> ... the prophetic anointing does not just declare what God wants do to (sic), but also carries creative power to bring what is declared into being. The testimony releases this anointing. When we declare what God has done, power is released to make that testimony happen again in the lives of those who hear it.[158]

The implication of this is that when we listen to or read the testimonies of others, we are able to claim the results of them (or similar ones) for ourselves, by using our faith to access the power of the prophetic to bring these things about. There is a unique supernatural power that is released when the acts of God are recounted, which goes far beyond the inspirational. This is closely related to the power of declarations that we discussed back in Chapter 3: Partnering with God.

Hearing testimonies of what God has done builds our faith, particularly in areas related to each testimony. For instance, if God healed a person of a broken arm through someone's prayer, the proclamation of this miracle builds up both the faith of people needing a broken arm healed and that of those who will be praying for such a healing. More generally, it will strengthen the faith of people for the healing of broken bones in other parts of the body, and also every other healing need.

For this reason, when I am praying for someone's healing, if I have seen their condition get healed before (especially if this has occurred recently) then I will let them know, in order to build their faith and thereby increase the likelihood of success. For instance, I've prayed for a number of people with arthritis and have probably seen the majority of them receive at least some degree of healing, on the spot. Therefore, every time I pray for someone who has arthritis, I will let them know that I've had a lot of success with this condition. And if I've seen a recent example, I might describe it to them in detail.

Testimony is also a great way to build someone's faith up enough to actually accept prayer in the first place. Frequently, when I offer to pray for a person in a public place, who has never even heard of healing prayer before, I will tell them of the multiple blind eyes and deaf ears that I've seen get healed through my own ministry. This conveys to them that I'm not joking, and that they have a really good chance of being healed if they receive prayer from me – particularly if their condition seems a lot less serious than blindness and deafness.

The power of the testimony not only works for one-on-one ministry; it can also be utilized very effectively on a much larger scale, such as from the platform at church, through audio/video recordings, social media/blogs, and in books – so that your breakthrough can become someone else's breakthrough, and their breakthrough can be yours. When we receive a miracle, it is our responsibility to share it with others so that God is glorified and other people are empowered to believe for similar things in their own lives.

While I have been concentrating on healing miracles in this section, the power of the testimony is certainly not limited to this area. It could involve finding a marriage partner, getting a new job, a loved one coming to faith in Jesus, a court case being resolved favorably, financial provision, hearing God's voice, and even raising the dead. Anything is possible with God!

Because the testimony releases prophetic power to repeat miracles over and over again, it creates a multiplier effect that allows the prevalence of the miraculous to snowball. Most of us would know that it is much harder to believe for something that we've never heard of before, or that occurred somewhere far away like Africa, many years ago. So when we hear of recent reports of certain miracles, especially in our country/city and through the hands of ordinary people like us, our faith to believe for them in our own lives can dramatically increase.

From a ministry perspective, therefore, instead of having to contend individually for every miracle, we can leverage the power of one miracle to cause a bunch of similar miracles to break out, creating momentum for ourselves in the miraculous. Obviously, this is far more time and energy efficient. As believers in Jesus, we often need to learn to work smarter rather than just harder. Many of us are already operating at full capacity, but still not achieving a whole lot. God is looking for increase rather than just effort in our labors for Him (cf. Luke 19:16-17 vs. Luke 19:18-19). The testimony is therefore an important shortcut to seeing more of the power of God manifest in our lives and ministries, which allows us to experience supernatural increase from our labors. Pam Spinosi, who is involved in documenting testimonies at Bethel, describes them very aptly as "the gift that keeps giving".[159]

At Bethel, one miracle that was unheard of a number of years ago was metal dissolving in people's bodies. And when Bill Johnson learned that itinerant minister James Maloney was seeing it occur in his ministry, he asked James for an impartation in this area. After receiving one, Bill started trying to replicate this miracle in his own ministry, and saw great results.[160] Then gradually over time, more people at Bethel tried it out and saw success as well. Today, this miracle is quite commonplace at Bethel. No doubt, the power of the testimony has played an important role in this.

Cancer is something that people also get healed from on a regular basis at Bethel (although still not regularly enough). The abundance of supernatural healing testimonies in this area helps those praying to pray with a stronger expectation of success, when dealing with this disease – even when it is classed as "stage 4" and "terminal". Such diagnoses present absolutely no barrier to God – unless we partner with the fear and intimidation attached to them, and thereby give them power.

You may, however, be wondering about how you and your church can exploit this power of the testimony I've been talking about, when nothing particularly notable has ever happened for you guys. To this, I would reply that you need to first start where you're at, by proclaiming what God has been doing in your lives, thanking Him for it, and continually going after the more. If you have only seen the occasional headache and sore back get healed then celebrate these things, for it is important to focus on what He is doing, rather than what He is not. And faithfulness in the small eventually leads to bigger things.

It is also important that you borrow the testimonies of other people, until you have a full set of your own. As Bill said in the first quote of his I made in this section, every story of every miracle that God has performed is yours, because you are related to Him. So therefore, just take these stories and use them in whatever ways you can, to build your faith and cause the supernatural to break out in your own lives. This is what I do, such as for raising the dead, which I've never seen before in my own ministry. The more I hear testimonies of others having done it, the closer I feel to seeing it happen for me. At the very least, I want to take every opportunity I get to have a go, for faith involves stepping out of the boat (Matt. 14:28-29).

"Releasing" a Testimony

A particularly effective way to impart the full prophetic power of a testimony is to actively "release it" to others. "Releasing" a testimony is something that has become part of Bethel jargon. It refers to a mechanism through which a testimony (i.e. its result, such as healing) can be transferred in faith, from one person to another person or a group of people. This can be as simple as just sharing a story of what God has done for you and allowing your listeners to receive it in whatever ways they choose to.

However, if people haven't been trained on how to receive something for themselves then their default will usually be to try to do so passively (e.g. by just listening) – which is usually not the best way, although God can still use this. An active approach is often far more effective in terms of causing the miraculous to occur.

At Bethel, you quickly get taught to carry out an act of faith pointing to a desired outcome, which is referred to as a "prophetic act" (i.e. this is an active approach to receiving). A prophetic act can involve both the releaser of the testimony and the one receiving it. For instance, the person sharing their testimony might say at the end, "I just release this to you now", and then hold up one of their hands and motion it toward those they're speaking to, as if they're throwing a ball of fire at them – which, in faith, they are. And those trying to receive that miracle might hold out their hands and say to God, "I receive this for myself, in Jesus' name. Thank you, Lord!"

Another example of releasing a testimony through a prophetic act would be the speaker at a church service inviting those seeking a particular miracle, which he or she had just testified about, to come up the front and have that miracle released to them individually, through the laying on of hands. This could involve these people holding out their hands and the speaker coming by one-on-one, laying his or her hands on theirs, and speaking the desired blessing over them e.g. "finances be released in Jesus name!" (if the testimony involved a miraculous increase in finances).

Even when the person releasing the testimony and those receiving it are not in the same room together, such as when the testimony is being shared on a video recording or blog, it can still be actively releasing to the audience. On video, you are able to do it in some of the same sorts of ways that you can in person. And for a written testimony, you could ask the reader to pray to receive the miracle. Alternatively, you could simply declare the miracle over every reader who is seeking it. There is, after all, no distance in the spirit – either in space or time.

The active approach to releasing a testimony is an attempt to create a "point of contact" for people to activate their faith, in order to receive something from God. The great healing evangelist Oral Roberts (1918-2009) used this term to describe how a person, object, or action can create a focus for someone's faith in order to help them believe for their miracle, just as the woman with the issue of blood believed that if she touched the hem of Jesus' garment then she would be healed of that condition (Matt 9:20-22). Another clear example of this in Scripture would be Peter's shadow, which people apparently believed had the power to heal anyone it fell on (Acts 5:15). I have even heard of people from Bethel who have drawn circles on the ground in chalk, and told others that they will be healed if they stand in the circle – which, I understand, has happened on a number of occasions.[161]

When you create a point of contact, it provides an opportunity for people to engage in the process of receiving their miracles – which makes it more likely that these miracles will actually happen, since action is an important part of faith (cf. James 2:14-26). This is, therefore, a particularly effective way to release a testimony.

Nevertheless, it must be recognized that there is no magic formula as to what exactly you should say and do when releasing a testimony. I would suggest seeking direction from the Holy Spirit, and letting Him inspire you to come up with some great ideas.

The most important thing, however, is that you at least start sharing the miracles and answers to prayer in your life with as many people as possible, so that this glorifies God, encourages others, and creates an open heaven to receiving more from Him. Then, over time, you can experiment with different ways of releasing your testimonies, as the number of them grows.

Whatever we do, though, we need to be careful that we don't become like the Ephraimites in the Old Testament, who serve as a sad example of what happens when we forget the acts of God in our life. These people failed to remember the signs and wonders that had God performed, in miraculously delivering them from Egypt and supernaturally sustaining them in the wilderness for many years (Psalm 78:11-20). Because of this they did not believe in Him or trust His power to save them (v.22), and as a result they turned back in the day of battle and broke His covenant (vv.9-10). What this story shows us is that by forgetting what God has done in the past, we lose access to the courage needed to fight our battles in the present and be victorious in them.

Psalm 78 highlights the importance of us making a record of the acts of God and passing it on to the next generation (vv.1-8), so that they will believe in God as we do (v.7). In this way, we leave a legacy such that our ceiling becomes their floor. This is something that is emphasized strongly at Bethel, not only for spiritual fathers and mothers toward their spiritual children, but also successive BSSM classes. Each generation should go further than the last, because the previous one paved the way for them by what they did and testified about.

Stewarding Testimonies

Due to the incredible power of the testimony to encourage people, build their faith, and cause the miraculous to happen, there is a strong emphasis within Bethel to "steward" testimonies that occur within the environment, such as at church, in BSSM, on the streets of Redding, and through the ministry of leaders and students as they travel.

Certain people within Bethel have the responsibility to collect and document what God has done, so that these stories can be disseminated as widely as possible – to glorify God, encourage Christians to step out in faith, help people believe for their own miracles, witness to those who don't yet know God, and in all of this extend the Kingdom of God on Earth.

A priority is placed on ensuring that these testimonies are as accurate as possible, so that God is not dishonored by anyone making exaggerated claims. Bill Johnson, in particular, prefers to err, if anything, on the side of understating the claims he makes of miracles in his own ministry. In view of this, effort is made at Bethel to tie some of the more significant miracles to supporting evidence, such as medical reports, if possible. And there has been a move to document some of these on video, so that the person who experienced the miracle can speak in their own words and share a first-hand account.

While Bethel relies heavily on self-reporting by the people claiming to receive miracles in its ministry, it is careful to not "jump the gun" by declaring ones that cannot be established without medical examination. For example, when a person with cancer receives prayer, they may perceive improvement in some or all of their symptoms (e.g. pain and/or the size of a lump has reduced/completely disappeared). But this does not necessarily mean that the cancer is either partially or totally gone. A doctor would need to declare the person healed for Bethel to publicize such a miracle. On the other hand, a doctor is not required to verify that someone with a frozen shoulder can move their arm well beyond the range of motion that they were able to before, or that a person's back pain has gone.

Bethel uses various means to get the testimonies out and turn them into resources for people. For instance, on their main website there is a testimony section, which contains countless written testimonies in various categories: bethel.com/testimonies/. And on Bethel TV, some high-quality video testimonies have been posted: bethel.tv/testimonies.

Several years ago, they also started publishing a professional-looking coffee table book (in volumes) called *Increase: Catalytic Stories*, containing testimonies sourced mainly from BSSM students. Since this book is not branded explicitly in terms of Christianity, it is something that you could strategically place as reading material in the waiting area of your service business (e.g. dentistry practice or hair salon). Alternatively, when you visit such a place as a patient or customer, you could "donate" a copy of one of these volumes to the pile of other reading material. The possibilities are endless!

The power of the testimony has proven to be so great that this truth has now become infused into the Bethel culture. Testifying of what God has done is now largely automatic, and something that happens on a regular basis. For instance, Bethel staff meetings always begin with an extended time of sharing testimonies of the amazing miracles that God has done recently in the life of the church. This creates the right atmosphere for leaders to make decisions in a spirit of faith, knowing that they have a big God, who is ready to back them up with all of Heaven's resources. Problems just seem a lot smaller when we frame them in terms of the God who created and sustains the entire universe.

If you go to the Bethel Healing Rooms on a Saturday morning, you will frequently hear a person on the microphone ask everyone to stop what they're doing and listen to the testimony of a notable miracle that has just occurred. Often following this, they will then "release" the testimony to everyone else with a similar need. And always after the Healing Rooms have finished for the day, the prayer servants will take turns sharing over the microphone some of the amazing things that they have seen God do through their ministry that morning.

At BSSM, there are regular opportunities for people to share what God has done in and through them, especially at their revival groups and City Service (outreach) sessions. Occasionally, there is also time for this during the main sessions when everyone is present.

Overall, the power of the testimony is significant in maintaining and building the culture of revival that exists at Bethel. This is something that every person and church can use to create a culture of revival for themselves, and cause a release of the supernatural that will eventually snowball. However, it takes intentionality and discipline to do so. Are you prepared to take up this challenge and give God a chance to move?

I will conclude this chapter with a testimony from Bethel staff members Dave and Taff Harvey, which illustrates extremely well the power of releasing a testimony and Bethel's revival culture in general:

One night, during a testimony sharing time at Dave and Taff's home group, someone mentioned a dream they had had about a friend depositing $1,000 into their bank account, and how the next morning they had discovered that this had actually happened in real life.

After this testimony was shared, Dave encouraged everyone to make some declarations about what they wanted God to do in their lives. Then, suddenly, he blurted out the words, "A thousand dollars for everyone!"

About five minutes later, they finished the group time and Taff went to the kitchen to organize supper. However, she came back straight away carrying an orange envelope, with a look of amazement and surprise on her face. This envelope, which had Dave and Taff's names typed on the front, contained $1,000 in cash!

If the story had ended there then it would have been pretty amazing. However, this was only just the beginning! By the next week, two other people from the group had each received $1,000. So they released the testimony again, and within another week two more people had each received multiples of $1,000. They then released the testimony a further time, resulting in four additional people receiving $1,000 during the following week.

Soon after this, Dave released the $1,000 testimony to his revival group at BSSM. One of his volunteers also declared, "And add a zero for Dave!" Then the next day, there was a knock at Dave and Taff's door, and when they opened it, a couple told them, "We have been trying to give money to an orphanage for months, but we couldn't find one we felt peace about. Then God gave us a vision of your house with a double story on it, and He said, 'This is an orphanage because they are breaking off the orphan spirit.'" Following this, the couple handed them a check for $10,000!

Ever since that time, Dave and Taff have released this testimony wherever they have traveled, and at the time this account was written for *Increase: Catalytic Stories*, they had shared it for 18 months to people around the world, and heard more than 70 first-hand accounts of people receiving either $1,000 or $10,000.[162]

I invite you, therefore, to participate in this testimony as well, by claiming these amounts for yourself. Then, when the money manifests to you, share your part of the story with others to encourage them. God is good and eagerly wants to bless you! Will you give Him a chance?

8. NOTHING IS IMPOSSIBLE!

There is one belief that is absolutely essential to unleashing the supernatural of God in our lives, and this is that nothing is impossible (Luke 1:37) - one of the four cornerstones of Bethel Church[163]. It may alternatively be expressed in the positive: all things are possible (Mark 9:23, 10:27).

However, what we need to be clear of is that this is not just positive thinking or about being self-confident, for God is the reason for our optimism and confidence. When we work with Him, the normal rules governing what is possible go right out the window, meaning that there are no limits!

The reason why this is such a key belief is that it unlocks the door to some other vital beliefs in the area of the supernatural - which we're going to look at over the course of this chapter. And when we possess this set of empowering beliefs, it leads to us boldly stepping out and taking action (i.e. risk), in order to see the impossible actually become reality - which is the process of faith. On the other hand, without these beliefs it is unlikely that we will pursue the miraculous in any meaningful way. Instead, we may end up embracing a set of elaborate, but erroneous theories as to why it won't work, and in the process discourage others from at least trying.

If we want to be used powerfully by God, it is vital that we let go of any skepticism about the supernatural that we may hold, and not allow anyone with such views to influence us. For it is a poison that will reduce us to a state of living well below God's best. He designed us to be supernatural beings, who violently enforce His rule on Earth against the kingdom of darkness (Mark 16:17-18; Luke 10:19). But He never intended us to be spectators who battle just to earn a living, along with everyone else.

At the very least, we need to open our minds to the limitless possibilities that exist with God, and embark on a process of exploring these with Him (and ideally others) – which will involve taking action. Although we may not start with absolute belief, we can move toward it over time as we progressively see more and more of the supernatural take place, for God works with us where we're at (Mark 9:20-27).

In this chapter, therefore, we will survey some of the key beliefs and mindsets that one needs to hold in order to successfully operate in the supernatural, on a consistent basis. But first, we will discuss the ones that will destroy our chances of ever doing so.

Beliefs and Mindsets that Limit the Supernatural

1. Cessationism: the supernatural gifts and the miraculous are not for today

Cessationism is the belief that the supernatural gifts of the Spirit (1 Cor. 12:8-10), and by implication, the miraculous, are things that we should not expect today, as part of the ordinary Christian life. This is a great example of how an incorrect theology can rob so many people of blessings that God desperately wants them to have.

Other than outright unbelief in the supernatural, there is probably nothing more destructive to the experience of signs and wonders than this particular theology, which we covered back in Chapter 1: God is Good. Ironically, it ends up being a self-fulfilling prophecy and vicious cycle for those who adhere to it: they don't believe in the supernatural gifts and therefore do not attempt to use them; consequently, they don't experience any miracles and this reinforces their belief that the gifts aren't for today.

2. Is it God's will?/Theology of suffering

Many Christians today question whether it is normally God's will to heal and perform the miraculous through us. It is their strong suspicion that He usually has a much better plan – one that involves people undergoing prolonged periods of suffering, in order for them to learn valuable spiritual lessons that are needed to form Christ-like character, such as patience, humility, and trust in God. This theology of suffering that they subscribe to, which in many cases is probably a response to past disappointments over unanswered prayer, betrays an unbiblical Greek dualistic mindset that spirit is good and the material world (including the body) evil.

God, however, sees everything He created as "very good" (Gen. 1:31), and this has not changed as a result of the Fall (1 Tim. 4:4), which corrupted humanity spiritually, and brought death and decay to the natural world – including the human body. He is equally committed to restoring both our body and spirit in the form of a resurrected "spiritual body" in Heaven (1 Cor. 15:44). Applying the "on Earth as it is in Heaven" principle (Matt. 6:10), we should therefore assume that God's desire is to heal us both spiritually and physically on Earth, not just spiritually at the expense of the physical.

While it is easy to see how cessationists would be inclined to doubt God's will to heal given their theology about the supernatural, this is by no means limited to them. A large number of other Christians also have this mindset (albeit to a lesser degree), including some Pentecostals and Charismatics. Although those from the latter two groups almost always accept that God does heal and perform other miracles sometimes, many of them are prone to believe that these events are unpredictable, uncontrollable, unexplainable, and rare – deserving, therefore, to be placed into the category of outlier, the exception to the rule. Furthermore, some of these people harbor unhealthy skepticism and cynicism toward both the supernatural and those believers who claim to operate in it. It is as if they don't want anyone rocking their theological boats, calling out their victimhood, and challenging them to greater deeds in their faith.

The sad result of all of this is that such people are unlikely to witness much of the supernatural in their lives – partly because they refuse to pursue it, by taking God at His word and stepping out in faith (e.g. offering to pray for those with healing needs and requesting prayer when they need healing). Worse still, they often infect others with their false beliefs in this area, causing those people to see God and the supernatural in the same limiting ways.

3. Fatalism

There is a view, which has strong relationships to the previous two we haveœ looked at, that also greatly limits the prevalence of the supernatural in the lives of those who follow it. This is that of fatalism.

The main tenets of this belief system are that whatever happens is God's will and whatever is God's will happens. Its adherents ("fatalists") are quick to proclaim devastating natural disasters as being God's judgment on the wicked and unrepentant.

In relation to the supernatural, they think that if God wants to act miraculously then He will do so – either sovereignly, or by directing a chosen human vessel to carry out a specific action (e.g. pray for the healing of another). But if neither of these conditions is met then they assume that it is not His will. On the other hand, taking the initiative in trying to work the miraculous, without clear direction from God, is often seen by them as being presumptuous, because we could very well be opposing His will.

This belief system is fundamentally flawed because everything that happens is not God's will, and God's will does not always happen – in fact, it often doesn't. For example, it is not God's intention that there be any sin in the world and yet there is plenty of it, as we all know. Furthermore, given that Jesus died for the sins of the world

(John 1:29; 1 John 2:2), God desires that none would perish and that all would come to repentance and be saved (2 Peter 3:9). However, most of humanity is heading to an eternity without Him.

What fatalists fail to take into account is that although God is all-powerful, Satan is the god and ruler of this world (2 Cor. 4:4; John 14:30), and his kingdom of darkness stands in direct opposition to God's Kingdom of light. Satan, therefore, has a large degree of influence over this world (Luke 4:5-6), including most of humanity and the natural realm.

While God could destroy Satan and his kingdom at any time He chooses, this would involve also destroying all of humanity who are part of that kingdom (i.e. everyone who is currently not a born again follower of Jesus, and living a holy and righteous life). But everybody who is alive on Earth, who is not currently part of God's Kingdom, still has the opportunity to be redeemed. Therefore, God, because of His incredible love for all people, is currently holding off on His great day of judgment (2 Peter 3:9-10) to avoid this massive collateral damage – in the hope that some of these people will eventually be saved.

In the meantime, though, He has a master plan: the Church. God wants to work through His people, those who have submitted to His rule, to destroy the rule of Satan. This way, His Kingdom can be advanced on Earth and many people freed from enslavement to the kingdom of darkness, without Him invoking the final judgment.

What this means is that God will normally work through individual believers in Christ rather than act sovereignly. His expectation is that we will follow His general instructions for building the Kingdom given to us in the Bible (e.g. proclaim the Kingdom, heal the sick, raise the dead, cleanse the lepers, and cast out demons (Matt. 10:7-8)), instead of always requiring special instructions. The implication is that we need to take the initiative, rather than wait for God to either specifically direct us, or do it all Himself (cf. Luke 19:11-27).[164]

Fatalists, along with those who are unsure of God's will, make the grave mistake of waiting for God to do what He is waiting for them to do. Their passivity prevents them from seeing the supernatural take place in their lives, because it usually only manifests when we step out in faith and take a risk (i.e. pray for someone's healing) - in a state of certainty that it is His will to work the miraculous through us in that situation. Unfortunately, however, what God calls faith and obedience, these groups often call presumption, especially when it pertains to going after healing, and therein lies the problem. In practice, these people are not very different to the non-absolutist (i.e. moderate) cessationists who allow for God to work the miraculous to a limited extent, and normally only in a sovereign way - which is seldom the way that He operates, particularly in such an atmosphere of unbelief.

4. God only uses "special" people

There are some Christians who completely accept that the supernatural gifts of the Spirit are for today, but believe that God normally only operates through "special" people, such as itinerant ministers, pastors, and possibly the associate leaders/elders of a church. What they end up doing is relying on those in authority to perform the supernatural for them when they need it (e.g. healing and deliverance). Meanwhile, they fail to recognize the abilities that God has placed within themselves and other regular believers.

These people have an unhealthy level of reverence for leaders in the Church, to the point of seeing authority figures as being intermediaries between themselves and God, who have special supernatural abilities that others don't possess. They go to their pastor as though he or she is the village shaman with magical powers to solve all of their problems. However, if the pastor's "magic wand" doesn't work, they will then try to get prayer from those they view as being even more powerful, who have noted signs and wonders ministries (e.g. Bill Johnson, Randy Clark, and Benny Hinn). And they will keep chasing such ministers until such time as they receive their miracle.

In essence, these people have an Old Testament view of the world, in that they believe that the Holy Spirit rests only on a few special people, who God has appointed to move in extraordinary ways. They fail to understand that God has poured out His Spirit on all flesh in these last days (Acts 2:17) - meaning that every believer is able to move in signs and wonders, regardless of whether or not they have any official position or designated role within the Church. Therefore, such people have an impoverished view of who they, and their fellow Christians, are in Christ, not recognizing that we are all mighty warriors with the power to change the world.

Sure, one can point to James 5:14-15, where sick people are instructed to go to the elders of their church and request prayer for healing. I have no issue with this and believe that there is blessing in spiritual authority. But our options are not limited to just this, as is indicated in the next verse (v.16), which instructs us to pray for one another that we may be healed. I do not believe that this is referring only to leaders. We all have this ability, and it might just be the case that God has appointed the little old lady sitting next to us on Sunday morning, to heal us. It is therefore important that we see people according to the Spirit rather than the flesh (2 Cor. 5:16), otherwise we might miss out on receiving our miracle.

At Bethel, there are a number of people who are probably just as good as Bill Johnson at healing in one-on-one situations (which he doesn't do a lot of these days; he normally leaves this to the ministry team). And dare I say it, there might even be some who are more effective than him, at least in regard to some conditions.[165] But it is hard to say with any certainty because many in this church move very strongly in healing, and no attempt is made to rank people's effectiveness. The point is that we don't need to go looking for Bill and other famous "healers" every time we're suffering from some ailment. For God has appointed many other people in the Body of Christ to fill these sorts of needs. If we want to receive our miracle then our first port of call should be those He has placed around us, particularly the ones who have made the decision to actively pursue the supernatural of God in their lives.

On the other side of the coin, He has also chosen us to fill such needs in the lives of others, and therefore we must to be ready to offer our services to fellow believers and anyone else who is in need. We could very well be the one that God has appointed to bring the solution to their problem.

Bill tells a story about how he noticed an ordinary couple at the church who had a significant anointing on their lives for finances – which he didn't at that time possess. So he humbled himself by asking them to pray for this to be imparted to him as well, and after they did, he saw God bless him financially to a much greater extent. This is a lesson that we all need to take to heart: recognizing what God has placed on the lives of those around us – including the ones who are not prominent. Neither should we forget to identify what He has placed on us.

We should, therefore, never see ourselves or anyone else as being too ordinary for God to use. We need to believe what He has told us in the Bible, that He wants to use everyone in powerful and significant ways – not just those we see on stage and Christian TV.

5. God would never use me – I'm not good enough

Another very common scenario is that people may fully accept that the supernatural gifts of the Spirit are for today, and that God operates in these ways through ordinary believers. However, they do not believe that God would ever use them, because they don't feel good enough. It might be that they don't think they're holy, smart, or educated enough. Alternatively, they may feel as though they are too old, haven't been in the faith long enough, or don't have enough experience. On the other hand, it could be that they're a woman, divorced, or "have a past" ... the list goes on.

These are, however, just a list of excuses, none of which disqualifies a person from moving in signs and wonders. In fact, there is nothing at all that can prevent you from operating in the supernatural other than yourself – through limiting beliefs, such as those we have just looked at above. Jesus, in Matt. 7:21-23, described how many people who had moved in great signs and wonders would not end up making it to Heaven, because there was no relationship between Him and them. If that is the case then every person who does know the Lord has absolutely no legitimate excuse. Remember, that God gives the Holy Spirit to everyone who asks Him (Luke 11:13) and rewards those who seek Him (Heb. 11:6). It is this Spirit who empowers us in the supernatural gifts (1 Cor. 12:11).

Soon after I started moving powerfully in healing, I was working to organize a team of people to help run a healing stall at a local New Age festival. I asked a guy I knew from my young adults' group if he wanted to be part of it. He declined, though, because he was still struggling in the area of alcohol. I responded by telling him that this didn't matter and that God would still use him. However, I was unable to convince him to change his mind. This was a pity because if he had seen God working the miraculous through himself then he would probably have gained more faith in God's ability to deliver him from his addiction to alcohol.

Unfortunately, Satan has tricked too many people out of moving in God's supernatural power through reasons like this. He knows their true power and is absolutely terrified that they might discover this and use it against him. But we can't allow this to continue. We need to understand our true identity in Christ as royal sons and daughters of God, who are righteous, powerful, and called to change the world (see Chapter 4: Saints, Not Sinners). We are worthy because He is worthy. End of story!

6. Double-mindedness

The sixth mindset that limits the activity of the supernatural in one's life is double-mindedness. This is the one that Pentecostal/Charismatic-type people, who have a strong understanding of what is available to them in and/or through the Atonement of Jesus, often seem to struggle with the most – including me. They know that Jesus provided forgiveness for all their sins, healing for all their diseases, provision for every one of their earthly needs, adoption into the family of God, a glorious destiny, peace and joy, the Baptism of the Holy Spirit, and many other wonderful things. In practice, though, their prayers invariably go unanswered. How could this be?

There are, of course, many potential reasons for this, and it is quite absurd to come up with any simplistic one-size-fits-all explanation like "lack of faith". Nevertheless, we cannot overlook a clear principle in Scripture explaining one particular possibility. Consider what James says about asking God for wisdom:

> If any of you lacks wisdom, let him ask God, who gives generously to all without reproach, and it will be given him. But let him ask in faith, with no doubting, for the one who doubts is like a wave of the sea that is driven and tossed by the wind. For that person must not suppose that he will receive anything from the Lord; he is a double-minded man, unstable in all his ways. (James 1:5-8)

This is a picture of a man who oscillates between faith and unbelief. He is not fully convinced that God will grant his request, and as a result, he forfeits the right to expect any answer from Heaven.

One might argue that the context of this passage is a request for wisdom. But it is clearly much broader than just this, as James generalizes it to "anything" in v.7, and therefore elevates it to a general principle of faith.

The following saying of Jesus corroborates this:

> Truly, I say to you, whoever says to this mountain, 'Be taken up and thrown into the sea,' and does not doubt in his heart, but believes that what he says will come to pass, it will be done for him. Therefore I tell you, whatever you ask in prayer, believe that you have received it, and it will be yours. (Mark 11:23-24)

And just to ram this home a bit further, let's look at another great biblical saying about faith:

> Now faith is the assurance of things hoped for, the conviction of things not seen. (Heb. 11:1)

What all of these passages are telling us is that if we want to receive from God then we must be fully convinced that He will grant our requests. But this requires us to know that the things we are requesting are His will for us:

> And this is the confidence that we have toward him, that if we ask anything according to his will he hears us. And if we know that he hears us in whatever we ask, we know that we have the requests that we have asked of him. (1 John 5:14-15)

When we are sure that it is God's will for us to have what we're asking from Him (which may require a personal word if it's not a general promise in Scripture), we can then pray with absolute certainty that He will grant our request. It is, for example, Bethel's view that it is always God's will to heal. However, it is almost certainly not His plan for every believer to be a billionaire in this life. This, of course, does not mean that He doesn't want each of us to prosper financially (as opposed to struggling to make ends meet). The Bethel community believes that God is a good Father, who desires to bless us in every area of our lives – including financially.

One thing that is important not to forget, though, is that when we make a legitimate request to God, Satan will invariably try to sow doubt into our mind. This will often be through flooding us with a list of reasons as to why it can't or won't happen, with the objective of causing us to move into a state of unbelief (or at least double-mindedness). If, for instance, we are believing for the healing of a major disease or injury in our body, the demonic realm will speak things like the following to us:

> How many times have you already prayed for this and it hasn't happened? So why is this time going to be any different? You need to just face reality and stop deceiving yourself that prayer is going to work. Learn to live with your illnesses like everyone else does. Other Christians, who are far more holy and faithful than you, have also prayed a long time for healing and haven't received it. If God was going to heal anyone then they would definitely come before you. Do you actually think you're better than them?

At this point, we need to decide who we're going to believe: God or Satan? What we face is a spiritual battle and to win this we need to take every thought captive to obey Christ, according to Paul in 2 Cor. 10:5. This means that we must challenge these demonic words spoken against us, by rejecting them and affirming the true words of God regarding our situation. For example, in this case of us believing for healing, we could say, "No, I reject these words" and declare various healing scriptures over ourselves, such as Matt. 8:17; 1 Peter 2:24b, Jer. 30:17, Prov. 4:20-22, and Psalm 103:2-3.

It might take a certain amount of time to get our breakthrough, but we must not give up if it doesn't come immediately. God is good, He is faithful, and He is willing and able to grant our requests. We need to have a calm assurance of His character and what He has promised to us.

However, if we allow Satan to get into our head and cause us to doubt God and His promises, we have made a decision to partner with his kingdom instead of God's. The result is that we should not expect to receive our miracle, as the scriptures quoted above have clearly warned us.

All of this equally applies when we seek to move in the supernatural gifts e.g. healing and miracles. There is every chance that we will fail to see much happen initially when we first step out and have a go. But we cannot give up and reason that God hasn't given us that gift. We must keep believing that we have it, and are called to do greater works than Jesus (John 14:12). Eventually, there will be breakthrough if we persist. This was the process that great revivalist John Wimber had to go through. Although he knew that God had called him to heal, he saw no evidence of this for 10 whole months. But he kept being faithful to the word of God until this truth manifested in the natural.[166]

Unfortunately, though, most Christians who pursue the supernatural gifts give up before the promise comes to pass. Often, just a few failed healing attempts are all that it takes to cause them to throw in the towel and leave healing to others, who they suppose are more qualified. And it is a similar story with revelatory gifts, like the word of knowledge and prophecy. The prophet Shawn Bolz tells people hoping to move in these:

> You're a wimp if you give up after ten times. It's going to take a thousand times before you have confidence because you have to learn the process.[167]

What a sobering thought this is! But if the process was so easy that it always worked perfectly the first and every subsequent time, then very little faith would be required and everyone would be doing it, wouldn't they? The question is, therefore, will you do what it takes?

Beliefs and Mindsets that Empower the Supernatural

Now that we have covered some common beliefs and mindsets that limit the supernatural, we will look at other ones that actually empower it in our lives.

1. Nothing is impossible[168]

If you want to see signs and wonders break out in your life then it is crucial that you embrace the foundational belief that nothing is impossible with God. This requires an absolute assurance in His ability and desire to bless not only us, as believers, but all of humanity. We need to trust that He never allows anyone to fall into any situation that is truly impossible and without hope (on this side of eternity); and that He always has a solution available for every problem that we face, whether through natural or supernatural means.

Most Christians would probably give mental assent to this idea that nothing is impossible, because it's clearly stated in the Bible and is a natural implication of believing in an all-powerful God. However, it appears that only a small proportion of all believers really do believe this in their heart of hearts, to the point of taking God at His word and actually going after it – which is what faith requires. Limiting beliefs and mindsets, such as those we looked at in the previous section, prevent most from doing so.

Let me ask you a question: when you see someone in a wheelchair, do you genuinely believe that God could use you to heal them, or does such a possibility seem too far-fetched to even consider? Your honest answer to this question will go a long way toward determining whether you will seize the moment by offering to pray for such a person, or whether you will just walk past them and carry on with your day. And this will in turn determine the extent to which you operate in signs and wonders.

If you do believe that such "impossibilities" are possible for you, through the power of God, and you're prepared to go after them, signs and wonders will begin to explode in your life – either sooner or later. This is where I started from: I didn't have any official position within my church and wasn't part of the ministry team. Therefore, I had no one approaching me for prayer and needed to go out and create opportunities for myself – which I did, often in real life situations outside of church contexts, such as at the gym or when I was shopping. My philosophy was that if I saw a need then I would go after it, and this led to a lot of success for me in the area of healing.

At the time of writing, I have probably seen several hundred people healed supernaturally through my own ministry. And I would guess that in the majority of these cases, I have approached the people concerned and offered my services. Only when I became part of the Bethel ministry and Healing Rooms teams did I start to have a lot of people approaching me for prayer.

The lesson in this, therefore, is to not wait for opportunities to come to you. You need to pursue them if you really want to move in signs and wonders. Also, don't wait until you feel ready, as you probably never will. Like everyone, you start with no track record, and only the word of God to go on – that nothing is impossible for you, when partnering with Him.

2. God wants to work the supernatural through every believer (including me!)

Building on the key belief that nothing is impossible, we need to believe that God wants to work the supernatural through each and every member of the Body of Christ, regardless of whether or not they're a recognized leader in the Church, male or female, young or old, rich or poor, educated or uneducated, black or white etc.

Even more so, we must have the assurance that He wants to use us personally (i.e. me!). However, many people will happily believe that God wants to use everyone other than themselves, as we discussed in the last section, on limiting beliefs and mindsets. This is an identity issue that needs to be resolved, otherwise it will become a self-fulfilling prophecy, through us not taking any action (e.g. offering to pray for people). Unfortunately, the devil tricks many believers out of God's best for them in this way.

3. Signs and wonders are normal

Thirdly, we should expect signs and wonders in our everyday lives as part of normal Christian living, both in terms of receiving for ourselves and helping others. For instance, we should never be shy about seeking supernatural fulfillment of any unmet needs that we may have. It is not a case of "naming and claiming it", as some critics allege, but accessing God's provision for us in accordance with the Scriptures (e.g. Psalm 34:9-10, 103:2-5; Mal. 3:10-12; Matt. 6:25-34;

Phil. 4:19). After all, He loves us and wants to bless us, just as any good father would.

This is not to suggest that faith allows us to be irresponsible in life, such as by expecting God to keep providing financial miracles to cover our laziness, instead of us getting a job and working. His supernatural power allows us rise above our challenges and limitations, reign in life, and bring His Kingdom to Earth.

If we are doing everything that we know to do and still can't pay our bills then it is legitimate to ask God for help (although it might be better to ask Him for a job, or a new, higher paying one, first!); ultimately, everything comes from Him anyway. There will always be times when our natural abilities and resources are stretched if we are living a life of faith, because faith requires pushing beyond who we think we are, what we have, and what we know how to do. It involves taking risk, such that God has to come through for us, if we are to be successful.

But if you want to live a life of safety and security, well within your own comfort zone, then don't expect to see much of the miraculous of God – at least not through yourself. The miraculous normally happens beyond our comfort zones, until such time as it becomes so normal that our comfort zone expands to include the impossible.

One area that we should particularly expect God to move in signs and wonders through us, is evangelism. The pattern that Jesus modeled to His disciples was that miracles should accompany the teaching and preaching of the Gospel, to authenticate the message (Matt. 9:35; Luke 6:17-19). He then sent them out to have a go at this (Matt. 10:7-8). This pattern not only continued after Jesus' ascension to Heaven, it became the new norm for all ministers of the Gospel – including every believer (Mark 16:20; John 14:12-14; Acts 5:12-16; Rom. 15:18-19; 1 Cor. 2:4-5; 1 Thess. 1:5; Heb. 2:3-4). For the Holy Spirit has now been poured out on all flesh (Acts 2:17), meaning that each of us has the power to move in the supernatural. Assuming that we are regularly witnessing for our faith, signs and wonders should therefore be normal for us.

In addition to all of this, God desires to move supernaturally through us in whatever spheres of influence that He has called us to. He wants to give us divine wisdom, ideas, and strategies to use in our careers, with our families, and in our finances etc. The question, though, is whether we will devote the time to seeking Him for these things. And if we do, will we act in faith on the information that He provides (which involves risk)?

4. If the miracle doesn't manifest immediately, it is still God's will

In addition to the above beliefs and mindsets, we need to have the assurance that if a miracle doesn't manifest immediately (and fully), that it is still God's will for the miracle to happen[169]. This requires having the same single-minded, persevering faith that Elijah had, when he prayed for rain to end a drought over the land of Israel (1 Kings 18:41-45), in response to a word from God (v.1). For him, it took a number of attempts before the first sign of the miracle manifested in the natural (v.44), but he never doubted or gave up.

It was a similar story with Jesus, when a blind man only got partially healed the first time He laid hands on him (Mark 8:22-24). He never even contemplated the possibility that this incomplete restoration of the man's eyesight was all that God wanted to do in the situation. Instead, He laid hands on him a second time, in absolute assurance that God's will was total healing – resulting in full restoration of his eyesight (v.25).

Like Elijah and Jesus, we must continue to believe for, and actively pursue, the miracle we're seeking, despite all evidence to the contrary. But if we give up because we're not seeing anything happen, we will end up aborting the process and fail to see the miracle come to pass. Then we might reason that it must not have been God's will, and make up some false theology around this (e.g. "God is far more interested in developing our character than healing our bodies").

This does not, however, mean that we should keep hitting our head against the proverbial brick wall if what we're doing is not working, after repeated attempts. We need to be flexible with our approach to pursuing the miracle, while never doubting that it is God's will. If, for example, we have laid hands on a particular person for healing several times and no improvement has taken place then it may be time to try a different tactic.

One alternative method that is commonly used in the Bethel Healing Rooms is to release peace over the person needing healing, particularly over the area of their body that is infirmed. Another approach sometimes used at Bethel is to laugh over the person (not at the person but their condition!). A third one is using the metaphor of an elevator. If the person is suffering from level 8 pain, you would ask them to imagine themselves on the 8th floor of a building and then stepping into an elevator, pushing the button for the ground floor, and going down to the bottom. As they "go down", you count down the floors for them: "8, 7, 6, 5, ... , 1, 0". The idea is to tie going down to the ground floor to their pain going down to level zero. So you tell them that, when they push the button and go down, their pain will respond in the same way. This has apparently worked many times before.

I mention these alternative approaches merely as examples that you could try, not as the official "Bethel Method" - of which, there is none that I'm aware of. The number of possible ways to effect healing is limited only to you and your God-inspired imagination. I have even heard of Bethel people using art to heal, such as through asking those seeking healing to look at a prophetic painting (cf. Num. 21:8-9). So there, I have given you a bonus method!

What could be even more effective, though, is to ask God for a word of knowledge regarding how He wants to heal, and then partnering with that (which, of course, presupposes that it is His will to heal). Have you ever wondered why Jesus often did some strange things to heal people, like spitting on the ground, making mud, and then rubbing it into a blind man's eyes (John 9:1-7)? In Scripture, He said that He only did what He saw His Father doing (John 5:19-20). So did God give Him a vision of rubbing mud into the blind man's eyes to heal him? Obviously, it is impossible to know for sure, but what we do know is that whenever He did something strange like this, it always worked[170].

Of course, instances of people doing different and unusual things to effect healing are not limited to the Bible and the ministry of Jesus. There are also many modern-day examples, such as the famous healing evangelist Smith Wigglesworth (1859-1947). On one occasion, Wigglesworth reportedly punched a man in the stomach who was deathly ill with stomach cancer, resulting in that man's dramatic restoration back to health. And today, the Nigerian prophet T.B. Joshua often heals through slapping parts of people's bodies with his open hand, apparently through inspiration of the Holy Spirit.

What these biblical and contemporary examples emphasize is the need to be open to the leadings of the Holy Spirit and partnering with them, rather than just always blindly applying our favorite cookie-cutter method e.g. the laying on of hands – which incidentally, is a principle strongly endorsed in Scripture (Mark 6:5, 16:18; Acts 28:8), but may not always be the best approach to effect healing.

Sometimes, however, the particular healing method may not be the issue. For instance, when the great John G. Lake (1870-1935) lived in South Africa, in the early 20th century, huge numbers of people came to his house seeking healing, and he would lay hands on all of them. Those who received immediate and full healing were then sent away, but those who did not were directed to another room. There, John's wife Jennie used her word of knowledge gift to determine why each person had not received their healing. When people dealt with these root causes, they would then typically be healed with a second round of prayer.[171]

Dave Hayes, who writes under the pen name "Praying Medic", believes, based on his own ministry experience, that emotional trauma is the one thing that holds people back more than anything else, from receiving physical healing. He has found that if a person gets healed of their emotional issues (e.g. emotional pain, guilt, shame, and anger) then it is much easier to get them healed physically.[172]

What these biblical and contemporary examples demonstrate, is the value of believing that the miracle we're seeking is God's will, persisting until we receive it, and if necessary trying different tactics. We are far more likely to receive under this methodology than if we just give up at the first sign of failure.

***

To summarize this chapter, therefore, when you embrace empowering beliefs and mindsets about the supernatural (and yourself!), and disavow any limiting ones that you have accepted, you place yourself in a prime position to operate powerfully in signs and wonders - assuming that you are prepared to back this up with appropriate action. Furthermore, when a group of people embraces these beliefs and mindsets (i.e. these beliefs/mindsets become part of the culture), it creates the potential for signs and wonders to break out on a corporate level - which is what has happened on a large scale at Bethel.

9. CULTURE OF EMPOWERMENT

Another incredibly important element of the Bethel signs and wonders culture is the culture of empowerment that exists within the environment. Put simply, Bill Johnson and his leadership team absolutely believe in their people. They empower them to be all that God has called them to be and to do everything He has called them to do.

At the most basic level, they recognize and validate each and every person as a unique individual, with important God-given callings on their life. Arising from this, they encourage everyone to be themselves and fully embody who God has made them to be. There is no desire to strip people of their individuality, in order to develop a military-style conformity. Nor is there any motivation to have people model themselves on others who are recognized as being successful[173], because each person has already been fearfully and wonderfully made, the way God intended them to be (Psalm 139:14). If He had wanted them to be another way then He would have created them that way in the first place.

Bill and the team see everyone at Bethel as being significant[174] and having a role to play, both inside and outside the church – by virtue of being made in the image of God, having the Holy Spirit living inside of them, and being placed by God at Bethel. Due to this, they provide their people with opportunities to be actively involved in various ministries and to receive training. A significant feature of this includes empowering women to such a degree that they have the same opportunities to be involved as men do, including in leadership.

"Be Yourself"

Before diving fully into this topic of empowerment in ministry, let's first discuss the area of empowerment in our individuality. There is a mindset common in the Church today, that we need to give up who we are in order to become more like Jesus, and reach greater levels of maturity in our faith. This "less of me, more of you Lord" philosophy arises from a misinterpretation of John the Baptist's statement to his disciples in John 3:30: "He [Jesus] must increase, but I must decrease."

To set the record straight, what John was actually saying was that his job of preparing the way for the Lord (Mark 1:2-3) was now complete, and therefore he had to step aside and give the limelight to Jesus. He no longer had a role to play in announcing the coming of the Messiah, because the Messiah had already appeared.

While we too need to draw attention to the Messiah, Jesus, rather than ourselves, our assignment is slightly different. Since Jesus has finished His earthly ministry and returned to Heaven to sit at the right hand of the Father (Col. 3:1), it is our job to declare what He has done on Earth and to proclaim His return. Furthermore, like His original disciples, He has sent us in His place (John 20:21) to carry on the same ministry to the poor, broken, and lost - which is everyone who doesn't know Jesus as their Savior, Healer, and Deliverer etc.

To complete this mission, by representing Him well, it is essential that we are Christ-like, in terms of being full of both the gifts (1 Cor. 12:4-11, 14:1) and fruit (Gal. 5:22-23) of the Spirit. But this does not mean that we have to give up our unique personalities - which God created and loves. The apostle Peter, for instance, did not. He apparently never lost his tendency to speak first, for any group that he was part of (e.g. Mark 9:5-6; Acts 2:14-40, 3:1-6, 12-26, 5:1-9) - often, it seems, before thinking. Surely, someone should have taken him aside and told him to be quieter, more humble, and to give other people a chance to express themselves?

But no, God used this personality trait of Peter's to work powerfully through him, as an influential leader in the infant Church. All that was required was for some of his rough edges to be smoothed out (e.g. Matt. 16:21-23; John 18:10-11; Gal. 2:11-14), and it is the same for each of us today. "Being ourselves" does not give us the right to hold onto our negative character traits/behavioral patterns and baggage in life, for that is not who we truly are anyway. When we let go of our "junk" and fully embrace our own individual personality and style, we become the best version of ourselves - which is the one that we were created to be and that God can work most effectively through.

As Bill Johnson says:

> What is needed is not less of us and more of Him. What is needed is *all of us covered and filled by all of Him!*[175] (emphasis original)

However, most of us are actually fearful to some degree of revealing who we truly are to the world, out of concern that we will be judged by others - particularly those we hold in high esteem. Therefore, instead of giving up aspects of our individualities, we actually need to more fully embrace the people who God designed us to be.

It is much easier, though, for a lot of believers to hide behind a "gentle Jesus, meek and mild" version of themselves - who is wishy washy, overly agreeable, never expresses their own opinions, won't say "no" to anyone, and who continually plasters a fake, cheesy smile on their face, to cover up how they really feel. This doesn't even sound much like Jesus to me, if that was the goal! For although He was the most loving human being who has ever lived, Jesus in His earthly ministry was a contrarian, who went around strongly expressing His divergent opinions and regularly offending people through during so (e.g. Matt. 15:1-20; John 8:12-59). He was often very blunt – not only with those who opposed Him, but also sometimes with His closest friends (e.g. Matt. 16:21-23; Mark 16:14) and those He ministered to (e.g. Mark 7:24-30). How many Christians try to imitate this? But we don't have to, as Jesus is Jesus and we are ourselves.

Neither should we attempt to be like other Christians. When Paul said to imitate him (1 Cor. 4:16) in the same way that he was an imitator of Christ (1 Cor. 11:1), he was not meaning that people should copy his personality and style, but his "ways in Christ" (1 Cor. 4:17) – which were his good character and conduct (cf. 3 John 11).

However, in the Christian world today, there are plenty of imitators out there. If you've been in the faith for any length of time then you probably know what I mean. For example, at some churches, all the speakers communicate in pretty much the same style. Sometimes they are what I call "shouting preachers", who are highly expressive, move around a lot, and constantly bellow at you as they make their points. But at other churches, they are all quiet, understated, and mellow. The point I'm trying to make is that people need to develop and embrace their own style, rather than copy those of others. For we are the greatest in the world at being ourselves, but, at best, a distant second at being anyone else. We must give up trying to be generic and instead be unique.

Of course, there is nothing wrong with looking at other people's strengths and trying to incorporate certain aspects of them into our modus operandi. For example, we can make a point of reading the Scriptures in a much deeper and thoughtful way, to mine some of the hidden nuggets of gold that Bill Johnson tends to discover. We can look to add a touch of humor into how we communicate, a la Kris Vallotton. And we can aspire to move in very detailed words of knowledge like Shawn Bolz. These traits and abilities can all be expressed through our own unique personalities. But we should never strive to be a carbon copy of these people, or anyone else for that matter. For God created each of us to be ourselves, not someone else. He is not after clones in the Church, either of Jesus or anyone else.

He wants individuals living authentically according to how He uniquely designed them.

Breaking news: you have permission to be yourself and "own it". That is who God created and loves. And this is the person that you will be in Heaven for all of eternity, so you had better get used to it! All that is needed is that you get rid of your junk, not your entire self!

Bethel, for its part, honors people for who they are, and actively encourages them to fully be themselves rather than try to imitate anyone else, in terms of personality and style – no matter how successful that other person is. God isn't looking for an army of "gentle, meek and mild" people. Nor does He need thousands of Bill Johnsons, Kris Vallottons, and Shawn Bolzes etc.; He only requires one of each of us. If you don't fully embrace who you truly are then the world will miss out on something really important. And most likely, this will mean that some people who could have been saved through your life and witness, won't end up making it to Heaven. You are that significant!

Bethel believes in empowering a team of individuals, who are each fully themselves. Individuality is not seen as a threat to anyone or an obstacle to effectively leading people – as long as it is not expressed in an arrogant, divisive, or dishonoring way. Rather, it is viewed as a gift from God and a valuable resource to be utilized. Of course, when you're on a Bethel team, you do have to follow the rules and protocols that have been set by leaders. But in these, there is invariably latitude to express yourself.

In general, great diversity of thought is allowed at Bethel. People are empowered to think for themselves, and no attempt is made to force anyone to accept certain theological, philosophical, or political beliefs. Their approach is that we gather together because we are family, not because we agree 100 percent with each other, on everything. That said, if you have vast differences of opinion over Bethel core values etc. then this church probably wouldn't be a great fit for you.

But everyone is welcome to attend, regardless of what they believe, as long as they don't behave disruptively.

The Power of Team

One key distinctive of Bethel Church that lends itself to the release of signs and wonders, is the strong belief in the power of team – which includes everyone, not just a clique of "special" or favored people. Like Jesus, Bethel empowers the ordinary and those who appear unqualified. A major part of this involves allowing, and even encouraging, their people to participate in the ministry of the church. The culture is therefore a very permission-giving one.

What we discussed back in Chapter 4: Saints, Not Sinners, regarding believers being seen as powerful world changers, is not just a set of empty words designed to build up people's self-esteem. At Bethel, the leadership team puts their money where their mouth is, so to speak, by actually employing regular believers in "real" ministry roles, such as healing and prophecy.

The reason that I put the word "real" in quotes above is that ministry includes many things in addition to serving on prayer teams. For example, chairs need to be set out and stacked, greeters at the door are needed to welcome people, and communion elements need to be distributed etc. In no way am I denying that any of these things are real ministry, as they absolutely are.

What I am trying to convey is that the Bethel leadership team trusts their people enough to allow them to minister in roles traditionally identified as being "ministry" and only for the professionals/those most mature.[176] They presume them to be of good character and full of the Spirit, such that those coming for ministry will be powerfully touched by God. After all, no special skills are needed to minister in the Spirit – only Him!

One thing that you often hear at Bethel is that there is no junior Holy Spirit, as God has poured His Spirit out on all flesh, making no distinction between different categories of believers (Acts 2:17-18).

Even a five-year-old can operate powerfully in all the supernatural gifts.[177] And unheralded "nobodies" can be just as effective at ministry as famous revivalists like Bill Johnson and Randy Clark. There are actually a number of ordinary people at Bethel, who either often or normally, see the miraculous occur when they minister. This is a significant feature of the way God is moving on the earth right now. He is choosing to use everyday men and women (as well as boys and girls), rather than primarily working through a small number of superstars, as in previous revivals.

John Wimber used to say that everyone gets to play and do the stuff. This is something that I have seen modeled better at Bethel than any church community that I've ever been a part of. The number of different opportunities to get involved in various areas is nothing short of spectacular. And personally, I have never felt so empowered as during those two years that I spent in Redding. That experience has truly helped me to come alive as a believer and the world changer that I'm called to be.

In a lot of other churches, however, regular people are either not allowed or not encouraged to minister to others. Instead, it is the leaders who perform the bulk of this ministry, while everyone else is largely confined to a spectator role.

The reasoning behind this is obviously that leaders are people who are known, respected, and trusted in the environment. Furthermore, they are typically viewed as being more qualified and experienced than others, due to their leadership/ministry experience, ministry/theological training, and because they are normally mature in terms of age. These factors are seen to address the safety issues that exist, regarding the potential for people to be hurt in a variety of ways, through substandard, misguided, and even abusive ministry. And in a positive sense, the belief is that ministry is likely to be most effective when carried out by a leader (cf. James 5:14-15).

Bethel, though, resolves these concerns in a different way – through training and accountability. The Bethel approach is that if you do the training then you are considered equipped and qualified to be on the team – until you prove otherwise, through things like inappropriate behavior and spiritually unhealthy lifestyle choices.

To serve in areas such as prayer ministry at church and the Healing Rooms, there is a process that every person must go through, in order to be approved.[178] This involves firstly putting in an application to join the team and then undergoing training on methodology and guidelines regarding that particular ministry. And for the Healing Rooms, applicants then have to do an online test to demonstrate that they have understood these things. Following this, they need to observe the Healing Rooms ministry being practiced by others for a few weeks, before actually being allowed to participate.

When applicants are approved, they are then issued an identification badge, which they are required to wear in order to minister. In the Healing Rooms, the ministry is normally carried out in teams of three or more (but at least two), always with one leader on each team, and ideally at least one man and woman. Higher-level leaders also monitor proceedings, and have the authority to direct team leaders and their teams when required.

The ministry team for church services (which is entirely separate from the Healing Rooms team) usually ministers one-on-one, instead of three-on-one. They are also involved in the Fire Tunnels[179], which usually occur at the end of the night services. Accountability for these teams is not as direct as in the Healing Rooms, although there are always church leaders present and paid security staff observing from positions on stage. Furthermore, ministry team members are usually tightly packed shoulder-to-shoulder along the front of the auditorium, as there are often hundreds of people seeking prayer after a service. Because every team member has a badge identifying them, any complaints regarding their conduct can be directed to leaders, who also normally wear identification badges.

In addition to the official Healing Rooms and church ministry teams, Bethel speakers will often involve the whole congregation in prayer ministry, during church services. The speaker will call out words of knowledge and invite people in the audience to stand if they have that particular prayer need (e.g. healing, breakthrough in finances, victory over fear). Following this, they will ask those around these people to pray for them, through the laying on of hands. Bill Johnson does this regularly for healing, and on these occasions a number of people are normally healed on the spot.

Overall, this release of ordinary people into prayer ministry type-roles seems to work extremely well. In fact, Bethel could not offer anywhere near the amount of ministry it does without the huge army of volunteers that it employs. Hundreds of people come to the Healing Rooms every Saturday morning (including virtually over Skype) to receive healing. And probably hundreds more over the course of each weekend line up for prayer after the church services (mostly on Sunday mornings). In addition to this, over a thousand would go through Fire Tunnels over a normal weekend, assuming that these are run on both Friday and Sunday nights – as they usually are. But this is not counting those who double and triple dip, by going through the tunnels multiple times (as I often did)!

Empowerment of Women in Ministry

One very significant feature of the ministry of Bethel Church that cannot be overlooked, is the role that women play. They are involved prominently in all aspects of the ministry (including teaching and leadership), contributing significantly to the success of the church, in terms of advancing God's Kingdom. At Bethel, there has been an intentional drive to empower women in ministry, so that they feel welcome and encouraged to pursue every opportunity that God is calling them to.

However, this topic of women in ministry, particularly the leadership side of it, is an area that has been quite controversial for a long time. Some churches and denominations have explicit rules as to what women can and can't do. More often though, there are unspoken expectations governing the degree to which they can be involved. Generally, this has meant that women have only been allowed to do things like serve in support roles, and teach other women and children. Recently also, an openness has developed to them occupying youth pastor/leadership positions. However, it has been assumed that senior leadership positions are for men, with their wives serving as add-ons to these roles. Similarly, itinerant ministry has not always been seen as an appropriate place for women – other than when operating alongside of their husbands, "under their covering".

In the Pentecostal and Charismatic movements, there have been some notable exceptions to these rules, which many of us would be familiar with, such as Maria Woodworth-Etter, Aimee Semple McPherson, and Kathryn Kuhlman. However, it seems to have been more a case of these women having such divine calls on their lives that they could simply not be denied. Heidi Baker is a great present-day example of a woman with a powerful ministry in her own right.

In my special report, *Women in Ministry: Examining the Case Against Female Leadership in the Church* (available as a free digital download, with this book), I analyze this issue in some depth from a theological point of view – particularly in relation to the two biggest "problem" passages: 1 Cor. 14:33b-35 and 1 Tim. 2:11-12. What I will say here, though, is that Bethel, as a movement, does not believe that there is any general scriptural prohibition against women ministering in church, that applies today. Their position is that ministry and leadership should be based on merit (e.g. calling, anointing, ability, and character), with gender not being seen as relevant to this.

Therefore, no distinction is made between men and women, in terms of suitability for these types of roles. Women are free to be involved in any area of ministry that men are; and for leadership positions, the best person for the job is chosen, regardless of gender. The result of this has been that women are heavily involved in ministry and leadership within the movement. In fact, when I was in BSSM Second Year, there were actually more female revival group pastors than male ones.

Empowering women in ministry (particularly leadership) not only means providing equal opportunities, it also involves proactively encouraging them to aspire to such positions and become involved. This is because many women assume, like the majority of the Church, that ministry and leadership is primarily (or exclusively) for men, and that to have any involvement they need to be married to a man who holds such a position. At BSSM, a significant amount of effort goes into teaching on this subject and encouraging women to become involved. There are even elective classes devoted to this topic.

It is vital that we as the Church fully empower women in ministry, especially considering that they make up the majority of our numbers (significantly more women than men attend church at this point). Therefore, failing to utilize them to their full potential means that we are wasting an incredible resource for extending the Kingdom. To give an example, if women weren't allowed to minister as prayer servants in the Bethel Healing Rooms then a large number of those who come for healing each Saturday morning would probably have to be turned away – due to lack of ministry staff. That would be a sad situation indeed.

To conclude this section, I have seen many women come alive through the opportunities granted to them at Bethel. Collectively, they will end up going into every major sector of society, extending the Kingdom of God and making a difference wherever they go. For some, this will involve full-time ministry in high-level leadership positions – even as senior pastors of churches. But regardless of where they end up, they have a tremendous amount to offer the world, as do all Christian women. I believe that Bethel's great success in the empowerment of women in ministry is a model that many other churches around the world will end up following, as women are an essential part of God's plan for global revival in the coming years.

Not a Spectator Sport

A natural consequence of the culture of empowerment that exists at Bethel, is that church is not a spectator sport. There is neither a culture of entertainment nor consumerism, although many people do leave the services entertained and satisfied – normally through active participation rather than passive observing.

The Bethel leadership team intentionally facilitates participation among the people, enabling everyone to be involved in some way during church services. To give some examples, very often at the end of worship, the service leader will ask everyone to give someone near them a hug as they return to their seat (a lot of people leave their seats to worship, such as by moving to the front, back, and sides of the sanctuary). The offering is often conducted actively, by having people "rush the buckets" at the front, rather than passively waiting for an offering bag to be passed along to them. Words of knowledge are frequently given for healing and other needs, and people who think that these words apply to them are invited to stand. Those who are near to these people are asked to gather around them, lay hands on and pray for them. Frequently also, when a speaker wishes to impart something over everyone in the audience through prayer, they will ask each person to place a hand on the shoulder of their neighbor (on both sides) and pray for that person. Then, finally, at the end of the service, there is the opportunity to go through a Fire Tunnel and/or receive prayer ministry – requiring the service of many ministry team members.

There is also a lot more happening at Bethel during the week outside of the official church services e.g. the Healing Rooms and the Prophetic Sessions. In addition to these on-site activities, evangelistic teams frequently go out on the streets sharing the Gospel of the Kingdom with others. All of these things represent opportunities for people to get involved in the mission of the church.

The culture at Bethel encourages people to be contributors rather than consumers. The end goal is not to entertain or "feed" people, but to have them worship God, experience His presence, and become world changers. However, many would agree with me that, in all of this, one finds great fulfillment and satisfaction. In my opinion, a good night at Bethel is usually a lot more entertaining than going to see a great movie or concert. When in Redding, I was always concerned that if I skipped a service, I might miss out on experiencing something powerful and significant. Very rarely are Bethel services mundane – at least that was my experience. Furthermore, being involved in the ministry of the church outside of the official services is usually just as fulfilling, and often even more so, as many lives are transformed through the power and love of God.

Advantages of Empowering People in Ministry

There are many advantages of empowering ordinary people to become involved in the ministry of the church, particularly supernatural ministry. Some of the most important ones are:

1. People get excited and take ownership

When you give people opportunities and encourage them to utilize their gifts and talents, they tend to get excited and take ownership. The church becomes theirs and they start to feel a personal responsibility for its success. This kills the consumerist mindset of "what can I get?" and leads to the commitment mentality of "what can I contribute?" (cf. Acts 20:35).

Bethel is a great example of all of this in action. Many people make use of the ministry opportunities that are made available to them and in the process actually end up discovering why they were created. This causes them to come alive on the inside and passionately serve God through the ministry of the church, giving up huge amounts of their spare time in the process. But to them, it usually doesn't feel like much of a sacrifice, as they absolutely love what they're doing.

To give an example, serving in the Healing Rooms can be very addictive, as you never get tired of seeing the amazing things that God does through you. I know this from experience, after having often served in this ministry. There was always a surprise waiting around the corner as God awed us with His power and goodness! This kind of excitement is a fuel that keeps the church running and continually moving on to greater things. Why else would people commit to regularly turning up at 8am on Saturday mornings to pray for others, without any form of (earthly) compensation?

Excitement is also viral, in that it can move from person to person very quickly. One excited person can infect many others with the same "disease", resulting in them becoming much more active in the ministry of the church. And when you have a number of such people together, the collective level of excitement rises even more along with expectation - which causes commitment levels to skyrocket. This leads on to the next advantage of empowering people: synergy.

2. Synergy is created

When people get excited and take ownership, it leads to incredible synergy being created, allowing everyone to operate at far greater levels than they ever could on their own. We all get to feed off each other's passion, learn from them, and benefit from their gifts - both in the spiritual and the natural. Running with powerful and passionate people strengthens us in many ways. As Prov. 27:17 says, "Iron sharpens iron, and one man sharpens another."

This reaches levels almost unparalleled when you have Davids and Jonathans operating together: same-sex friends who have a special bond with each other (see 1 Sam. 18:1-4). At BSSM, I witnessed at least two examples of this sort of relationship - both of which were female ones. These women, who (I believe) in both cases did not know each other before coming to Bethel, became almost inseparable and spurred each other on to great things in God. One of these pairings operated very powerfully in ministry together, especially the prophetic.

But whether it is the rare case of a David and Jonathan relationship, or the more common situation in which like-minded people work together, synergy is, I believe, a large contributor to why Bethel is known around the world as a great signs and wonders movement. It is not that there is any magic happening at this church, but the power is in the empowering environment that exists, in which excited people inspire and spur each other on to greater deeds in God. Nowhere is this more evident than in BSSM, where there exists a strong positive peer pressure toward being a world changer who influences the course of history.

This was one of the biggest reasons why I loved being part of the Bethel movement. It helped me to operate closer to my potential and even stretch beyond what I thought was possible for myself. I got shocked out of my comfort zone when I saw so many people operating at similar levels to myself, and some at much higher ones in a few areas.

For example, before I arrived at Bethel, I had seen a lot of healings in my ministry but didn't have a lot of experience using the revelatory gifts, like prophecy and the word of knowledge. This didn't concern me, though, because very few people around me were moving in these gifts and therefore I had only limited appreciation of their power and usefulness. I was content to just do what I knew best – healing the sick and infirmed, which I was seeing great success at.

But when I got to Bethel, I was confronted by a prophetic and revelational culture, the like of which I had never experienced before. It was for many people fairly normal to hear specific words from God regarding their everyday lives. There were also some who were using the word of knowledge, prophecy, and healing together on the streets in an evangelistic context, and consistently leading people to Jesus through doing so. For instance, they might walk by someone and sense that this person has a sore neck. They would then ask them if they have a sore neck, and if the person says "yes" offer to pray for their healing. And when the person is healed, they would then tell them about Jesus and offer them a chance to receive Him as their Savior.

After seeing other Christians operating in this degree of revelation, I could no longer remain in my comfort zone of just praying for the healing of those who had obvious healing needs or who had expressed health issues to me in conversation. I now had to risk in getting words of knowledge for less obvious healing needs. The result was that I experienced some success and a lot of failure, but I grew (and am still growing) through the process.

On the other side of the coin, I am sure that some of these people who inspired me to step out in the revelatory gifts, were also inspired by my simple belief that we can pray for any healing need and expect to see healing - without any special word from God. Furthermore, I know that others who hadn't seen much healing through any approach, were inspired by my example to pray for people - with the expectation that God wants to heal through them too.

This is how synergy works: we inspire and spur each other on to more in God. And there always is more, because God is an infinite God who desires to fully manifest His divine power in and through us. We cannot rest on our laurels until at least reaching the benchmark set by Jesus and His ministry. But even that may not be enough, as He said that we will do greater works than Him (John 14:12).

3. More gets done

An obvious advantage of the people being empowered in ministry is that much more gets done, in terms of ministry outcomes. The results of the many will far exceed those of the few. But it is more than just a case of many hands making light work. For God has designed the world in such a way that interdependence is required. No one is an island unto themselves, such that they can do everything on their own without needing others, and this is no truer than in the Church. Paul's metaphor of the Body of Christ emphasizes that each and every believer has an important role to play, because they have different and complementary gifts to others (1 Cor. 12). Without them playing that role, their church, the Church, and humanity in general is missing out on something very significant.

However, when only a small percentage of a church body is involved in the ministry of that church, most of the gifts, ideas, and creativity that God has endowed that church with, are wasted. The ministries that do exist will typically only reflect the gifts and interests of those who are leading - especially the senior leadership team. What these leaders do not feel strong in will typically not be emphasized in the life of the church. For example, if the pastor is gifted in teaching then this is likely to be a major focus of the church. But healing, prophecy, and evangelism may have little place within that congregation.

God, of course, does not expect every person to be involved in every area of ministry. It would be a disaster, for instance, if I was required to serve on the worship team, as I have no special talent or interest in that area. But together, we can cover all the bases with our unique gifts, and get far more done in terms of extending God's Kingdom on Earth.

Bethel understands this by empowering people to run in the areas they feel called to. The result is that a number of different ministry hubs have developed, such as in the areas of business, prophecy, healing, evangelism, music, helping the poor and disadvantaged, fighting human trafficking, and "creative" endeavors.

At Bethel, there are now so many opportunities to get involved, that almost anyone can join the church and quickly become part of the ministry in some way that utilizes their gifts and talents. Square pegs go in square holes and round pegs in round holes. As mentioned earlier, Bethel could not offer anywhere near the amount of ministry that it does without its people being as heavily involved as they are. This is a church of and for the people.

4. Leaders have more time for doing what they do best

A flow-on benefit of leaders empowering their people in the ministry of the church is that they end up with more time to do what they do best – which is usually leading, teaching, and training. They no longer have to be everything to everyone.

To give the example of Bill Johnson, I remember him saying once that he no longer gives a lot of personal prophetic words to people, because he recognizes that there are many other people who are good at this. It is not that he can't, but that it is just no longer necessary.

He and his team have empowered others to operate at high levels in this area – which allows him to focus his energy on the things that are more central to his calling. Bill is a leader who is secure enough in himself that he doesn't need to be the "go-to" guy for everything. Furthermore, he trusts his people.

5. Believers are equipped for ministry outside of church

Finally, and perhaps most importantly, when believers are empowered in signs and wonders ministry, they can then utilize these skills outside of the four walls of the church, such as at work, when they go shopping, and literally anywhere they happen to be. It is now fairly normal for ordinary people from Bethel to get others saved, healed, and delivered out in the community, through supernatural ministry. And when such testimonies are shared, it encourages even more people to get out there and have a go, resulting in a snowball effect.

Practicing supernatural ministry outside of the Church is absolutely vital if we want to see the Kingdom of God advance in any significant way. We must go out to the unchurched world, rather than require them to come to us. This is the essence of the new apostolic age that Kris Vallotton is talking about (i.e. sending rather than gathering).[180] The idea that we have to somehow devise a set of grand strategies to get multitudes through the doors of our churches is fundamentally flawed. We should only expect people to come to church after they receive Jesus, not to receive Him. This is how the Church grew so rapidly in the first few centuries, as the Gospel was shared in the marketplaces and on the trade routes of the ancient Roman Empire. Regular Christians were largely responsible for the explosion of this new faith.

***

Given these advantages of empowering the full Body of Christ in ministry, it is difficult to understand why so many churches limit the involvement of their people. Maybe it is tradition, in that the leadership team sees themselves as responsible for the ministry of the church. Possibly it is a lack of understanding that God has given His Holy Spirit to all His people and appointed each of them as priests, to minister to others. Alternatively, it could be out of fear that someone might make a mess, which they would end up being responsible for, and the associated belief that the only way to guarantee something is done right, is to do it yourself. Whatever the case, no church can reach its God-given potential and fulfill its purpose without empowering all of its people in ministry. A few people can never accomplish what the many can. As I explained in an earlier chapter, the purpose of five-fold leaders is to equip the saints for ministry. It is not to monopolize the ministry themselves.

But what should you do if the leaders of your church are not open to empowering you, and insist on restricting the ministry to themselves and a select few? Outside of praying whether it's God will for you to move to another church where you would be more adequately empowered, you could empower yourself by gathering a group of friends together and practicing ministering to each other.

Even better, why not go out and minister in your everyday life? No leader can stop you from praying for and prophesying over people on the streets, at the supermarket, the gym, and work etc. That is actually your job as a Christian anyway. And this was largely how I developed my healing ministry.

No matter who we are, each of us as a Christian has ministering in the Spirit as an important part of our job description. Personally, I find it not only a responsibility, but also a great privilege. It enables us to make a difference in the world that no one else can, which leads to opportunities to share the Gospel of salvation with people. Otherwise, we will always be incredibly frustrated about having the greatest message in the world but that no one is interested in hearing it.

If you are a leader reading this book, I urge you to take a chance by empowering your people into this sort of supernatural lifestyle. And if you're a regular believer, who is not currently being empowered by anyone, I encourage you to empower yourself in this area. Either way, you won't be disappointed. I can promise you that!

10. CULTURE OF RISK

There is one final secret of the Bethel signs and wonders culture, as to why the power of God moves so strongly at this church, and through its people, wherever they go. This is Bethel's culture of risk, which is the ultimate in empowerment.

Over the previous nine chapters, much of what we've discussed has related to the beliefs and mindsets that underpin the release of the supernatural in our lives. This chapter, though, concerns the application of these things along with everything else we've discussed – through real-world action.

The reason why this is so important is that you can believe that God is good, that you are powerful, and that nothing is impossible with God etc. But until you actually put these beliefs into practice, by getting out there and applying them on a regular basis (e.g. praying for the sick and prophesying), it is unlikely that you're ever going to see much happen, in terms of signs and wonders.

This goes a long way toward explaining why miracles are still the exception rather than the rule, in most of the Church today. While plenty of people possess many of the beliefs necessary to see the supernatural break out in their lives, they just aren't putting feet to their faith.

A big issue in this regard is that stepping out in faith requires taking risk – which means sometimes experiencing failure and rejection. And this is enough to scare a lot of people off, as we have all been conditioned by society to believe that failure is something bad and to be avoided at all costs. Many of us would rather just remain in the safety and security of our prayer closets, reading book after book on revival. Then occasionally, we may venture out to attend a conference on the supernatural.

The secret hope is that someday God will "blast" us so that we suddenly feel powerful and anointed, and the supernatural becomes effortless: everyone gets healed and delivered instantly, words of knowledge are always 100 percent accurate in every minute detail, and prophecies come to pass every single time – meaning that we never have to experience any level of failure. This is why some of us have become conference junkies, seeking the "magic" impartation that will allow us to move in the supernatural like one of the greats in the faith, but without paying the same price to do so – including the embracing of a lifestyle of risk.

Unfortunately, this is a delusion that is extremely unlikely to ever happen. Of course, with God, you can never say never; He reserves the right to break all of the rules at any time He chooses. The thing is, though, the supernatural gifts of the Spirit operate by faith, which involves trusting God despite what our natural senses are telling us. In other words, risk is necessary because we're not fully in control – which we don't like!

So if this is the case, then how can those of us who feel a bit timid be encouraged to step out into our destinies, both in the supernatural and every other area of our lives?

Bethel's solution to this problem has been to create a culture of risk that promotes, empowers, and normalizes a lifestyle of courage, in which people are constantly challenging their fears by going after the things they're not completely comfortable doing – especially those that are totally impossible without God's help e.g. moving in the miraculous. In support of this, an environment has been established where risk is encouraged and celebrated, regardless of the outcome – creating a positive peer pressure. When failure occurs, it is not punished. Instead, it is seen as a necessary part of the process toward eventual success, and this helps to remove some of the fear factor.

Without this freedom to fail, you end up instead with a culture of fear, in which people are reluctant (or even totally unwilling) to take risk, as Kevin Dedmon points out.[181] Playing it safe then becomes the motto, which leads to the death of all creativity, innovation, and excellence. This scenario rarely results in any significant achievements; it usually only preserves the status quo, an outcome that too much of the Body of Christ has settled for today, due to their fear of failure.

The problem, as Bill Johnson argues, is that:

> The Church has an unhealthy addiction to perfection: the kind that makes no allowances for messes.[182]

He contends that:

> The goal of many in ministry is no messes. And that becomes the measure of success. I remind you, graveyards are orderly and clean. Nurseries filled with babies are not. One is alive, and the other is dead. If you want increase, get a shovel, and learn how to patiently work with people who are in process.[183]

The following Old Testament proverb (which he cites[184]) illustrates this principle well:

> Where there are no oxen, the manger is clean, but abundant crops come by the strength of the ox. (Prov. 14:4)

Interestingly, Jesus made the "risky" decision to work with people in process when choosing His disciples and ministry associates. They were completely unqualified and ill-prepared for the roles that He was soon going to assign them. What is more, He only gave them a crash course in ministry in observing Him for a relatively short period of time, before He sent them out on their own to have a go! None of this fazed Him, though, as He saw the bigger picture of the people they would eventually become through these opportunities.

Unsurprisingly, when they got their chance, they were far from perfect, and Jesus was forced to spend some time along the way correcting them – particularly for wrong attitudes and impure motives (e.g. Matt. 16:5-12, 21-28; Mark 9:33-37; Luke 9:51-56, 10:17-20). Eventually, though, all but one of His inner circle of 12 apparently matured into the powerful ministers and leaders that they were called to be. Everyone reading this book has been affected by their ministry, as it totally changed the world and altered the course of history.

The key lesson is that we must give ourselves, and those we lead, the chance to learn and grow through the process of taking risk, making mistakes, and failing. Risk is required to move in the supernatural and reach toward our God-ordained destiny, just like Peter when he stepped out of the boat and tried to walk on water (Matt. 14:22-31). These things, though, will typically not happen when the desires for safety and security are allowed to override the objectives of growth and achievement. This is actually a state of fearfulness, which is the absolute antithesis of faith and something quite displeasing to God (Num. 13:1-14:12; Heb. 10:38-39; Rev. 21:8).

Faith is Spelt: R - I - S - K

John Wimber used to say that faith is spelt: R - I - S - K, an idea that Bethel has taken and infused into their culture to such a degree, that it has become inseparable from everything else they do. They see risk as the point where the rubber meets the road, in terms of our actions reflecting what we claim to believe regarding the promises of God (cf. James 2:14-26). Nowhere is this more essential than moving in the supernatural, because it involves trying to do things that are utterly impossible with only our natural abilities. If God doesn't come through for us then failure is 100 percent certain.

To give an example, Jesus said in Mark 16:17-18 that one of the signs that will accompany those who believe is that they will lay hands on the sick and they will recover. This means that every time we cross paths with someone who is sick or suffering from an injury, we face a choice: to either to step out into our God-given calling as a believer in Christ by offering to pray for that person, or to avoid this calling by doing nothing. However, anyone who has prayed for healing knows that, for whatever reason, healing is not always the outcome. It therefore takes risk to step out, knowing that the result is not necessarily guaranteed. In fact, many people discover when they're getting started, that their "failures" overwhelm their "successes", as I indicated in back in Chapter 8: Nothing is Impossible!

This was the case for evangelist Todd White, who had to pray for around a thousand people before he saw the manifestation of first healing through his own hands (3½ months averaging about 10 people per day).[185] Now, though, he probably has one of the highest success rates of anyone in the world at effecting healing – all because he fanned into flame the gift of God that was in him (2 Tim. 1:6).

But how many people facing those same circumstances would have given up long before the first healing occurred, and concluded that they just don't have that particular gift? I suspect most would – before they even reached failure number 20. In fact, a lot of people do not even get started at all!

I am absolutely convinced that there are many, many Christians out there who are sitting on some incredible supernatural gifts, without even the slightest inkling that this is the case. These gifts are in a dormant state and just need to be activated, through getting out and having a go. The issue is that such people have probably never been adequately encouraged to do so. This is one of the things that Bethel excels at; not only do they consistently encourage their people to have a go, they actually provide them with safe platforms on which to do so (e.g. the Healing Rooms for healing and the Prophetic Sessions for prophecy). The Bethel leadership team makes it so easy for each person to move in the supernatural, that the only way for anyone not to experience this in their life, in my opinion, is by them deciding to be a spectator rather than a participant.

Stories like Todd's illustrate extremely well how essential risk and failure are to moving powerfully in the supernatural gifts of the Holy Spirit. One thing that is important, though, is to put this process of risk into proper perspective. Unless we are extremely unwise, there should not normally be any significant downsides to "failing", such that we might lose the shirt off our back, so to speak. Often, it will be like going to a casino where all the gaming machines have been set to free play: when we "lose", we lose nothing other than our time, but when we win, the winnings are real.

If this is the case, why would we not want to keep trying as often as possible, like Todd obviously did in praying for an average of 10 people per day over an extended period of time (which is quite an achievement, by the way, especially when no one was getting healed)? His incredible success in the realm of supernatural healing could probably be attributed largely to just a couple of key reasons: he believed God's promise in Scripture that he would heal the sick in Jesus' name; and he had the courage to fail faster and more than just about anyone else, until he saw evidence of the promise coming to pass.

It appears that achieving proficiency at supernatural gifts like healing is nothing more than a decision – whether or not we will choose to do what is required to be successful. As I've heard people say, salvation is free but everything else in the Kingdom requires work on our part. Sure, there are some who are more naturally gifted at certain things than others, but just like the Olympics no one wins a gold medal on ability alone. Everyone has to work (and work hard!) to become really good at what they do. Remember also, that it is a Kingdom principle that when we are faithful in using what we do have, we get given more (Matt. 25:14-29). Of course, we don't work from a performance mindset to earn favor, but out of our identity as sons and daughters of the King – who we have the amazing privilege to co-labor with.

The Process of Improving Our Ability to Operate in the Supernatural

As I have indicated above, becoming proficient at operating in the supernatural is a somewhat of a process. Despite what many people think, it is not the case that "you either have it or you don't". The supernatural gifts of the Spirit normally come in seed form, and need to be planted, watered, and grown – through consistent use (i.e. taking risk) (cf. 2 Tim. 1:6). For example, you may possess the ability to operate very strongly in the gift of prophecy, but never have clearly discerned the voice of God before. You should expect that becoming good at the prophetic will require a lot of practice, in learning to hear God speak. But without undergoing such training, you might never end up giving anyone a true word from God.

This explains why people who come from cessationist backgrounds will sometimes ask, "Well, if God has bestowed such amazing supernatural gifts on the Church then where are all these people who are moving in signs and wonders? I don't know anyone who is healing the sick, raising the dead, or accurately predicting the future." But this is like saying that no one you know can ride a bike when none of them has ever tried to ride a bike, let alone experienced the multiple falls required to get good at doing so.

Of course, these cessationists and the people they know, all have the ability to move in the supernatural gifts, just as much as anyone else. But they are not doing so because they have not gone through the required process. And a big contributor to this is that they're believing the lie that God has withdrawn these gifts from the Church, so that moving in them is no longer possible.

There are actually four major elements to the process of improving our ability to operate in the supernatural – all of which we have direct control over when we are taking action:

1. Learning distinctions (i.e. gaining knowledge and experience)

Just like in the natural (e.g. learning to ride a bike), an important part of improving at the supernatural gifts is learning new distinctions[186], through trial and error (and being taught by others). As we practice moving in the gifts by taking risk, we will see finer and finer distinctions that will lead to greater and greater success, when applied. For example, when we practice trying to hear God's voice in the pursuit of revelatory gifts like prophecy and the word of knowledge, we learn to distinguish the difference between God speaking to us, and our voice and the voice of the enemy.

It is helpful, therefore, to think of learning distinctions as being the process of gaining knowledge and experience. But it is important to weight this process heavily toward the practical, as opposed to theory (e.g. book and seminar learning). After all, you have not truly learned something until you can apply it in practice; and experience can never be gained through learning from others.[187] If all you do is receive teaching from others then you will likely struggle to successfully apply it in practice, when called upon. Furthermore, you will probably forget most of that information in a very short space of time anyway. For these reasons, it is therefore vital that any theory that you learn is applied, and applied quickly, otherwise you will have largely wasted your time and effort.

To give a personal example, the process of learning distinctions was very important for me in improving at deliverance ministry (i.e. the removal of demonic influence from people's lives). For a couple of years, I was in a living situation where I had a lot of opportunities to practice the skill, with two extremely demonized people around and things that were going bump (or more accurately, BANG!) in the night. Most notably, one of my housemates, who I will call Josh (not his real name), was so demonized that he couldn't even sing at church without manifesting strongly in the demonic. Unfortunately, there was no one at his church who was able to help him. Neither did he get any freedom from an itinerant healing and deliverance minister, whose meeting I took him to on a very cold winter's night. During the ministry time, when the minister asked him what he wanted prayer for, Josh suddenly started roaring at the top of his lungs and manifesting so strongly, that two men each had to grab one of his arms to restrain him, until the manifestations subsided. The minister, however, did not spend much time on Josh before giving up and moving on to other people who were waiting for prayer. Obviously this was quite disappointing.

It turned out that Josh also let me have a go at practicing deliverance on him at home. Over the course of a few months, I performed several intense sessions of ministry on him, admittedly with limited success, although I was always able to manage the situation so that it did not get out of control (the demons would always stop manifesting and "go down" when I commanded them to do so). However, I did learn a lot from those experiences, which helped to prepare the way for my future success in this area.

In case you're wondering what eventually happened with Josh, one day he felt God tell him to no longer allow other people to perform deliverance ministry on him, and to instead do self-deliverance.[188] This morphed into him spending a lot of time in his room worshiping God, and gradually the demons dropped off him one-by-one, over a long period of time (years, I think, from memory). As a result, he came to experience increasing levels of freedom in his life from demonic oppression.

One key lesson from his experience is that to gain freedom from demonic oppression, it is very helpful to do the things that demons don't like, such as worshiping God, expressing thanksgiving to Him, and praying in faith[189]. Resist the devil and he will flee from you (James 4:7)!

In Josh's case, it was very easy to see that the demons oppressing him hated his worship of God, because they manifested so strongly in reaction to it. The manifestation of demons (e.g. hissing, screaming, and violent outbursts) is usually an expression of the torment that they are experiencing, the anger and fear that they feel as a result, and a desperate attempt to intimidate their victim into ceasing the activity that they don't like.[190] They prefer to be left alone, to quietly go about their business of destroying a person's life, behind the scenes. But if you keep doing what they don't like then it becomes so torturous to them that they will eventually have to leave when they can stand it no longer. This is how Josh progressively flushed his demons out.

It is also worth mentioning that on the other side of the coin, there are some things which demons do very much like, which attract them to a person and allow them to strengthen their hold on that person. Probably the four most significant categories of these things are sin, fear, unbelief, and unforgiveness. In order to get rid of demons and keep them off yourself, it is therefore very important to also avoid doing these things, and to stop doing them if you already are.

Another thing that needs to be pointed out is that Josh's experience does not invalidate the ministry of deliverance through other people – which if effective, should dramatically speed up the process of removing the demonic influence from a person's life. Instead of being an arm wrestle for control, it becomes more like an execution.

Anyway, back to my story! Fast forward a few years, and I found myself in a situation where a lady I was ministering healing to manifested demons to the point where they completely took over her body, just like in the movies. She was left merely as an observer while they interacted with me (I described what happened in an endnote to Chapter 6: Complete Five-Fold Ministry. This was the lady who spontaneously started speaking in tongues when I prayed for her healing). I didn't finish the job that night as the demons were being very defiant[191], it was getting late, and the lady was extremely drained from hours of intense ministry. But I came back and successfully delivered her on another occasion. It was a very clunky process at best, in which I had to keep referring back to a cheat sheet on deliverance methodology that I had constructed by watching YouTube videos on the subject[192]. I had hidden this cheat sheet inside my Bible, and turned my back to the demons every time I needed to refer to it. This was to prevent them from realizing how much of a newbie I was! Anyway, it was satisfying to find out that even though I was a novice (and in hindsight I'm sure that the demons knew this!), the power and authority that I had in Jesus Christ was enough to cast those suckers out, through a proven approach.

I knew that this was a watershed moment for me; I had now learned enough distinctions of deliverance ministry to enjoy a certain measure of success, although I was obviously still far from an expert. The power was there and I had sufficient knowledge, but the main things I lacked were the experience and belief systems (see below) needed to apply them. These could only be acquired by going after more opportunities, and in the process suffering further failures and setbacks. Practice makes perfect as the saying goes! So I looked forward to every future opportunity to minister in this area.

Fast forward again to recently, when a woman who had been tormented for 20 years by spirits, came to me for ministry. These spirits were causing random sensations of pain and strangulation in her neck area, multiple times a day. Although the demons tried various strategies to obstruct me, I knew exactly what to do and was able cast them out relatively easily. While this was very satisfying, I couldn't help but think how sad it was that for two whole decades this poor lady had apparently not found anyone with the skills to deliver her (i.e. who had learned enough distinctions of deliverance) - especially considering that it ended up being a relatively simple process. Hopefully many more Christians will see the great need out there for deliverance ministry and do what is required to become part of the solution to the diabolical problems many around them are facing. Will you be one of them?

2. Expanding our belief of what is possible with God

Another part of the process of improving our ability to operate supernaturally is expanding our belief of what is possible with God (i.e. what He can do through us) - which occurs incrementally, as we step out and have a go. And usually, the more action we take, the faster this happens – as long as we continue to take risk, and never allow ourselves to settle into any comfort zone.

It is important, however, to understand that there is a huge difference between knowing something in our head and actually believing it in our heart of hearts. While being able to quote all the right Bible verses on faith is a great start, this does not automatically equate to having the corresponding belief system. Real world action and experience are also necessary.

To give an example, it says in Mark 9:23 that all things are possible for one who believes. But the reality is that for some things, we will not have a high level of expectation, possibly because we have never seen such a miracle occur. It may be that someone we know has been diagnosed with cancer, and when we consider offering them prayer for healing, our doubts scream out at us: e.g. "I've never seen anything big like cancer get healed before."; "I'm sure lots of people have already prayed for him and it obviously hasn't worked, so why would it work for me?"; "I should just leave it to those who have a recognized gift of healing."

Whenever we're in these sorts of situations, however, it is imperative that we do not avoid praying for the people in question. Eventually, if we persist, there will be a moment when we experience a bit of success, which we can then build on. Then, the next time we pray for someone with that same condition, we will have a higher level of belief that they'll get healed – which makes healing more likely. Over time, we should therefore see more people healed of that condition, and progressively gain higher levels of faith in that area. This is the process of risk and incremental improvement that will one day lead to us operating like our heroes in the faith.

To give a personal example, for a long time I experienced very little success at praying for the healing of hearing conditions e.g. deafness. I had one instance of "beginner's luck" and then nothing for years. However, during my final year at Bethel, I got to pray for quite a few people with hearing issues and that all changed. Several got healed from conditions like partial deafness and tinnitus. Now, I would say that when I pray for someone with hearing issues, I often see something happen. In short, I persevered until I achieved a measure of breakthrough – which then increased my level of expectation for this category of need and led to increasing success in this area. There are, of course, other areas that I'm still contending for breakthrough in, and I will keep going until I either get these breakthroughs or die trying.

3. Spiritual warfare

There is also, I believe, a process of spiritual warfare going on in the background that we must win, in order to gain our next level of breakthrough in the supernatural. I am not suggesting that we need to devote time to actively praying against various spirits that might be standing in our way. It is actually about the act of stepping out and taking risk, and then continuing to believe God, and persevering when the results are not matching up with His promises in Scripture.

After all, the mere act of moving toward these promises, by taking risk, is an act of spiritual warfare, in that it is a direct assault on spirits of fear (especially the fear of man) – which scream at us to not do it, and threaten us with consequences if we do, such as that it won't work, and that we'll embarrass ourselves in front of others and be criticized.

In relation to these threatened consequences, a big demonic strategy in the area of healing (particularly in an evangelistic context) revolves around the worry about what we will say to a person if they don't get healed. And the corresponding one in the revelational realm is the concern about how we'll handle it if we give an incorrect prophetic word/word of knowledge. However, what I've discovered through experience is that these fears are completely unfounded. People usually don't have any great expectations when you minister to them, and therefore they won't react in any negative way if it doesn't work. Quite often, they are very appreciative that you spent the time trying to help them.

When we push through these fears and go for it, we expose them as complete lies and smash the influence of the associated demons over us. We then realize that the only power these demons have over us is the power we give them, by believing their lies and thereby accepting the fear generated by these lies.

The other part of the equation is perseverance. Although we may defeat spirits of fear by taking action, this does not mean that we will automatically achieve the intended result (e.g. the person we pray for gets healed). Very likely, it will take multiple and potentially numerous attempts before we see the first sign of the promise being fulfilled. At this point, spirits of discouragement will step in and become our chief adversaries. They will tell us that we haven't got that particular gift, and that therefore we're wasting our time, because it's never going to happen!

To defeat this type of spiritual adversary, we just need to keep going and not give up. The issue at stake is whether we will continue to believe God despite the results not lining up with His promises, or alternatively, whether we will decide to agree with the enemy against Him – effectively calling God a liar.

When we are battling fear, discouragement, or any other spiritual opposition, the key to victory, therefore, is that we need to stay focused on the promise and continue to take the necessary action to achieve it. As Bill Johnson often says, "... physical obedience brings spiritual breakthrough."[193]

As we are obedient, through taking action, the first two parts of the process of improving our ability to operate in the supernatural come into play. That is, we learn greater distinctions (i.e. gain knowledge and experience), which when applied will lead to success. And secondly, we expand our belief of what is possible with God, when we eventually enjoy a bit of success – which leads to greater and greater success. In addition to this, part of the breakthrough comes solely through winning the spiritual battles against fear and discouragement, as we take action. That is, we make gains that cannot be attributed to either an increase in our knowledge and experience, or a higher level of belief. In fact, higher levels of belief may partly be the result of this aspect of breakthrough.

4. Frequency of action

There is a fourth element to improving our ability to operate supernaturally, which is the frequency of our action. It should come as no surprise that the more action we take, the more we will improve. This affects all three of the other elements, in that we learn more of the key distinctions, expand our belief of what is possible with God, and win a greater number of spiritual battles.

However, the relationship between action and growth is not just a simple two-dimensional one. Rather, the amount of growth we experience will be greater the more quickly we complete a given amount of activity. For instance, we should be closer to our next breakthrough in healing, after praying for 30 people, if we do it in a month rather than a year.

Going back to Todd White's experience of only seeing the first healing after praying for around 1,000 people in three and a half months, it might have actually taken him 1,500 people if his frequency of action was far less. This is because it is more difficult to identify patterns and learn when we only occasionally take action, and we are more likely to forget some of the lessons we have already learned. Furthermore, the longer it has been since our last breakthrough, the more difficult it is to steward that breakthrough and make use of it in the future. This is because, for example, the greater the length of time since we last saw someone's blind eye opened, the less real it seems, and therefore the more difficult it is to believe for the next blind eye to be opened. Essentially, we are talking about the power of momentum, which should never be underestimated. It is an incredible force that we need to harness in our lives, for Kingdom purposes.

I believe that this is part of the reason why (ordinary) Bethel people minister in such power, authority, and revelation. They are people of action and risk-takers, who run toward opportunities rather than waiting for opportunities to come to them. Consequently, they greatly shorten the process to becoming powerful in the various supernatural gifts. It is not that there is anything special about them or magical about Bethel Church. The secret, rather, is in the Holy Spirit operating through those who have decided to be go-getters! And this can be reproduced anywhere on the planet.

***

What all of this underscores, is that process of stepping out and taking risk is something that we are going to need to keep repeating until we achieve 100 percent success, all the time - at everything we do. Therefore, we had better get used to risk, failure, and perseverance. The only way to avoid these things is to sit on the sidelines, an option which too many Pentecostal and Charismatic Christians are choosing today. Not to mention the countless numbers of believers in other parts of the Church, who simply have no idea that moving in signs and wonders is even possible for them - due to what they've been taught (or haven't been taught)[194].

Case Study: A Safe Prophetic Culture

At this point, I would like to take you through a case study, to illustrate how Bethel creates an environment where people are free to step out in the supernatural gifts and hone their skills in these - but with safeguards in place, to protect others from being hurt when failure occurs.

The area that we're going to look at is the prophetic, which is probably the gift that has the greatest potential to cause harm - given that prophecies, by their very nature, are usually not directly testable, and need to be carefully weighed. A potential danger zone therefore exists in which incorrect information could be conveyed, received, and acted upon, to the detriment of the recipient. This is particularly the case at the earliest stages of a person's development, in both exercising their prophetic gift and evaluating prophecies given to them by others. With this in mind, we will be exploring what a safe prophetic culture looks like, through the example of Bethel.

There is one thing that is absolutely critical if you want to develop a powerful prophetic culture like Bethel's, and this is that the culture you are hoping to create must be safe for those operating in it, otherwise such a culture will never get off the ground in the first place. This is something that Bethel understands acutely, in encouraging and celebrating risk in the prophetic, regardless of whether it comes off or not. They recognize that a learning process is required to become proficient at operating in this gift. Therefore, there they are more than willing to allow people the space to practice, get it wrong, and grow.

As with anything, if you want a particular outcome (e.g. a powerful prophetic culture) then you need to strongly encourage and actively reward the behaviors that will lead to it (i.e. action and risk). But if, in the case of the prophetic, you punish failure then you are actually discouraging action and risk, which will likely prevent any prophetic culture from developing. This is what happens in church environments where one could be rebuked, removed from a ministry team, or even labeled a "false prophet" if they give an incorrect prophecy. The result is that everyone will be too afraid to prophesy, or at least prophesy anything that is testable.

Bethel leaders, however, not only encourage and celebrate risk in the prophetic, they personally model this lifestyle - sometimes even to the point of giving prophetic words on stage, in front of hundreds of people and potentially many thousands more online, when the service is streamed on Bethel TV. They are not overly concerned about the possibility of failure, as they know that it would not damage their credibility. Quite the contrary, their standing in many people's eyes would likely improve because they had a go rather than played it safe, since the culture rewards the risk more than any positive result arising from it.

This modeling of risk by leaders is vital to developing and maintaining a culture of risk, because it greatly empowers everyone else to also have a go without fear of missing the mark. As a leader, you can't expect others to do something that you're not prepared to do yourself. Leadership is not just about making decisions and telling people what to do. It is also involves leading the way by going first and demonstrating a desired behavior, so that others are inspired to follow.

At this point, though, someone might ask the completely legitimate question, "What is the point in practicing prophecy and taking risks in it? God either speaks to a person or He doesn't, and you shouldn't try to come up with something when He's not speaking."

In response to this, I would say that in practicing prophecy, we are definitely not trying to force God's hand in any way, or make anything up. The belief at Bethel is that God is always speaking to us[195] and that He delights in responding when we seek after Him. What we are attempting to do, therefore, is hear what He's saying - which takes practice given all the other "noise" that is coming at us (both internal and external), particularly in this modern world where the presence of electronic devices and social media is so ubiquitous. Most of us today have developed a certain level of attention deficit disorder (ADD), and this has reduced our ability to discern God's still small voice (cf. 1 Kings 19:12, NKJV).

What is important to point out is that God very, very rarely communicates to most of us in a crystal clear, unmistakable way, as in an audible voice or through an open vision - neither of which has ever happened to me, that I can recall. If we are looking for this then we will almost certainly come to the conclusion that He never speaks to us, other than through the words of Scripture (and possibly circumstance) - which is what many Christians actually do believe.

Far more often, He actually communicates to us in subtle impressions, thoughts, pictures, words, repetitions of ideas/numbers/phrases/events that we hear and see in life, and Bible verses that jump out at us etc. These things will normally flash by us so quickly that those who are untrained will usually miss them.

The problem, though, is that not every subtle impression, thought, and picture etc. is God speaking to us. These things can also come from the enemy and, of course, originate from us (e.g. our own thoughts/imagination, desires, and internal dialogue). The difficulty, therefore, is in discerning between these different sources (i.e. God, the kingdom of darkness, and us). Often, when either God or evil spirits are speaking to us, we will confuse this with our own thoughts etc. On the other hand, sometimes when we particularly want to do something (e.g. marry someone), we will mistake our own desires for what God is saying – which is why getting second opinions from people we trust is so crucial, when making very important life decisions. It takes practice and experience to get this right on a consistent basis.

What all of this means is that there exists great potential to make errors in hearing God speak, and therefore to give people incorrect prophetic words when ministering to them. To compensate for this possibility, and to more generally ensure that prophetic ministry is conducted in the way God intended it to be, Bethel has put a few protocols in place for best practice:

1. Prophetic words need to be encouraging

Before we consider the possibility and potential consequences of errors, it is helpful to first consider the purpose of normal New Testament prophetic ministry, through the gift of prophecy. According to Kris Vallotton:

> The primary purpose of the gift of prophecy is not to *direct or correct* the Body of Christ, but rather to **encourage the church.** We should never allow people who are ministering in the gift of prophecy to speak negatively into the lives of others. The *goal* of the gift of prophecy is to **bring out the best in people!** [196] (emphasis original)

Prophetic words at Bethel therefore need to be positive and encouraging, rather than directive or corrective. Our goal is to find the gold in those we minister to, through calling out their identity, destiny, and special talents etc., as we discussed back in Chapter 4: Saints, Not Sinners. If, however, we discern something negative (e.g. a person struggling with pornography), we can phrase it in a positive way (e.g. "I believe that God is calling you to a new level of purity").[197]

Along these lines, we should not be predicting any negative events (e.g. financial difficultly or a person's death), as this can bring about fear and distress, and even in some cases literally cause such an event to take place. Remember that death and life are in the power of the tongue (Prov. 18:21).

There is, though, one exception to the rule that prophecies need to be encouraging. It involves recognized five-fold prophets in the Church (according to Eph. 4:11). As Kris notes:

> Prophets have the authority to correct and direct because they are part of the government of God.[198]

Their job description is much broader than the average Christian; it includes the responsibility to equip the saints for the work of the ministry (Eph. 4:12), and build them up to maturity in the faith (Eph. 4:13-14). For these purposes, prophets have the authority to speak the truth in love (Eph. 4:15), through use of the prophetic and other means.

Five-fold prophets, by their very nature, are people who are experienced, tried, and proven over time, otherwise they would (hopefully) not have been recognized by their church (and possibly the wider Christian community) in this area of ministry. We should therefore have much greater confidence in the reliability of what they say prophetically than, for example, someone who only is just starting to learn how to hear God speak. This is part of the reason why prophets enjoy more latitude than others in conducting their prophetic ministry. However, this does not mean that they have the right to embarrass people in front of others, such as by proclaiming someone's sins in public. If the prophetic word is of a more sensitive nature then they should almost always deliver it in private.

One of the dangers of regular people using prophecy to correct or direct others is that they could seriously mess people up if they get it wrong – which will be a frequent occurrence to most when they're getting started. The thing is that not everyone is mature enough to evaluate a prophetic word properly; some will swallow everything whole. However, an encouraging prophetic word that is wrong should not present too much of a danger to most recipients.

2. Prophesy in a natural, low-key way

Bethel people are strongly encouraged to prophesy in a natural, low-key way, avoiding the use of common embellishments like "King James English" and shouting – neither of which adds any informational content or makes a prophecy more authoritative[199]. In fact, using King James English can actually obscure the message, as our recipients may not completely understand what we're saying. Shouting is not helpful either if everyone can hear us at a normal volume. We should, therefore, not attempt to make a prophecy more dramatic, or draw unnecessary attention to ourselves, through such means.

It is also important that we preface a prophetic word in an appropriate, low-key manner. For example, "I feel the Lord might be saying ...", "I sense God is saying ...", or "I believe I have a word for you ..." etc. This leaves a sufficient amount of room for people to evaluate and potentially reject that word.

However, if you preface it with something overly authoritative like "Thus saith the Lord ...", "I, the Lord, say unto you ...", or "The Lord says ...", you can intimidate a person into accepting it, as few believers want to be guilty of rejecting what God is saying to them. This sort of practice is extremely discouraged at Bethel, and could possibly invite correction from leaders, if they find out about it – particularly if you do it to a visitor while serving on the ministry team.

Normally only insecure people will say something like this[200], as their identity is tied up in their ability to prophesy, and therefore their self-worth is threatened by anyone rejecting a prophetic word from them – which is equivalent to them being personally rejected. Their attempt to artificially bolster the word is designed to make it more difficult to reject.

Mature people, who have identities strongly rooted in their relationship to God rather than their giftedness, have no need to pull this sort of stunt because being wrong is no threat to their self-worth. In any case, the culture at Bethel is such that a prophetic word given in this sort of manner would normally raise a huge red flag, which might cause it to be rejected out of hand – the opposite of what was intended.

Yes, some of the Old Testament prophets prophesied in this way, but they had a very different commission to most New Testament believers today. They were an extremely small and select group of people who had almost exclusive access to God's spoken word in those days. Their role was to serve as intermediaries between Him and other individuals, groups, and even entire nations, conveying His very words – which needed to be received as such.

Since these prophets were the direct mouthpieces of God to people with little or no ability to Hear His voice for themselves, the prophetic words that they gave had to be inerrant, and thus He spoke very clearly to them – most likely audibly, or through a very distinct internal voice. It was therefore not possible to unintentionally get the word wrong, unlike today, when God very rarely speaks to us in this sort of clarity. The only way that an incorrect prophetic word could be given back then was through deceit (i.e. lying and false prophets). This, combined with the fact that a false prophetic word could have had serious consequences if accepted, was likely the reason why the penalty for getting it wrong was so severe – death (Deut. 18:20).

New Testament believers, by contrast, all have the Spirit of God living inside of them, and therefore they all have the ability to hear God speak, without the need for any go-between (John 10:27, 16:13; 1 Cor. 2:16). In fact, God primarily wants to speak to them in a one-on-one way, rather than via an intermediary, as in the Old Testament, through the prophets. He does not want to interfere with this relationship by consistently giving other people clearer and more reliable information than what they are receiving from Him themselves. Otherwise, believers would then look to those who are moving strongly in the prophetic to hear from God, rather than primarily hearing from Him themselves (which unfortunately, some people try to do anyway).

What God does want to do, though, in allowing the prophetic to continue (albeit in a less authoritative form), is establish some level of interdependence within the Body of Christ, so that it is never just "me and God". He created us for community, such that we need each other to be fully successful. He also gave us the gift of prophecy so that non-believers will be convicted that there is a God (1 Cor. 14:24-25).

That said, there may still today be a few very special prophets, who have commissions approaching those of some of the great Old Testament ones, giving them the right to speak with something resembling that level of authority. But even they must be very careful to only say exactly what God is saying, when using a phrase like "Thus saith the Lord". It is therefore important that they differentiate between what they know for certain that God is saying, what they feel He is saying, and any interpretations they place on a word.

3. Prophecies need to be evaluated

Thirdly, Bethel teaches its people to evaluate the prophecies they receive from others and any interpretations provided, to determine the truth and accuracy of these words (1 Thess. 5:20-21; 1 Cor. 14:29; cf. 1 John 4:1). Those that ring true[201] should be documented in some way for easy reference, such as in a journal. The ones that don't currently make sense can also be documented, but they are to be metaphorically placed on the shelf until a later time when, in the light of new information, they may make more sense. And those that are clearly wrong are to be flushed, especially if one discerns that the prophecy is being given out of a wrong spirit – such as hurt, jealousy, or the desire to manipulate (e.g. "God told me that you're going to marry me.")

However, even if a prophecy is perceived to be incorrect, the person who gave it should not be rejected as a false prophet or scolded for getting it wrong. Assuming that they gave it out of the best of intentions, they should rather be celebrated for having a go, and encouraged to keep trying, until they become more proficient at using this gift.

What we must keep in mind is that unlike in OT times, the test of a true prophet is not whether their prophecies are always accurate and comes to pass. Instead, Jesus said that we will recognize them by their fruits (Matt. 7:15-20) – which is what they produce in life.[202] The accuracy of a prophet today only really indicates their current level of skill in the prophetic.

Often, though, it is not a case of a prophecy being either right or wrong, true or false. Some elements of it can be true and others false, since many prophecies contain multiple details, all of which need to be evaluated. It is therefore helpful to offer point-by-point feedback to the person who gave the prophecy, evaluating the particular details of it. This allows them to see where they got it right and wrong, so that they are able to improve faster. For someone new to this, it can often be very encouraging to see that they got even one thing right!

Risk Does Not Just Involve "Spiritual" Things

Thus far, we have looked at the concept of risk mainly in terms of operating in the supernatural gifts of the Holy Spirit, particularly healing and prophecy. However, the culture of risk at Bethel is much broader than just acts of faith in the area of supernatural ministry. It is about consistently stepping outside of our comfort zones toward greater opportunities, in every area of our lives. This might involve us joining Toastmasters to improve our public speaking skills, quitting our job and going back to school to pursue our dream career, or even asking out someone of the opposite sex if we're single and wanting a relationship.

There are two really important things to keep in mind. Firstly, that God is a good Father, who desires to bless us in every way imaginable – both for our benefit and that of others, who we will in turn bless. And often these blessings require us to partner with Him in some way – which will invariably involve some level of risk, such as when He freed the Israelites from slavery in Egypt (Exod. 1-14).

Secondly, being a supernatural Christian is not just about running around healing people and giving out prophetic words. As we discussed in Chapter 5: Optimistic and Victorious Eschatology, God has assigned us as the Church the task of bringing Heaven to Earth, in every sphere of society, so that He can release His life, peace, and prosperity over the whole world. Doing this to the degree He that is expecting obviously requires supernatural enablement, and it is faith expressed through risk that attracts this special enablement (cf. Dan. 1:20; 2:16-19). His supernatural power added to the natural skills and abilities that we possess, can literally change the world.

Speaking of our natural skills and abilities, we need to also increase these, through a process of taking risk, in order for God to use us in the way that He desires, just as David had to fight lions and bears before he got his chance to face Goliath (1 Sam. 17:34-36). For example, God may have called us to become a pioneer in medicine, who "discovers" the cure for cancer through divine inspiration or revelation. But we still must do our medical training to become qualified and gain access to the resources needed to conduct our research. Until we do, He cannot use us in this way.

The BSSM leadership team sees this "big picture" view, and therefore equips their students to be successful in every area of their lives, through a lifestyle of stepping out and risking – no matter what they're doing. One thing that really stuck in my mind was the advice that Gabe Valenzuela (Senior Overseer of BSSM Second Year) gave us on the first day of Second Year. He said that we need to take enough risk so that we don't succeed 100 percent of the time. The idea was that if we are not failing at least occasionally then we're playing too small and not operating anywhere near our potential. This echoes philosophies from the business world, such as at Facebook, where employees are told that the biggest risk is to not take any risk. There, they are encouraged to move fast and break things, for if you never break anything then you are not moving fast enough.

The levels of growth and success that we are capable of simply cannot be achieved within our comfort zones, where we enjoy high levels of competence, control, and confidence. Great things can only be achieved by taking significant risks, and in the process, becoming bigger people. It is no different than going to the gym, where we try to lift more weight than we have before, and train to failure, in order to get bigger and stronger.

Risk is an important part of the process of becoming all that God has called us to be and achieving everything that He has assigned us to do. Our attitudes toward risk and fear will therefore determine to a large extent how successful we are in fulfilling our personal destinies. Will we run in the opposite direction every time we feel uncomfortable, or will we feel the fear and do it anyway?

To reach our full potential in life, we need to come to the place where we're comfortable with being uncomfortable, such that we pursue growth and opportunity, while fully embracing change. As Kris Vallotton often says, "The dogs of doom stand at the doors of destiny". Like the Israelites (Num. 13) and later David (1 Sam. 17) found out, we will normally have to fight and kill giants in order to enter into our promised land, and this will require great strength and courage, as God reiterated to Joshua (Joshua 1:6-7, 9). However, when we understand the strength of our God and how much He desires to work through us with His wonderworking power, it gives us great reason for confidence, enabling us to be as bold as a lion (Prov. 28:1).

Therefore we need to be eager to "cross the chicken line" every chance we get. The "chicken line" is an imaginary personal line which courage is needed to cross, and that the fearful usually stay well behind. Crossing this line involves doing something a long way out of our comfort zone, which threatens our sense of safety and security. Every man who has ever asked out a woman he's really interested in, knows this experience. Kris laments, though, how:

> [Fear] has been disguised in the Church as "stewardship," "wisdom," and a bunch of other spiritual words, reducing the Christian experience to simply holding the fort.[203]

Fear, which he identifies as being the most socially accepted sin in the Church[204], ends up paralyzing many Christians. It prevents them from stepping across the chicken line to take the sort of risks that would propel them into living as the world changers that they're called to be.

What Kind of Risk are We Talking About?

The kind of risk that we're talking about is not doing stuff that we know is immoral, unethical, or foolish, such as shoplifting, driving through a stop light, or climbing into the lion enclosure of our local zoo. Generally, we are referring to things that involve us stepping out of our comfort zone, by challenging our fears and moving toward areas of personal destiny. When we do this, there will normally be no guarantee of success, and possibly some limited potential for harm. Often the first steps we take will be baby ones, which will naturally involve a bit of stumbling and falling down.

When taking risk, it is wise to apply the minimax principle from decision theory, which is to minimize the maximum possible loss (i.e. the worst case scenario). That is, we need to protect our downside and ensure that we can tolerate failing, losing, and being wrong – without suffering catastrophic consequences, like the loss of life or limb. It is all about creating a safe place for ourselves to take risk in, just as an infant is placed in a playpen to allow them room to develop their skills, without hurting themselves.

This is precisely the approach taken at BSSM, which is structured in such a way that requires students to regularly face their fears and take risks that will lead to personal growth and success – while ensuring that these risks are not fatal. I am now going to give some examples of this, to give you a feel for how you could pursue risk in your own life, and potentially establish a culture of risk in your own church community:

Within the first few months of school, all First and Second Year students go with their revival groups on a "Ropes Course", in Weaverville, California. This involves working with a small team to navigate through various obstacles, while walking on tightropes that are suspended high in the air. There are often scrapes and bruises, but each person wears a harness to protect them from any catastrophic fall. While no one is forced to complete the course, most people have to overcome some level of fear to do so. In the process, many experience some significant "aha" moments. This obstacle course therefore serves as a great metaphor for the risk-taking process that we are highlighting in this chapter.

As you might expect in a supernatural ministry school, students receive many opportunities to practice their word of knowledge and prophetic skills, starting right from day one of First Year. On that first day of school in September 2014, our class of 1,100 was asked by Kris Vallotton to come up with supernatural information about one of the people sitting next to us, such as the names of their family members etc. And over the next two years that I was at BSSM, I received a number of other opportunities to practice these skills, often through fun games. For instance, one day in revival group, our First Year pastor Ben Fitzgerald placed some mystery items in boxes and asked us to "guess" what was in each box. Another game that we played involved us dividing into two equal-sized groups and forming two circles out of them, one around the other. Members of the inner circle would close their eyes and the outer circle would keep rotating around them until a leader (who was not part of the circles) said "stop" – at which point, each member of the outer circle would stand in front of the closest member of the inner circle to them. The inner circle (who still had their eyes closed) would then have to come up with words of knowledge about certain characteristics of their outer circle partner, such as their gender, age, height, and hair color. After this, each inner circle person would open their eyes and check with their partner as to how well they did. Following this, the inner circle moved out to become the outer circle so that the roles were reversed, allowing the others to also have a chance to hone their word of knowledge skills.

There were, of course, quite a few real opportunities to come up with words of knowledge and prophetic words about people, both at Bethel and on mission/ministry trips. Speaking of these trips, the school itself takes a huge risk in sending out groups of students who, outside of the training they receive in class, are often complete novices in areas like teaching, preaching, and supernatural ministry. But like everyone else at Bethel, the leaders of BSSM embrace the culture of risk that is needed to grow people into the world changers that God has called them to be.

In Second Year, the opportunities to risk are considerably greater than First Year. For example, students are required to do an assignment that involves asking others for feedback on them as a person, including the identification of areas of weakness. Probably few people could do an exercise like this for the first time without encountering some level of trepidation. But the BSSM leadership team wants to develop people who are comfortable with receiving feedback from others, and who will even proactively seek it out, for the purpose of personal growth. At Bethel, a high value is placed on feedback, including the brutally honest kind. Obviously, it is risky to participate in this culture of feedback, not only for the person receiving the feedback, but also the one giving it, as there is no guarantee that it will be received well.

Each First and Second Year student participates in a program called *City Service* (normally on a weekly basis), which is basically an outreach that involves things like evangelism and serving the community in practical ways. In this, the Second Years get to practice their leadership skills by acting as team leaders over the First Years.

"Messes" happen on both sides, and you are taught to clean up those that you create.

In Second Year, I chose an elective class called *Church Leadership and Planting*, taught by church leadership experts Steve Backlund and Michael Brodeur. Part of the class involved running experimental church services one night of each week, during which we got to practice ministering to others, while exploring different ways of doing church. One week, our team, *Campfire Church*, would lead the service, while another team would act as the congregation. Then the following week, the roles would be reversed, although we wouldn't be paired with the same team. The team leading the service would be responsible for performing roles such as leading worship, taking up the offering, teaching and ministry – just as in any regular church service. One week, our team even had the honor and privilege of going to a nearby town, Red Bluff, to conduct a service for a church group there.

Another Second Year elective class that I was involved in was *Heaven in Business*, led by Andy Mason. Like *Church Leadership and Planting*, there was the opportunity to practice what we were learning, outside of regular class hours. For this, most of the class decided to become involved in creating hypothetical start-up businesses, which at end of the school year would be pitched to potential investors. To date, I know that at least one of these proposals has already been turned into a real-world business.

There are also a number of other opportunities within BSSM (and the wider Bethel environment) to lean into this culture of risk. Many of these are not mandatory as part of the school and therefore require a student to be proactive, by choosing to go after them. But this is a far more realistic real-life scenario, as we all need to be self-starters who are intentional about pursuing our own growth. While leaders and mentors in our life can be invaluable in guiding us along the path to our success, there comes a point where we must take responsibility for our own growth, rather than totally relying on others to point us in the right direction. This is an important aspect of becoming a person of maturity.

The Fruits of a Culture of Risk

When a culture of risk (with an emphasis on the power of God) develops in a Christian community, it strongly encourages people to go after the supernatural and to pursue their God-ordained destinies. What those who take up the challenge discover, is that far more is actually possible for them than they ever imagined (Eph. 3:20). Signs and wonders begin breaking out and become normal expressions of their faith. Furthermore, their work and everyday lives move from being mundane, boring existences to exhilarating journeys with God – in which they are transforming the world wherever they go and in whatever they do, through bringing Heaven to Earth.

In the process, they become people burning with passion and excitement, who have an insatiable appetite for more of God in their lives, accompanied by an unshakeable hope for a far better tomorrow. Instead of reaching a certain level and then camping there, they continue pushing the boundaries of what is possible with God, until that which is written on the pages of Scripture becomes their normal experience (e.g. Luke 7:22; John 14:12-14); nothing else is acceptable to them. Paradoxically, though, before seeing the big successes they celebrate the small ones, giving thanks to God for these, while anticipating the future increase. They are people of ever-increasing faith who pull many others into this reality, causing the whole thing to snowball.

This is effectively what has been happening at Bethel over the last two decades. It is not a church whose success has been built on the "man of God" model of the past, in which everyone gathers around one extremely gifted and anointed individual, who does all the ministry themselves. Instead, it has been about equipping and empowering the regular people to go out and "do the stuff". An army of the saints sent out into the world will always be far more powerful than a single man (or woman) of God, operating exclusively in one building, one day of the week. This was what Jesus demonstrated by equipping and then sending out others to operate like Him in ministry. Unfortunately, the Church, over its two thousand year history, has generally missed this and instead focused almost exclusively on leaders. And these leaders have typically raised up passive followers, who participate mainly as consumers and spectators.

As is the case at Bethel, a culture of risk facilitates the growth of people into the world changers that they're called to be. After all, the most effective way to learn is by doing, and this will involve making many mistakes and experiencing failure on numerous occasions. Granted, it is often not very fun when we're in the middle of this process. But this is the price that we must pay to eventually enjoy the kind of success that we've dreamed about. In the end, we will see that the struggle is more than worth it – even a hundred times over! The alternative is, of course, to play it safe by continuing to do what we've always done and getting exactly the same results. I, for one, have decided that this is no longer acceptable, and I hope you will too. Let's change this world together, through the power of God!

CONCLUDING THOUGHTS

Now that we've come to the end of the book, I strongly recommend that you read it through at least once or twice more, in order to get the most out of it. Also, it is even more important that you immediately start implementing the principles we've discussed, which have all been proven over a number of years at Bethel, and now many other places around the world. I am confident that they will work incredibly well for you too, when you take advantage of them. Without this kind of decisive action, though, you risk wasting the time and money that you've spent on the book. There is little to be gained from treating it as just an academic exercise.

Furthermore, don't forget your special bonus report: *Women in Ministry: Examining the Case Against Female Leadership in the Church*, which is available at: gregjtaylor.com/bethel-book-bonus

Finally, I realize that not everyone reading this book will necessarily be a believer in Jesus. Therefore, if you don't currently have a faith in Him, I want to give you the opportunity right now to make this important decision – so that you too can embark on the life and journey that we have discussed over the last 10 chapters. Each of us must be born again to enter the Kingdom of God (John 3:3) and become a new creation in Christ (2 Cor. 5:17), who has the ability to move in the kind of signs and wonders that Jesus did (and even greater ones! (John 14:12)). So if you would like to experience this second birth, I invite you to pray the following prayer:

> Jesus, thank you for dying on the cross for me. Right now I claim you as my Lord and Savior, and ask you to forgive me for everything that I've done wrong over my life, in offending against others and hurting you. Likewise, I make the decision to forgive each and every person who has wronged me in any way, as you require.
>
> Father God, please fill me with your Holy Spirit, and transform me into the righteous son/daughter of God and powerful world changer, that you've created me to be. Amen!

If you have just prayed this prayer and done so sincerely, you can now consider yourself a child of God and born again follower of Jesus, who is righteous and powerful. The next step is to find a good church community to be part of, where you will be encouraged and supported in your journey with God. It is also important to get a Bible and read it regularly, as this is one of the major ways that God speaks to us.

APPENDIX: SIGNS AND WONDERS

What are "Signs and Wonders"?

The term "signs and wonders" is one that is frequently bandied about in Pentecostal/Charismatic circles, but without ever being precisely defined. So what exactly are these signs and wonders, according to Scripture?

"Signs and wonders" is a phrase that is found 20 times in the ESV translation of the Bible: nine in the Old Testament and 11 in the New Testament. It first appears in Exod. 7:3, referring to the miracles that God would perform through Moses and Aaron in the land of Egypt, to free the Israelites from Egyptian slavery. Six out of the other eight occurrences of this term in the OT also refer to those particular miracles. The remaining two instances are in the Book of Daniel: King Nebuchadnezzar appears to use the term to refer to both the miraculous deliverance of Shadrach, Meshach, and Abednego from the fiery furnace, and the interpretation of his dreams by Daniel (Dan. 4:2). King Darius also uses it to refer to the preservation of Daniel in the lions' den (Dan 6:27).

Regarding the NT, "signs and wonders" is used four times in Acts (4:30, 5:12, 14:3, 15:12), and once in both Rom. 15:19 and Heb. 2:4, to convey the performing of miracles – which interestingly all took place in the context of evangelism. Healing is specifically mentioned in relation to the first two of these usages (Acts 4:30, 5:12-15). Outside of these six instances, the term is used three times to denote miraculous activity through the power of Satan, which appears to directly precede the second coming of Jesus (Matt. 24:24; Mark 13:22; 2 Thess. 2:9). The final two occurrences are in John 4:48 (by Jesus, when asked to heal an official's son) and 2 Cor. 12:12 (Paul's signs of a true apostle).

There are also a number of variants of, and additions to, this term in the Bible, which appear to usually be roughly synonymous, such as "sign(s)"[205], "wonders", "wonders and signs", "signs and wonders and various miracles", "signs and great miracles", "mighty works and wonders and signs", and "signs and wonders and mighty works". When all of these occurrences are added together, we see that there are at least one hundred clear usages of this basic concept in Scripture, related to the miraculous.[206]

To give some specific examples in the NT:

The apostle John, in his Gospel, mentions various signs of Jesus, such as the turning of water into wine (John 2:1-11), healing the sick (John 6:2), multiplying food (John 6:1-14), and raising the dead (John 12:17-18).

In Acts 3:1-8, Peter healed a man lame from birth, and this was referred to as a "notable sign" (Acts 4:16) and a "sign of healing" (Acts 4:22).

Philip the Evangelist cast out unclean spirits and healed many who were paralyzed or lame in Acts 8:5-8, and these occurrences were referred to as "signs" (v.6) and "signs and great miracles" (v.13).

Mark 16:17-18 lists certain "signs" that are supposed to accompany those who believe in Jesus, such as casting out demons, speaking in new languages, and healing the sick.

We can therefore establish that the phrase "signs and wonders", and related terms, usually refer to the miraculous activity of God[207], which in the life of a believer occurs through the power of the Holy

Spirit (Rom. 15:19). In the NT, healing is a prominent component of this. It apparently also includes tongues, prophecy, and most likely the exercising of other revelatory gifts (1 Cor. 14:22-25; cf. Deut. 13:1-2).

For these reasons, I use "signs and wonders" in this book as a catch-all phrase, denoting supernatural activity of every kind, through the power of God. I alternate between this and certain synonymous terms like "the supernatural", "miracles", and "the miraculous".

What are these Miraculous Activities of God Signs Of?

The next question that we need to answer is: what are these miraculous activities of God signs of?

First and foremost, they are signs of His reality and His absolute power and authority, that He is the one true God, who is above all and has no equal (Exod. 7:5, 14:4-31; Mark 9:2-7; Luke 8:22-25).

When performed through a person (as God normally does cf. Col. 1:15-16), miracles signify the activity of God through that individual (Luke 7:11-16; John 14:8-14). In conjunction with this, they are signs of that person having been appointed by God, indicating the truthfulness of their message (i.e. the Gospel) (Mark 16:20; 2 Cor. 12:12; Heb. 2:3-4; cf. John 9:16, 33).

For John, in particular, the miracles of Jesus were signs that glorified the Lord and pointed to Him as the Messiah of Israel and Son of God, causing people to believe in Him (John 1:47-50, 2:1-11, 23, 4:46-54, 11:1-48, 20:24-31). The Synoptic Gospels also make this point (Matt. 14:22-33; Mark 9:2-7; Luke 5:17-26), as does Acts regarding the miracles that followed His ascension to Heaven (Acts 2, 5:12-16).

Matthew and Luke often picture miracles as signs of the Kingdom of God that accompany its proclamation (Matt. 4:23-24, 9:35, 10:5-8, 12:28; Luke 9:1-2, 11, 10:9). Mark makes this a normative experience for believers in Jesus (Mark 16:15-18, 20), as does John (John 14:12).

Similarly, Paul believed that demonstrations of God's power should be an integral part of proclaiming the Kingdom (1 Cor. 2:1-5, 4:19-20).

Finally, it is vital that we do not miss a very important point, which is that miracles are normally signs of the goodness of God, in terms of His compassion for those who are in need and/or suffering – as demonstrated in the life of Jesus (Matt. 14:14, 15:32-38, 20:29-34; Mark 1:40-42; Luke 7:11-15; John 11:1-44). Since we, like Jesus, are representatives of God, it is our responsibility to show that same level of compassion toward those in need, via the miraculous (and other means), so that people will also see the goodness of God through us.

What Are the Purposes of Signs and Wonders?

Given that we have now answered the questions of what signs and wonders actually are and what they are signs of, the final question that we now need to address is: what are the purposes of these miraculous signs? This naturally follows on from the second question, regarding what they are signs of. They are intended to display God's reality, power, and authority – which brings Him glory and creates reverence for Him (Matt. 15:29-31; Mark 2:1-12; Luke 7:11-16, 9:37-43, 18:35-43); endorse the people that He works through (and their message); reveal His Kingdom; demonstrate His goodness; reveal Jesus as the Messiah and Son of God, and in the process lead people into believing in Him.

REFERENCES

Dedmon, Kevin and Chad Dedmon, *The Risk Factor: Crossing the Chicken Line into Your Supernatural Destiny* (Shippensburg: Destiny Image, 2011).

Goodrick, Edward W. and John R. Kohlenberger III, *Zondervan NIV Exhaustive Concordance* (Grand Rapids: Zondervan, 1990, 2nd ed.).

Johnson, Bill, *Face to Face With God: The Ultimate Quest to Experience His Presence* (Lake Mary: Charisma House, 2007).

Johnson, Bill, *God is Good: He's Better Than You Think* (Shippensburg: Destiny Image, 2016).

Johnson, Bill, *Hosting the Presence: Unveiling Heaven's Agenda* (Shippensburg: Destiny Image, 2012).

Johnson, Bill, *Strengthen Yourself in the Lord: How to Release the Hidden Power of God in Your Life* (Shippensburg: Destiny Image, 2007).

Johnson, Bill, *When Heaven Invades Earth: A Practical Guide to a Life of Miracles* (Kindle Version) (Shippensburg: Destiny Image, Expanded Edition, 2013).

Kittel, Gerhard (ed.), *Theological Dictionary of the New Testament* Volume I, Translated by Geoffrey W. Bromiley (Grand Rapids: Eerdmans, 1964).

Liardon, Roberts, *God's Generals: Why They Succeeded and Why Some Failed* (Tulsa: Albury, 1996).

Moo, Douglas J., *The Epistle to the Romans* (Grand Rapids/Cambridge: Eerdmans, 1996).

Sakenfeld, Katherine D. (ed.), *The New Interpreter's Dictionary of the Bible* Volume 1, edited by Katherine D. Sakenfeld (Nashville: Abingdon Press, 2006).

Vallotton, Kris, *Basic Training for the Prophetic Ministry* (Shippensburg: Destiny Image, 2005).

Vallotton, Kris, *How Heaven Invades Earth* (Bloomington: Chosen, 2010). NB. This book has previously and subsequently been published as *Heavy Rain.*

Vallotton, Kris, *Spirit Wars: Winning the Invisible Battle Against Sin and the Enemy* (Minneapolis: Chosen, 2012).

Vallotton, Kris and Bill Johnson, *The Supernatural Ways of Royalty: Discovering Your Rights and Privileges of Being a Son or Daughter of God* (Shippensburg: Destiny Image, 2006).

Vine, W.E., *Vine's Expository Dictionary of Old & New Testament Words* (Nashville: Thomas Nelson, 1997).

Wimber, John with Kevin Springer, *Power Healing* (London: Hodder & Stoughton, 1986).

ENDNOTES

Introduction

[1] It has in recent times, though, been moderated by the influence of postmodernity, which is far more open to spiritually, albeit in a pluralistic sense. However, despite what many people claim, modernity still has a very strong hold on our society.

[2] What is important to understand is that the same thinking that led to the development of modern science actually fed into modernity resulting in them having much in common philosophically. Modern science later became associated with modernity through the great emphasis modernity placed on it.

[3] None of these philosophical principles in conflict with faith and the supernatural, though, are actually required to allow science to do its job of investigating physical phenomena and making sense of the observable world. For example, empirical analysis (i.e. scientific research) can be carried out effectively without assuming that it is the only way to assess truth (empiricism); it is merely one particular way.

[4] The extreme form of them is scientism – the self-defeating belief that only science is able to determine objective truth and reality.

⁵ But logically, how could there be any physical evidence of an afterlife, for example? This speaks far more about the limitations of science than the likelihood of the phenomenon in question.

⁶ There is, however, no contradiction between science and faith. The only contradiction is actually between modern science (with its unverifiable anti-supernatural presuppositions) and faith. Can you see the difference? It is also worth pointing out that these unverifiable presuppositions contradict empiricism – modern science's own presupposition that we have to verify something (through observation) to be able to label it is "true". Modern science's philosophy therefore does not even satisfy its own requirements. Furthermore, if it is allowed to embody unsubstantiated "beliefs" in faith (e.g. nothing exists other than the physical world) then why can't Christianity also (e.g. something does exist other than the physical world – God)?

⁷ John Wimber with Kevin Springer, *Power Healing* (London: Hodder & Stoughton, 1986), p.29. NB. Wimber's definitions of healings, miracles, and signs and wonders are apparently different to the ones used in this book where "signs and wonders" and "miracles" are synonymous terms and healings are a subset of these. See Appendix: Signs and Wonders.

⁸ By "modern secularism", Wimber is essentially referring to what I am calling "modernity".

⁹ John Wimber with Kevin Springer, *Power Healing*, pp.29-30.

¹⁰ The excluded middle is the unseen supernatural (i.e. spiritual) dimension of this world (e.g. angels and demons on Earth and the ability to effect miraculous healing). The other two parts are the seen physical world which we are most familiar with and the unseen otherworldly supernatural dimension (e.g. Heaven and Hell, and the heavenly realms where spiritual entities reside. See Eph. 6:12; Col. 1:16).

¹¹ This is not to suggest that there is anything wrong with getting medical treatment; there isn't. And if you're experiencing a medical emergency it is foolish not to seek immediate medical advice. The issue, rather, is in whether we will involve God in the process through seeking out prayer for healing and prayerfully considering various treatment options (if appropriate). We are often too quick to pop a pill or reach for the phone to call the doctor before consulting God and giving Him a chance to heal us directly. Unfortunately, many Western Christians have little or no faith that He will heal them supernaturally and this, I believe, is a major problem.

[12] By "Bethel people", I am not only meaning those who currently attend the church and ministry school. I am also referring to those who have been at Bethel for a significant period of time, taken on its teachings and values, and subsequently moved away to implement what they've learned there in other places. All of this, of course, includes both the leadership and rank and file.

[13] The word for "church" in the New Testament, *ekklēsia*, literally means "to call out". Therefore, expressed as a noun, this refers to "those who are called out". As Edward W. Goodrick & John R. Kohlenberger III, *Zondervan NIV Exhaustive Concordance* (Grand Rapids: Zondervan, 1990, 2nd ed.), p.1546, explain: "In the NT a church is never a building or meeting place".

[14] It is particularly notable that at Bethel, the elderly are full of life and purpose – which comes from being valued and included, instead of being put out to pasture.

[15] It is important to understand that this Bethel signs and wonders culture which I am describing is a subset of the overall Bethel culture that relates specifically to the supernatural. Furthermore, the key components of it that I identify are the most important differences to other churches not seeing the supernatural manifest to a similar extent. These things therefore explain why some key elements of the Bethel culture appear to be missing from my list, such as the "culture of honor" and "culture of worship". Many churches, for example, have cultures of honor and worship and yet see little of the supernatural manifest. On the other hand, there are churches around that see a lot of miraculous activity without having cultures anywhere near as honoring as Bethel's.

Regarding worship, I do believe that it is an important amplifier of the supernatural. But when most people refer to worship they are thinking mainly of music. At Bethel, true worship is a lot deeper than this; it relates to a valuing and seeking after the presence of God of which music is only one entry point. Many churches sing a lot of songs, however not all of them have the same level of passion for the presence of God. This is why one of the secrets of the Bethel signs and wonders culture is being "Focused on His Presence" (Chapter 2) rather than having a "Culture of Worship". In conclusion, therefore, I would argue that if you removed any one of the 10 components of the Bethel signs and wonders culture that I have identified, it would have a significant impact on the level of supernatural activity that you experience.

Chapter 1: God is Good

[16] Bill Johnson, *God is Good: He's Better Than You Think* (Shippensburg: Destiny Image, 2016), p.150.

[17] Bill Johnson, "Kingdom Core Values: God is Good"; Bethel TV, February 1, 2017 https://www.bethel.tv/classes/kingdom-core-values/segment-1/5307, 57:16.

[18] The four cornerstones of Bethel Church are: 1. God is good; 2. Nothing is impossible; 3. The blood of Jesus paid for everything; 4. We are significant. (http://www.bethel.com/about/; accessed July 5, 2018.)

[19] The 13 core values of Bethel Church are: God is good; Salvation creates joyful identity; Responsive to grace; Focused on His presence; Creating healthy family; God's word transforms; God is still speaking; Jesus empowers supernatural ministry; His kingdom is advancing; Free and responsible; Honor affirms value; Generous like my Father; Hope in a glorious church. (http://www.bethel.com/core-values/; accessed July 5, 2018).

[20] http://www.bethel.com/core-values/; accessed July 5, 2018.

[21] To be sure, many people will actually end up in Hell. However, it was never God's plan for this to happen as He desires everyone to be saved (1 Tim. 2:4) and that no one will perish (2 Peter 3:9). People end up in Hell when they choose to reject God's offer of salvation through faith in Jesus, and instead follow the desires of the flesh (Rom. 8:5-8).

[22] We need to be clear, though, that God doesn't need to find any pretext to bring judgment on us. If that was His intention then He never would have sent Jesus to die for our sins, in order to save us. It would have been perfectly holy and righteous of Him to destroy each and every one of us – which He could do in a heartbeat anytime He chose to.

[23] Bill Johnson, *God is Good*, p.30.

[24] Bill Johnson likes to point out that Jesus didn't tell us to pray for the sick, but to heal them (Matt. 10:8). We don't need to ask God to heal when He has already given us both the authority and mandate to do so – which will often be through laying on of hands and speaking to the person's condition, commanding healing (Matt. 8:2-3; Mark 7:31-35); sometimes, though, it will be through an act of faith (Mark 2:3-12, 3:1-5). The other dimension of this is that we need to approach the situation in faith that the person is going to be healed rather than just give it a go and hope that it works (cf. James 1:6-8). As Yoda once said, "Try not! Do or do not. There is

no try." Nevertheless, in this book I am going to continue to use the terminology of praying for the sick because it is familiar to most of us and the grammar of not using it can become awkward.

[25] Bill Johnson, *When Heaven Invades Earth: A Practical Guide to a Life of Miracles* (Kindle Version) (Shippensburg: Destiny Image, Expanded Edition, 2013), p.51.

[26] Faith is a very abstract term that people have differing views about. My definition of it would be: a trust in God's character and word (in both the Bible and personal revelation) that rises above our natural doubts and fears to the point where we are willing to take action based on it.

[27] In retrospect, I am sure that God did actually rescue many people from the devastation of that tsunami. The statistics of the number of casualties don't tell us how many people escaped from the jaws of death. But most of those stories will probably remain untold and never correctly be attributed to the hand of God.

[28] Actually, there are multiple faiths for healing: one for healing others through your own prayers, another one for receiving healing for yourself from others through their prayers, a third one for receiving healing through your own prayers, and a fourth one for receiving healing through standing on the word of God (e.g. biblical promises), etc.

[29] Practicing our gifts is the "exercise" required for building up capabilities in them. A lot of people, though, go from conference to conference trying to receive impartations of power from great men and women of faith, but without spending enough time exercising the gifts they hope to operate in. Therefore, usually they don't move powerfully in these gifts no matter who has laid hands on them.

[30] I am referring more to mountain-moving faith here than the kind of faith that only believes that we will go to Heaven when we die.

[31] To be clear, I am not saying that we earn greater faith and power through works. Rather, when we use what we do have and stretch ourselves, we improve our abilities and gain confidence in using them. This actions the Kingdom principle, that as we are faithful with what we do have, we are given more (Matt. 25:14-30). To give a personal example, in recent years, I have been tested on numerous occasions in seeing God provide accommodation for me (especially in Redding, for BSSM!), often under difficult circumstances (e.g. time and financial pressures). The result of this has been

that I now have much greater faith in seeing the supernatural provision of God in this area, without getting unduly stressed out.

[32] John Wimber with Kevin Springer, *Power Healing*, pp.59-60. As an example, he quotes Irenaeus from the second century who mentions the casting out of demons, the healing of the sick, the raising of the dead, and the practicing of prophetic gifts in his day.

[33] See Appendix: Signs and Wonders, for further discussion on these matters.

[34] Passages such as Rom. 5:3-5 and 2 Cor. 12:7-10 are cited in support of this view.

[35] There is actually a huge difference between the legitimate blessings God offers us and the excessive claims made by a relatively small number of "faith" teachers.

[36] Obviously, though, if we're martyred for our faith there will be no earthly victory over this condition due to its finally – unless of course someone raises us from the dead, which is absolutely possible with God! (cf. Acts 14:19-20)

[37] What this reference to nakedness probably means is the lack of adequate clothing for the conditions (e.g. cold weather) rather than a total lack of clothing.

[38] Bill Johnson, *Face to Face With God: The Ultimate Quest to Experience His Presence* (Lake Mary: Charisma House, 2007), p.106.

[39] This includes the bondage to sin.

[40] The New Covenant, which believers in Jesus are under today, offers the promise of full physical healing (Matt. 8:17; 1 Peter 2:24). Similarly, faithful believers under the Old Covenant had the promises of protection from harm and healing (Exodus 15:26; Psalm 91, 103:3). However, it is likely that Job lived even before the time of the Old Covenant, when no healing promises were in effect – meaning that God would have been under absolutely no obligation to either prevent the attacks against him, or eventually bring healing and restoration.

[41] Of course, if after ministering to them, we feel that they are ready to make a decision to follow Jesus then we should present this opportunity. The point is, though, that this should not be our main objective in going into the interaction.

Chapter 2: Focused on His Presence

[42] Bill Johnson, *Face to Face With God*, p.214.

[43] This, of course, assumes that we are living a healthy lifestyle, which includes eating the right foods, exercising regularly, and getting enough rest and sleep. If any one of these factors is out of balance then some of our issues might be self-inflicted. Also, chemical imbalances in the brain can be responsible for things like depression and other mood disorders, in some people.

[44] Bill Johnson, *Face to Face With God*, p.60.

[45] Bill Johnson, *When Heaven Invades Earth*, pp.151-152.

[46] Kevin Dedmon and Chad Dedmon, *The Risk Factor: Crossing the Chicken Line into Your Supernatural Destiny* (Shippensburg: Destiny Image, 2011), pp.188-190.

[47] Note, the assumption is that He is definitely going to provide for us. The only question is how.

[48] Bill Johnson, *Face to Face With God*, p.20.

[49] Bill Johnson, *Hosting the Presence: Unveiling Heaven's Agenda* (Shippensburg: Destiny Image, 2012), pp.138-139.

[50] Kris Vallotton, *Spirit Wars: Winning the Invisible Battle Against Sin and the Enemy* (Minneapolis: Chosen, 2012), p.62.

[51] Kris Vallotton, *Spirit Wars*, p.25.

[52] Kris Vallotton, *Spirit Wars*, pp.152-154

[53] Kris Vallotton, *Spirit Wars*, p.154

[54] Bill Johnson, *Hosting the Presence*, p.29.

Chapter 3: Partnering with God

[55] Bill Johnson, *Hosting the Presence*, p.150.

[56] Bill Johnson, *Hosting the Presence*, p.97.

[57] Bill Johnson, *Hosting the Presence*, p.97.

Chapter 4: Saints, Not Sinners

[58] Kris Vallotton, *Spirit Wars*, p.42.

[59] Kris Vallotton and Bill Johnson, *The Supernatural Ways of Royalty: Discovering Your Rights and Privileges of Being a Son or Daughter of God* (Shippensburg: Destiny Image, 2006), p.69.

[60] Kris Vallotton and Bill Johnson, *The Supernatural Ways of Royalty*, pp.69-70.

[61] Notice that, in this book, I utilize this same technique most of the time when referring to Bible scholars/theologians, biblical writers such as Paul, and Jesus.

[62] Douglas J. Moo, *The Epistle to the Romans* (Grand Rapids/Cambridge: Eerdmans, 1996), pp.464, 474-476, argues that for the phrase, "law of sin (and death)" in Rom. 7:23, 25, 8:2, "law" should be translated as "binding authority" or "power" (e.g. "power of sin (and death)"). This phrase should not be equated with the "Law of God" (Rom. 7:22), i.e. the Mosaic Law, since v.23 indicates that the "law of sin" is "another law", v.7 clearly affirms that the Law (of God) is not sin, and vv.12-14, 16 state that the Law (of God) is holy, good, and spiritual.

[63] Some people point out that this verse actually says that the Spirit "convicts" (*elegchō*) the world of sin, not believers. However, the same Greek word is used in Heb. 12:5 ("reproved" ESV; "rebukes" NIV2011) and in Rev. 3:19 ("reprove" ESV; "rebuke" NIV2011) when speaking about what God does to believers.

[64] Two of his other major roles are to deceive (Rev. 12:9) and accuse (Rev. 12:10).

[65] This includes non-believers as well. Their sin nature is caused not by their physical bodies, which God originally created good (Gen. 1:31; 1 Tim. 4:4), but by the flesh, which has gained control over their bodies and thereby created an overwhelming compulsion toward sin (Rom. 7:20, 23). That is, the sinful desires of the flesh have become the desires of the body, such that a person has a body of sin/death (Rom. 6:6, 7:24), which they cannot control.

[66] Kris Vallotton and Bill Johnson, *The Supernatural Ways of Royalty*, p.67.

[67] Kris Vallotton and Bill Johnson, *The Supernatural Ways of Royalty*, p.72.

[68] John Wimber with Kevin Springer, *Power Healing*, p.89.

[69] There are consequences to our actions that remain despite the fact that we've been forgiven by God. For example, if we spend time watching porn and then repent, we have at the very least completely wasted that time, which could have been spent on things far more productive.

[70] Kris Vallotton and Bill Johnson, *The Supernatural Ways of Royalty*, pp.22-23.

[71] Kris Vallotton and Bill Johnson, *The Supernatural Ways of Royalty*, pp.23-24.

[72] Kris Vallotton and Bill Johnson, *The Supernatural Ways of Royalty*, p.35.

[73] Kris Vallotton and Bill Johnson, *The Supernatural Ways of Royalty*, p.36.

[74] Nevertheless, the reality is that He provides for most of His children through the same ways that others earn their income – working a job or running a business. The difference, though, is a mentality: the job or business is not our source, God is. And we don't earn it; He gives it to us. Therefore, we do not need to be slaves to our job or business (i.e. effectively money cf. Luke 16:13) and don't need to fear losing that source of income (e.g. losing our job), because God is still our provider. We can trust that He will just provide through some other means. This, of course, does not imply that we should all quit our jobs and "live by faith" – which, if He hasn't called us to this sort of life, would be putting the Lord to the test (cf. Luke 4:9-12). For some, "living by faith" is actually a cover-up for sheer laziness and irresponsibility, disguised in spiritual terminology.

[75] Kris Vallotton and Bill Johnson, *The Supernatural Ways of Royalty*, p.156.

[76] Kris Vallotton and Bill Johnson, *The Supernatural Ways of Royalty*, p.104.

[77] Kris Vallotton and Bill Johnson, *The Supernatural Ways of Royalty*, p.106.

[78] Kris Vallotton and Bill Johnson, *The Supernatural Ways of Royalty*, p.80.

[79] Kris Vallotton, *Basic Training for the Prophetic Ministry* (Shippensburg: Destiny Image, 2005), p.13.

[80] Kris Vallotton and Bill Johnson, *The Supernatural Ways of Royalty*, p.106.

Chapter 5: Optimistic and Victorious Eschatology

[81] There is, however, no official position on eschatology that I am aware of beyond the belief that God's Kingdom is advancing on Earth and will continue to do so right up until the return of Jesus, transforming society and revealing God's love and goodness to the world.

[82] The same scenario applies if we die before His coming in that our service to God will be evaluated.

[83] Synonymous parallelism is a literary device in which the same idea is expressed in two different ways.

[84] The fact that Matthew, in his Gospel, has a strong preference for the term "Kingdom of Heaven" rather than "Kingdom of God" further strengthens this argument that God's will being done is associated with the coming of Heaven.

[85] Bill Johnson, *God is Good*, p.67.

[86] Edward W. Goodrick & John R. Kohlenberger III, *Zondervan NIV Exhaustive Concordance*, p.1500, give the meanings of *shalom* as, "peace, safety, prosperity, well-being; intactness, wholeness; peace can have a focus of security, safety which can bring feelings of satisfaction, well-being, and contentment".

[87] W.E. Vine, *Vine's Expository Dictionary of Old & New Testament Words* (Nashville: Thomas Nelson, 1997), p.842.

[88] Kris Vallotton speaking in BSSM First Year, October 8, 2014.

[89] Kris Vallotton, *How Heaven Invades Earth* (Bloomington: Chosen, 2010), p.203. NB. This book has previously and subsequently been published as *Heavy Rain*.

[90] Kris Vallotton, *How Heaven Invades Earth*, pp.201-216.

[91] Shortly after this, theologian Francis Schaeffer also reportedly received a similar revelation.

[92] Notice that Daniel requested a meeting with the king to reveal the interpretation of the king's dream before he had even received the interpretation by God (Dan. 2:16-19). That is faith!

[93] Bill Johnson, *God is Good*, p.177.

[94] It does not matter whether or not you believe that any of these practices deliver what they offer. The important thing is that many people do and are willing to pay a lot of money for these deliverables.

[95] Two other potential contributors to this are an <u>identity of persecution</u>, which may have developed and been passed on through the centuries to successive generations of Christians; and <u>ascetic traditions</u>, which have always existed within the Church. Both of these lead to positive views of suffering and defeat, and to great suspicion regarding success and popularity.

[96] Bill Johnson, *God is Good*, p.52.

Chapter 6: Complete Five-Fold Ministry

[97] This maturity includes the "unity in the faith" and "the knowledge of the Son of God" mentioned in the passage.

[98] The word "missionary" is actually derived from a Latin word for "send". And as we are about to discuss below, the word "apostle" is derived from the Greek word for "send".

[99] It is interesting that in many streams, every senior and associate leader is given the title of "pastor". This has set an expectation that church leaders are going to function primarily in pastoral capacities – which appears to be part of the problem in terms of why apostles have ended up in inappropriate positions.

[100] W.E. Vine, *Vine's Expository Dictionary of Old & New Testament Words*, p.55.

[101] Karl H. Rengtorf, "ἀπόστολος", in *Theological Dictionary of the New Testament* Volume I, edited by Gerhard Kittel and translated by Geoffrey W. Bromiley (Grand Rapids: Eerdmans, 1964), p.407.

[102] Terence Donaldson, "APOSTLE", in *The New Interpreter's Dictionary of the Bible* Volume 1, edited by Katherine D. Sakenfeld (Nashville: Abingdon Press, 2006), p.206.

[103] Terence Donaldson, "APOSTLE", in *The New Interpreter's Dictionary of the Bible* Volume 1, edited by Katherine D. Sakenfeld, p.206.

[104] Karl H. Rengtorf, "ἀπόστολος", in *Theological Dictionary of the New Testament* Volume I, edited by Gerhard Kittel, p.407.

[105] Karl H. Rengtorf, "ἀπόστολος", in *Theological Dictionary of the New Testament* Volume I, edited by Gerhard Kittel, p.407.

[106] Karl H. Rengtorf, "ἀπόστολος", in *Theological Dictionary of the New Testament* Volume I, edited by Gerhard Kittel, pp.407-408.

[107] Terence Donaldson, "APOSTLE", in *The New Interpreter's Dictionary of the Bible* Volume 1, edited by Katherine D. Sakenfeld, p.206.

[108] Karl H. Rengtorf, "ἀπόστολος", in *Theological Dictionary of the New Testament* Volume I, edited by Gerhard Kittel, p.408.

[109] They may, of course, have used the term in multiple ways. For example, in 2 Cor. 8:23 *apostolos* is translated as "messengers" in the ESV and there is certainly reason to believe that those referred to here are not apostles in

the same sense as people like Peter and Paul who were recognized as significant leaders within the Church.

[110] The apostle John also positioned himself as a father in the faith on multiple occasions (e.g. 1 John 2:1, 3:7, 5:21), although only once outside of his first letter (3 John 4). The apostle Peter did once as well (1 Peter 1:14) - assuming that he is referring to his readers' status as his spiritual children rather than as God's children.

[111] This, however, still does not explain their function or purpose.

[112] But this view does not imply that the senior leader of every church is automatically an apostle or "apostolic". This is because, as is going to be argued below, a distinguishing mark of the apostle is their focus on sending their people out to bring the Kingdom (with the expectation that many of these people will not end up coming back to rejoin the congregation). And if this is not the primary focus of a senior leader then they are not an apostle. For instance, if their main objectives are to gather people and build a large congregation of happy, healthy believers then they are most likely a pastor instead.

[113] Based on 1 Cor. 3:10-11, this foundation is almost certainly the one laid by the apostles and prophets (Jesus Christ) rather than the apostles and prophets themselves.

[114] Kris Vallotton speaking in BSSM Second Year, March 23, 2016.

[115] But the most effective evangelists, while focusing on the individual and their spiritual needs, will not neglect people's physical needs, and that is why healing and evangelism work so well together. Remember, it is about the Gospel of the Kingdom rather than just the Gospel of salvation, as we discussed in the last chapter.

[116] Kris Vallotton, *How Heaven Invades Earth*, Chapter 2: "The Emerging Apostolic Age", pp.57-74.

[117] Kris Vallotton, *How Heaven Invades Earth*, pp.68-70.

[118] Kris Vallotton, *How Heaven Invades Earth*, pp.63-64.

[119] Kris Vallotton, *How Heaven Invades Earth*, p.64.

[120] Kris Vallotton, *How Heaven Invades Earth*, p.67.

[121] Kris Vallotton, *How Heaven Invades Earth*, p.69.

[122] Kris Vallotton, *How Heaven Invades Earth*, p.64.

[123] Pastors equip people for ministry as well (Eph. 4:11), but in a more indirect way, by caring for them so that they are healthy on the inside.

[124] Kris Vallotton, *How Heaven Invades Earth*, p.66.

[125] Another reason is that people are often not praying in the most effective way to impart healing. From my own experience, a person is many, many times more likely to get healed if we pray for them when they are present (which includes them being on the phone or Skype with us etc.) than when they are absent and don't know that we're praying for them at that particular time. The laying on of hands is also very important (cf. Mark 16:18), ideally on the sick/injured area(s) of their body if this is appropriate. Thirdly, it is vital that we assess the results after prayer (i.e. ask the person if there is any change in their condition etc.) and pray again if necessary. Most people, though, skip this step because they are either afraid of being told that nothing has happened, or they are simply not expecting anything to happen.

[126] By a "Bethel effect" I am meaning the tendency for Bethel's reputation, as a signs and wonders ministry, to raise expectations (i.e. faith) for healing.

[127] Admittedly, though, I probably only prayed for about three or four people on our team regarding healing needs.

[128] There are, of course, other factors involved as well and therefore we should never conclude that a person doesn't have enough faith if we pray for them and they don't get healed. After all, it could actually be our lack of faith that is the problem!

[129] Kris Vallotton, *How Heaven Invades Earth*, pp.69-70.

[130] Kris Vallotton, *How Heaven Invades Earth*, p.70.

[131] Kris Vallotton, *How Heaven Invades Earth*, p.68.

[132] Kris Vallotton, "Kingdom Core Values: Hope in a Glorious Church"; Bethel TV, January 25, 2017, https://www.bethel.tv/classes/kingdom-core-values/segment-1/5306, 45:54.

[133] This is not to suggest that no events should ever be put on to get non-Christians along to church. Bethel, for example, organizes community meals, like its holiday feasts and Sunday morning breakfasts, to appeal to the poor and disadvantaged. Its Healing Rooms could arguably also be placed in this category of events used to get non-Christians along to church. We need to be doing as many things as possible to share the Gospel with people. The key, though, is in not being dependent on secondary strategies, like entertainment and getting people into our physical church buildings, in order to present the Gospel to them. The Church, after all, is the people

of God, not a set of buildings. And we need to take the Church (i.e. us) to the world, not rely on attracting the world to "church".

[134] Another option is that these leaders don't actually believe in their people, that they're capable of doing evangelism out in the real world, effectively.

[135] Kris Vallotton and Bill Johnson, *The Supernatural Ways of Royalty*, p.152.

[136] Sadly, it is not popular nowadays in most Christian academic circles to discuss the supernatural, in terms of it happening today. Often you will be seen as extremely naïve and unsophisticated if you do. The expectation is that if you are going to talk about this subject, it will be to downplay what is possible and criticize those who have faith in this area, as being overly triumphalistic or simply deceived.

[137] What they are really saying in this is that it almost always is not God's will to heal because, in their experience, He usually doesn't.

[138] Bill Johnson, *When Heaven Invades Earth*, p.97.

[139] To finish off this story, things then got even stranger when I sensed, via word of knowledge, the presence of evil. And as I placed my hand on the woman's head to pray for her, her personality and demeanor instantly changed and she started speaking in a very different tongue to before, one that sounded harsh and aggressive - unlike any earthly language that I had ever heard. Clearly a demonic spirit had just manifested and totally taken over her body. I proceeded to command it to speak in English and it did! After this, I tried to cast it out and encountered strong resistance. Eventually it got very late at night (after multiple hours of ministry) and the lady was becoming quite drained spiritually. So, I commanded the spirit to go back down and decided to finish the job another time - which I did, casting multiple demons out of her. In Chapter 10: Culture of Risk, I go into some more detail of the actual deliverance.

[140] Bill Johnson, *When Heaven Invades Earth*, p.92.

[141] Of course, the kingdom of darkness does operate in the supernatural as well - which is normally easy to discern e.g. demons appearing, pictures falling off walls, and televisions turning themselves on and off when they are not even plugged in.

[142] Bill Johnson, *Face to Face With God*, pp.7, 122-123.

[143] Prophets embody elements of both emphases and could therefore be seen as acting as a bridge between two.

Chapter 7: Culture of Revival

[144] Bill Johnson, *When Heaven Invades Earth*, p.99.

[145] Bill Johnson, *When Heaven Invades Earth*, p.99.

[146] bethel.com/about/; accessed July 3, 2018.

[147] This is the BSSM definition of a revivalist from *Seeds of Revival: Bethel School of Supernatural Ministry Core Values Journal*, 2015-2016 Version, p.2.

[148] Obviously though, it would take a lot longer to drill down deeper into more complex topics like Sozo (Bethel's inner healing methodology).

[149] Bill and Kris, especially, have been great spiritual fathers; I will forever be grateful for what they've poured into me.

[150] http://deadraisingteam.com/our-director/; accessed June 29, 2018.

[151] The sacrifice that many people have made to be part of Bethel (especially BSSM) may also be an important contributor to the strength of the community, through raising the level of commitment. For instance, a lot of people have left their homes and loved ones to travel from different parts of the country or world, to come to Redding.

[152] A church can have a big vision, but if no viable strategy to achieve this is being pursued then it won't inspire anyone and is simply a waste of time. In contrast, the vision conveyed in Bethel's mission statement, that we looked at earlier in the chapter (i.e. revival, on a global scale), is extremely bold, but the means by which it is being pursued (i.e. God's presence - expressed through the people of God) is very feasible, which therefore moves many people to buy into it.

[153] Bill Johnson, *When Heaven Invades Earth*, p.123.

[154] It is, of course, true that we as the Church have lost relevance to our world and desperately need to regain this. However, in my experience, when Christians talk about the need to be "more relevant", what they are often actually advocating is watering down our core message, by doing things like trying to be entertaining, avoiding discussion on unpopular topics (e.g. sin and judgment), and adopting some of the world's values (e.g. relaxing some of our moral standards). But these sorts of things tend to have the opposite effect to what is intended, by actually making us LESS rather than more relevant to society. For we don't attract the world by becoming more like them, but by offering them something of value which they lack. To truly be more relevant, what we need to do is start preaching the true Gospel of the

Kingdom (with power! See 1 Cor. 2:4-5, 4:20) and represent God accurately, rather than offering an incomplete and distorted gospel that offers people little that they do not already have. After all, God is always the most relevant one around, given that He is the embodiment and source of all life, love, intelligence, wisdom, wealth, creativity, knowledge, truth, and power. When we reveal Him to the world, we should therefore expect that many will come running.

[155] Perhaps this is a reason why Christians in the West don't see as many miraculous healings as they would like to. The medical treatments that are available today are often so good that it is usually much easier to just swallow some pill or have an operation to fix a problem; we don't need to depend on God. However, many of our brothers and sisters in poorer nations do not have the same level of access to this sort of care, and therefore they have no choice but to rely on God to heal them (and He does!).

[156] Having said this, though, the manager of the apartment complex would not have approved this woman as a tenant due to her history, and therefore the only way I could have given her my apartment would have been by not telling the manager that I had done so.

[157] Bill Johnson, *Strengthen Yourself in the Lord: How to Release the Hidden Power of God in Your Life* (Shippensburg: Destiny Image, 2007), p.108.

[158] Bill Johnson, *Strengthen Yourself in the Lord*, p.109.

[159] From a Skype interview I conducted with her for this book, on June 1, 2017.

[160] This information was provided by Michael Van Tinteren from Bill Johnson Ministries.

[161] Technically, though, none of the three examples of acts of faith used to create "points of contact" that are cited in this paragraph count as prophetic acts, because they do not act out the receiving of the miracle. They could instead be considered "symbolic acts". All prophetic acts are symbolic acts, but not all symbolic acts are prophetic acts. In order to eliminate any confusion, I will give you another example of a prophetic act, one that is very clear. Sometimes a leader at Bethel will ask people gathered (more likely in a training session, rather than a church meeting) to imagine themselves holding a barrel full of Holy Spirit "wine", and then turning it upside down and drinking all of the contents so that they get drunk in the Holy Spirit (Eph. 5:18).

[162] This is a summarized version of the article "$1,000 For Everyone!" in *Increase: Catalytic Stories* Vol. 2 (which I have used with permission from Dave and Taff).

Chapter 8: Nothing is Impossible!

[163] http://www.bethel.com/about/; accessed July 5, 2018.

[164] This is not in contradiction to what we discussed in Chapter 3, about partnering with God. We don't need any special divine strategy or instructions to know, for example, that we need to pray for the sick and evangelize – which in both cases is clearly spelled out in Scripture (James 5:16; Matt. 28:19-20).

[165] The level of effectiveness of particular people can be different for different conditions. For example, person A may have greater success in healing cancer, while person B may be more effective with hearing issues.

[166] John Wimber with Kevin Springer, *Power Healing*, pp.66-69.

[167] Shawn Bolz on "Sid Roth's It's Supernatural"; October 22, 2017 https://sidroth.org/television/tv-archives/shawn-bolz-2/; 11:37.

[168] As I wrote this chapter, the phrase "nothing is impossible" started jumping out at me all over the place, and not always where you might expect – including the title of marketing podcast episode, which had absolutely nothing to do with Christianity. I believe this indicates that it is something that God particularly wants to highlight to you, as a reader of this book.

[169] We know that something is God's will if it lines up with His revealed will in Scripture and/or a personal word that He has given to us. For example, God's desire to heal is extremely well established (Psalm 103:3; Matt. 8:17; Mark 16:18). However, in general, we should assume that He is happy for us to believe for most things that don't specifically violate His revealed will (Mark 9:23; 11:22-24) – as long as we have the right motives (James 4:3).

[170] There was the one case, though, that I mentioned above in which it only partially worked (Mark 8:22-25). He spat on the blind man's eyes and laid hands on him, but needed to lay hands on him for a second time to fully restore his sight.

[171] Roberts Liardon, *God's Generals: Why They Succeeded and Why Some Failed* (Tulsa: Albury, 1996), pp.180-181.

[172] https://prayingmedic.com/2019/03/31/supernatural-saturday-when-youre-not-healed/; 11:53; accessed April 8, 2019. Hayes also has a very

simple but effective method of emotional healing, which is as follows: 1. Recall a traumatic event in your life; 2. Identify the emotion(s) resulting from it (e.g. shame); 3. Ask God to take away that emotion (or emotions), and heal the associated wound. 4. Think about this event again, and if you can do so without the negative emotion(s), you have been healed. But if not, go through the process again until you receive full healing (15:28).

Chapter 9: Culture of Empowerment

[173] Of course, they do believe that we can all learn from others.

[174] This comes from the fourth cornerstone of Bethel, which is "We are significant". See https://www.bethel.com/about/; accessed July 19, 2018.

[175] Bill Johnson, *Hosting the Presence*, p.80.

[176] This does not include teaching/preaching in official church services, which are roles only performed by recognized Bethel leaders and invited visiting speakers.

[177] Often, they can even be more effective than adults, as they don't tend to have the same concept of it potentially not working e.g. someone not getting healed when we pray for them.

[178] The requirements for BSSM students are often less than ordinary church members, due to the equivalent ministry training that they have already received in the school. For example, Second and Third Year students are automatically church ministry team members. However, there are additional requirements for them to become prayer servants in the Healing Rooms.

[179] A "Fire Tunnel" is a prayer tunnel in which ministry team members form two lines facing each other. When people walk through the middle of these two lines they receive prayer on both sides, from each team member, usually through the laying on of hands.

[180] Kris Vallotton, *How Heaven Invades Earth*, p.68.

Chapter 10: Culture of Risk

[181] Kevin Dedmon and Chad Dedmon, *The Risk Factor*, p.77.

[182] Bill Johnson, *When Heaven Invades Earth*, p.186.

[183] Bill Johnson, *God is Good*, p.126.

[184] Bill Johnson, *God is Good*, p.126.

185 "Todd White - Interview - What if No One Gets Healed?"; https://www.youtube.com/watch?v=LE96DqEDAfQ; 0.37 and 7.44; Todd White - Lifestyle Christianity You Tube channel; Accessed November 3, 2017.

186 A distinction is knowledge about what works as opposed to what doesn't work, and in which situations.

187 To give an example, who learns to drive a car just by reading books or attending a series of lectures on the subject? However, many Christians attempt to do this with important aspects of their faith, such as operating in the supernatural.

188 It was amusing when I walked past his room sometimes and heard him shouting commands to the demons inside of himself, with hideous screams and shrieks immediately following this. It sounded like someone was in the process of being murdered on the other side of the door!

189 The reason I say "praying in faith" rather than just "prayer" is that the devil does not mind prayer that is done in an attitude of fearfulness or complaining - which is absolutely no threat to him (if anything, it actually helps him to tighten the screws on his victims).

190 This does not mean that it should be our goal as deliverance ministers to cause the manifestation of demons, or that we should allow such manifestations to continue if they happen to arise. Manifestations are not necessary to successfully deliver a person, and often it will not be appropriate to allow them to occur, as they might scare other people (and distract them from what is happening at a church service). As deliverance ministers, we can tell demons to "go down" or "be quiet" whenever we want, and the manifestations should stop. This, however, is no indication that their torment has ceased; we are just forbidding them from using the person's body to express how they're feeling, and from trying to intimidate others in the process. Neither does the cessation of manifestations necessarily indicate that the demons have gone.

191 I said to the demons, "Do you know what I'm going to do to you?" They replied, "We will fight you!" I then tried to cast them out by simply saying something like, "I command you to leave her in Jesus' name". However, when nothing had happened after a couple of minutes of doing this, the demons taunted me by saying, "Haha, it's not working, is it?"

192 This is an example of how to use theoretical learning correctly. When my real-world efforts came up short, I did research on the area that I lacked

knowledge in, and then went straight back and applied what I had just learned.

[193] Bill Johnson, *Strengthen Yourself in the Lord*, p.69.

[194] Many, for example, have had little or no exposure to any teaching on this subject, and therefore haven't been empowered to operate in the supernatural gifts. Furthermore, some have been explicitly taught that moving in the supernatural is not possible today, such as through cessationism.

[195] Kris Vallotton, *Basic Training for the Prophetic Ministry*, p.31.

[196] Kris Vallotton, *Basic Training for the Prophetic Ministry*, p.20.

[197] Kris Vallotton, *Basic Training for the Prophetic Ministry*, p.20.

[198] Kris Vallotton, *Basic Training for the Prophetic Ministry*, p.21.

[199] Kris Vallotton, *Basic Training for the Prophetic Ministry*, pp.70-71.

[200] However, in some churches (especially Pentecostal ones), this sort of language is part of the culture.

[201] Three of Kris Vallotton's criteria for evaluating prophetic words are: they must be congruent with Scripture and the heart of God; they must bear witness with our spirit; their fruit must be that we are brought closer to God and His people (*Basic Training for the Prophetic Ministry*, p.55). I would also suggest that it is helpful if they line up with what God has said to us in the past (including through previous prophetic words) and is saying to us at the moment (including through recent prophetic words).

[202] This, of course, does not mean that we should measure someone solely according to their outward success, such as their ability to perform miracles, cast out demons, or even come up with true prophecies, as the next verses clearly state (Matt. 7:21-23). How they treat people, their ethics, and the sort of followers they produce are also important things to consider.

[203] Kris Vallotton and Bill Johnson, *The Supernatural Ways of Royalty*, p.160.

[204] Kris Vallotton, *Spirit Wars*, p.62.

Appendix: Signs and Wonders

[205] Occasionally, this word has different connotations that clearly have nothing to do with the miraculous, as in Matt. 26:48, Luke 1:22, 2:12, and 2 Thess. 3:17.

[206] I found 103, by adding together the references in the ESV to "signs and wonders", "signs", "sign", "wonders" and "wonder" (double counting was

avoided). When "signs" and "wonders" or "sign" and "wonder" appear in close proximity to each other, as in Deut. 4:34, Dan. 4:3, and Acts 2:43, they were only counted as one occurrence. Not included were the numerous references to signs non-miraculous in nature, particularly in the OT, such as the sign of circumcision (Gen. 17:11) and the sign of the Sabbath (Exod. 31:16-17). Debatable references, such as 1 Sam. 10:7; 2 Kings 20:9; and Luke 21:11, were also excluded.

[207] The exception is the term "sign" in the OT, which on only a few occasions refers to miraculous signs.

ABOUT THE AUTHOR

Greg Taylor is from Christchurch, New Zealand, and a graduate of the Bethel School of Supernatural Ministry (BSSM). He has been active in signs and wonders ministry (particularly healing) since 2006, with a focus on practicing it outside of the church - in both everyday life and evangelism. One of his greatest passions is equipping people in this kind of ministry.

Greg has ministered in several countries around the world, including New Zealand, the United States, Mexico, Israel, Germany, and the United Kingdom. Signs and wonders follow him wherever he goes.

Greg holds a graduate diploma in theology from the Bible College of New Zealand (now Laidlaw College). He has also earned BSc and MCom degrees in economics, from the University of Canterbury.

Greg has worked professionally as a demographer at Statistics New Zealand (New Zealand's national statistics agency) and a researcher in economics at Lincoln University. At the moment, he is involved in online marketing.

www.ingramcontent.com/pod-product-compliance
Lightning Source LLC
Chambersburg PA
CBHW021935290426
44108CB00012B/847